KADER ASMAL

Politics in My Blood

To Finn & Maire

With deep gratitude
for love and support
which is much appreciated

Love

Graham & Anne

KADER ASMAL

Politics in My Blood

A Memoir

by Kader Asmal and Adrian Hadland

with Moira Levy

First published by Jacana Media (Pty) Ltd in 2011

10 Orange Street
Sunnyside
Auckland Park 2092
South Africa
+2711 628 3200
www.jacana.co.za

ISBN 978-1-77009-903-6 (Soft cover)
ISBN 978-1-4314-0257-1 (Hard cover)

Job No. 001558

Cover design by publicide
Cover photograph credit: Benny Gool
Set in Stempel Garamond 10.5/14.5 pt
Printed and bound by Ultra Litho (Pty) Limited, Johannesburg

See a complete list of Jacana titles at www.jacana.co.za

For my mother, my father, Louise and my family,
and for all those in South Africa and elsewhere
who have inspired me

Contents

An Appreciation
by President Nelson Mandela

Kader Asmal is one of our most valued comrades. He has demonstrated a remarkable ability to grasp a broad range of complex issues, and to pursue challenges with rare insight and vigour.

As Minister of Water Affairs and Forestry in our historic government of national unity, he alerted the entire nation to the huge environmental challenges we faced; under his guidance innovative programmes were developed to conserve scarce water resources and restore indigenous plants so vital to our environment.

As Minister of Education he displayed a similar capacity for innovation and creativity. Furthermore, such was his dedication to good government that he soon became known amongst his colleagues in my Cabinet as the Minister of All Portfolios.

As well as being an astute political leader, he is a renowned academic and thinker who has made his mark on our country and internationally. Above all, his honesty and integrity, his willingness to challenge orthodox thinking when necessary, is something we should cherish as South Africans.

We thank him for what he has meant to South Africa and for what he has contributed to the wider world.

Acknowledgements

This work is not an autobiography nor is it a straightforward memoir. It is, rather, the account of my life, from growing up as the son of a shopkeeper in a small country town in KwaZulu-Natal, moving to England to study and then to Ireland to teach law, and finally returning to a free country, where I played a part in devising a new constitution and served as a Cabinet minister for two terms. Along the way I have learnt much from books, from encounters with many and various people, and from my experience of life in South Africa, England and Ireland. I have not attempted to include every last detail or nuance. That would require a very much larger work, and this one is already quite large enough.

I acknowledge the work of David Chidester, Thomas Alberts and John Young in ordering my files and documents over a number of years and in preparing earlier drafts of sections of this manuscript.

I am grateful to Guy Preston, Albie Sachs, Allan Taylor, Nasima Badsha, Linda Chisholm, Ahmed Essop, Richard Harvey, Wilmot James, Brenda Leibowitz and Bronwen Levy for their willingness to be interviewed for this book or to provide material that has been useful in its writing. Enuga Reddy, Rushni Salie, Eberhard Braune, Jackie Hadland and Micah Faure were immensely helpful and supportive in the process of research and writing. I also owe a great debt to Moira Levy for the interviews she conducted and for the invaluable work she did at the final stages of preparing the script for publication.

Prologue
The First Day

The day that South Africa convened its first, democratically elected, non-racial Parliament, 9 May 1994, was one of the most important days of my life. As I sat at my desk on the leather-covered benches of the government side of the National Assembly in my new suit and Trinity College Dublin tie, I saw the order paper was titled 'First Session, First Parliament'. It was as if the previous three hundred years of illegitimate state oppression had melted away at the hand of an astute parliamentary officer with a keen sense of history. I wondered who had arranged for this re-ordering of history on the order paper. Orthodox parliamentary protocol suggested this should have been the first session of the tenth Parliament (since the formation of the Republic of South Africa). Instead, this was the first day of the first Parliament. And, in many ways, that was exactly right.

I looked over at the benches of the National Party, the political party that had presided over more than forty-five years of oppression, and its leader, former State President F.W. de Klerk. I felt the exhilaration of a victor and the vindication of the just. The regime had fallen and with it three hundred years of racism and injustice.

Nelson Mandela, who was soon to be chosen by Parliament as South Africa's first democratic President, had often talked to me about the importance of forgiveness and tolerance. I sometimes found this hard to accept. I was courteous towards our opponents during the negotiations for political power because it was correct and productive to do so. But I never forgot with whom I was dealing.

All the same I didn't feel vindictive or angry even as they sat across the floor in the opposition benches, grinning and patting each other on the back. Instead, I asked myself: What had we won? State power had been wrested from the grasp of the unjust by the will of the people.

Now I was sitting there, a minister in Nelson Mandela's first Cabinet, and thinking of what we would have to do to overcome the awful legacy of colonialism and apartheid.

This, for me, was the real beauty of that first election and the government it produced. It was a compact of unprecedented historical dimensions. If I was religiously inclined I would call the first democratic poll, and all those that followed, a sacrament of democracy. It was a ritual of high moral currency. Voting confers great dignity on people who have previously been denied a role in their own governance. There is a grace that is close to the divine in enjoying this for the first time. Can there be a more fundamentally democratic act than taking up your right to vote and claiming your stake in determining who rules?

A pamphlet circulated by the African National Congress (ANC) at that time captured much of what many of us were feeling. 'So much hope, pain and suffering have been expended in the achievement of this dream,' it said. After nearly four years of negotiations, much of which had taken place far from the lives and preoccupations of ordinary people, a peaceful transfer of power to a legitimate government had finally taken place. 'Legitimacy entitles us to say proudly: this is our government, not this government or this illegitimate regime. The mistakes we make will be our errors. Neither hostile nor even benign prescriptions can any longer be imposed on us. We will share in decision-making.' The pamphlet went on to say that our struggle had been bound together by the 'golden thread of non-racialism', a thread that had held us together in exile, in the torture chambers and in the hell-holes of our prisons. It was this thread, as well as the just nature of our cause, that had also inspired the rest of the world to set up solidarity movements without parallel in history.

On the first day of voting in that famous election, 27 April 1994, I was an hour or two up the east coast from Cape Town in the fishing village of Hawston, close to Hermanus, monitoring the election there on behalf of the ANC. As at many of the thousands of polling stations across the country, the logistics of our first democratic election in Hawston were problematic. There weren't enough ballot papers or officials. Voters queued for many, many hours almost without exception and almost without complaint. There was no water or food available, neither for the voters nor for the polling station staff. But, as anyone who was there or who has read about those most amazing of days will recall, the people of South Africa waited quietly, with dignity, to share in the sacrament of democracy. They would not be denied. They had waited too long, given too much.

On the second day of voting I was in Bellville, in Cape Town's northern suburbs, which is traditionally a stronghold of white Afrikaners. It was a very tiring day. There were so many emotions swirling around within all of us. People queued for hour upon hour, white middle-aged women standing patiently next to their African maids in their pink or light-blue overalls. Officials went without food and water and didn't seem to mind or notice. The people waited. Our people. They waited and they smiled and they seized their right with both hands. There was hardly a person there who didn't realise the importance of making their mark on the ballot paper that day.

Can there be a more important human condition than dignity? Without it, we are bitter, downtrodden, unheard, humiliated, embarrassed and disempowered. With dignity, we are peaceful, collegial, kind, compassionate and even at times cohesive. The notion of dignity resides at the very heart of our constitutional settlement here in South Africa and is fundamental to our bill of rights. It is implicit in the right to equality. It is assumed within the right to political association, in our freedom of speech and in our freedom of movement. How can we have dignity if we cannot go where we wish, say what we want and join with others who share our passions and our dreams? Along with equality, freedom and justice, dignity is one of our most important principles. Apartheid stripped our dignity away every bit as brutally and systematically as it curtailed our other fundamental rights. Voting in a real election gave it back again.

In Parliament on that first day of the first session I thought of those whose sacrifices had brought us to that air-conditioned hall filled with singing, happy, colourful people. I thought of my struggling, generous father. I would have given anything to have taken his hand that day and led him up Parliament Street. How proud he would have been along with scores of other parents and compatriots.

And I thought too of the other reason, or rather the other person, who made this moment so very special. He sat not far from me in a navy suit and white shirt with more gravitas and dignity than seemed possible for a living person. Nelson Rolihlahla Mandela. Madiba. To be a minister in the first Cabinet of Nelson Mandela was almost too much to grasp, even in the midst of the pomp and ceremony. The election that brought Madiba to the presidency had been an extraordinary event. South Africa had stood on the brink of war and catastrophe, divided against itself. Now we all sat in the same parliamentary chamber, united in a government of national unity led by our Madiba.

I sat at my bench that late autumn afternoon in Cape Town and readied myself to recite my affirmation of office rather than the oath. A torrent of emotions and thoughts coursed through me. Here, at this moment, was the death knell of apartheid. Here, at this moment, was the birth of a legitimate state acting on behalf of its people for the first time.

It may have been Day One, but the roots of this moment are to be found far back in South African legal, constitutional and political history. 'One person, one vote' was adopted by the African National Congress as official policy in 1943. This policy of universal suffrage found powerful and indeed indelible expression in the Freedom Charter, which was drawn up by South African democrats in 1955 following an extensive, nationwide consultative process. The vote was the *leitmotif* of freedom fighters' demands and the core issue of the liberation movement's legal and constitutional struggle for justice. The central issue was not the creation of a bill of rights, nor was it equality, nor was it even the freedoms black people didn't have. At that momentous time, it wasn't even about the need to overcome poverty, provide services and dismantle the other shameful trappings of apartheid. On those two days on which we South Africans voted for the first time, the central issue was universal suffrage. The vote was the prime determinant of the kind of society we wanted to build. Its eventual expression in those two days in late April 1994 was a glorious, spiritual affair that held the world in awe. Apart from my own personal feelings, I was deeply aware of the enormous importance that moment would have in determining the kind of South Africa the ANC would create. After three hundred years, freedom had arrived and, with it, the chance to put into practice at least some of the ideas on social justice, dignity and constitution making that I had been gathering and developing over the years, as these memoirs will make clear.

Although this work is not intended to be strictly autobiographical, some of the personal events and relationships that marked my life have shaped the way in which I think about things and help explain my passion and interest in different notions. If, for instance, I had never sat in the cinema as a boy watching a newsreel depicting the liberation of Auschwitz, I would not have taken such a special interest later in the Nuremberg Trials and their applicability to South Africa. My career grappling with international law, participating in UN conferences, proposing a truth commission and helping to author a country's constitution has its roots in a piece of scratchy black-and-white cinematography that has haunted me for my entire life.

It is also true that my family and social environment have had a powerful impact on me. They have shaped how I feel about intimate things such as one's right to privacy, about education and the power of the word, about religion, about dignity and about duty.

When I was a boy, the family toilet was situated at the far end of the yard. Getting there was dark and unpleasant and scary. This was not particularly unusual for a South African then, nor is it even now, but when I joined the Cabinet as minister responsible for water, my early experience of sanitation resonated in every policy I established.

In my twenties, I was prevented from attending a residential university because my family couldn't afford it. Instead I became a teacher. This instilled in me a deep appreciation of the privilege of learning and a love of engaging and growing young minds. As Minister of Education, how could such experiences not weigh on me as I mulled over the restructuring of the higher education sector?

This memoir is not all rose-coloured recollection and fanciful idealism. There are aspects of my life of which I am not proud, decisions I have made that I regret and people I have encountered whom I should have stood up to or fought off.

The ANC that has been my whole life may have wavered in its mission in recent years. The heady principles and morals we championed even unto death appear to have been tarnished by the complacency and acquisitiveness of power. Some leaders have become greedy, self-serving and cynical, and the serpents of ethnicity and populism have wound their powerful coils around our ankles. I have no doubt that there are many South Africans, of all colours, who retain the fundamental values of the Freedom Charter and our Constitution, but we shall need to assert ourselves. I only hope that in time the ANC as an organisation will recall and revere the things that created and inspired it. Perhaps this book will help.

This is a story of many journeys. It is the story of my own journey to adulthood and comprehension. It is the story of the ANC's victorious struggle against apartheid. But most of all it is the story of my country's journey from the darkness of injustice to the dappled sunlight of freedom.

1

Formative Years

I was born on 8 October 1934, in a small country town called Stanger (now KwaDukuza), which lies about seventy kilometres north of the port city of Durban. It's a small, unremarkable town surrounded by sugar-cane fields. Everything grows well in Stanger. Flowers bloom in the gardens, lawns are neatly cut, and trees line the streets. Outside beautiful, spacious houses, maids and servants loiter and chat in the sunshine. The cricket square is meticulously prepared and the tennis courts are well maintained.

But I didn't grow up in this Stanger. That was the Stanger where the white residents lived, the forbidden zone on the mountain side of Durban Road. I would never have dared go there as a child, even though it was a short walk from the small, cramped house where my family stayed. There were no tree-lined streets or neat pavements in the part of Stanger in which I spent my first nineteen years.

It wasn't that the police stopped you from going to the white side of town, unless you were African, nor were there fences or walls. Such was the effect of racialism that proscriptive measures like these were transmitted by a kind of osmosis. I knew, instinctively, that the white suburbs of Stanger were out of bounds. Only on my return from exile, when I was fifty-seven years old, did I venture into the forbidden zone for the first time. By then, of course, everything was changing.

The part of Stanger in which I grew up was an area of great poverty. There were ten of us in the Asmal family, my parents and eight children, and we lived in a small, two-bedroomed house. The toilet was a bucket located outside in a wooden shack. We had to pick our way through the chicken run to get to it – an ordeal for me especially at night or when a subtropical storm blew in from the Indian Ocean.

My father, Ahmed, came originally from a town called Kathor in Surath, India. In 1898 he and his family sailed to South Africa to join his grandfather Ebrahim, who was already settled there and had a thriving merchant's business in Durban. Grandfather Ebrahim was famous in Durban for his acute business sense and for zooming around town on a big, noisy motorbike. He must have passed some of his daredevil genes on to my father, as he too never shirked a challenge or failed to stand up to bullies. On one occasion the white mayor of Stanger was about to hit my younger brother with a sjambok when my father grabbed it and pulled it away from him. On another occasion he nearly knocked down a well-known lawyer. Towards the end of his life he was charged for punching the dustman and paid an 'admission of guilt' fine. The dustman was never again quite so sloppy when it came to emptying our 44-gallon drum of rubbish. But my father was also extraordinarily generous and caring of those around him.

My mother, Rasool, was South African-born and -bred. She and my father were brought together by a matchmaker, as was the custom then. They were married in 1918. After their marriage my parents moved from Durban and settled in the not-too-distant town of Stanger, where my father opened a grocery shop specialising in fruit and sweets. By the time war broke out in 1939, our financial situation had not improved: we owned neither our house nor a car. We were perhaps 'discreet lower-middle-class'. My father's grocery shop sold the best homemade ice cream in town. He relished making it in a big tub almost as much as we enjoyed sampling it. The counter top was always full of long jars crammed with chocolate-covered coconut sweets and other delicious goodies. We sold icicles for one penny each. I am sure that's where I developed my sweet tooth.

We lived upstairs from the shop in Reynold Street (now renamed Chief Albert Luthuli Street), in a tin-and-wood structure. It was often hot and usually crowded. The lavatories were outside, three of them. Anyone in the street could use them and they were open to the road beyond. From an early age I began to value privacy very much indeed.

As I suffered terribly from asthma as a child, my parents decided against sending me to school until I was nine. They wanted me where they could keep an eye on me during the day and my bed was moved to a small space under the shop counter. Here, equipped with a pillow and blanket, I spent much time listening to the world around me, to people coming and going and interacting with my shopkeeper father. I learnt a great deal in this way. Though I only started school at the age of nine, I completed my matric at eighteen, having received 'double promotion' because of the knowledge acquired in my father's shop.

Every now and then, the local police sergeant used to come into the shop, after lock-up time. The sergeant was an Afrikaner and, like other Afrikaans-speaking public officials, he caused some trepidation as he walked around Stanger. The Afrikaners were somehow more intimidating than their English-speaking counterparts.

But here was the police sergeant sitting down with my father to listen to the crackling, screeching sound from the radio. As a seven-year-old, invisible to the sergeant, I was intrigued by the apparent friendliness of my father, who did not speak Afrikaans. The two sat listening to what I subsequently discovered were pro-Nazi broadcasts from the Zeesen radio service, produced by a South African expatriate, Erik Holm.

As I collected material for my scrapbook on what was called 'the war effort', I discovered that Zeesen's obsessively anti-Semitic broadcasts were meant to mobilise Afrikaner sentiment against the war. My father did not approve of the war against Hitler though he was no anti-Semite. He thought it illogical that while the French, the British and South Africa's Prime Minister, General Smuts, demanded support for the anti-Nazi campaign, in their empires or at home they maintained racist and colonial systems based on violence.

I realised from listening to the two men discussing the radio broadcasts that, though my father was not a formally lettered man, he knew all about the latest news and current affairs, and he enjoyed reading newspapers, something I learnt from him. He and the sergeant debated the news heatedly. My father talked about colonialism and about recent political developments in our own neck of the woods. In his own way he was an anti-colonialist. This was a real education for me.

In the lead-up to the Second World War, the 'Fusion' government had held sway in South Africa. This was a parliamentary alliance forged in the 1930s between the United Party of Jan Smuts and the National Party headed by General J.B.M. Hertzog. It was during this period that legislation was enacted that consolidated and entrenched the process of segregation and strengthened the foundations for apartheid. Qualified Africans in the Cape were removed from the common voters' roll, a right they had held since 1853, and ownership of land by Africans was pegged to a mere thirteen per cent of South Africa's landmass.

My father was a serious-looking man, forbidding even. He wasn't tall but had a commanding voice. He obtained a driving licence in 1932, and I have a photo of him sitting proudly at the wheel of his Oakland, with three of his cronies. He inculcated in us a sense of curiosity and whetted my interest in the world. He also had an extraordinary generosity. As a shopkeeper he gave credit to everyone, especially to those white women whose husbands were fighting in North Africa or Italy, even though he didn't really believe in the war. He not only extended them credit, but he gave them food parcels to send to their husbands at the front.

A local white lawyer who knew that my father's generosity had pushed him to the edge of financial ruin came round one day and spoke to him. 'Ahmed, so many people owe you so much money, yet you won't make them pay you,' he said. 'How can I bankrupt these women?' my father replied. Before long, he lost everything. If he had been more ruthless, he could have evaded the ignominy of bankruptcy. Perhaps if he had been less scrupulous about cheating African people, a common business stratagem in the 1940s, he would have kept his beloved grocery shop for a little longer. The sugar-mill owners in the area were anything but scrupulous about exploiting their workforce. They would load dozens of their workers at a time into the company lorries and drive them down to a 'friendly' shop. There they would be encouraged to run tabs and borrow to buy the overpriced bread, milk, sugar and blankets that were on offer. The employees had no choice. The prices were fixed, and the shopkeepers and the mill owners pocketed generous profits.

My father never condoned such schemes, but being a humanitarian had its downside. To be a successful businessman, my father once told me, you have to be tough, hard-hearted and a bit of a bastard. After all, the Catholic patron saint for rogues and brigands and for merchants, he added, is the same! So maybe it was for the best that his grocery store went under. If it hadn't, my brothers and I might have remained in Stanger selling fruit and ice cream, and all that I have seen and done would be somebody else's story.

The bankruptcy had an immediate and profound impact on our family's fortunes. The car went. The shop was gone and my father left Stanger to seek work. He took on piecemeal jobs as a shop assistant or salesman in distant towns and sent home what he could. He was gone for long periods, though when he returned there was much joy and excitement. No one was more pleased than I was to see his familiar frame in the doorway; his red beard, his rough face and his kind eyes.

Though my father never read a book, he appreciated both their power and his bookish son's love for them. He brought me home books so often from his travels that he had to order a specially built bookshelf with a glass door. I have no idea where he got the books from, perhaps from Durban or second-hand markets he happened across on his travels. One or two of them were first editions that I devoured with the relish of an acolyte. Others were tattily covered tomes rescued from the bonfire. I built up a wonderful collection of books, all of which were later scattered as my role in the exiled liberation movement became known and the apartheid regime stepped up its harassment of my family.

Following the bankruptcy, we left our house and moved about a hundred yards away to an even smaller house in Reynold Street. If the flat above the shop had been hot and crowded, our new rented home was much worse. By now my sisters had left home but there were still nine of us living together. My eldest brother, Ebrahim, and his wife shared one of the bedrooms; my second brother, Mohammed, the other; and the rest of us slept in the remaining bedroom. Even when we moved again to Colenbrander Street on the outskirts of Stanger, my parents had to put up partitions which reached about two-thirds of the way to the ceiling and didn't really provide any privacy at all.

We slept under heavy eiderdowns that intensified the stifling Stanger summer heat. The eiderdowns soon smelled rank and, in the morning, were gathered up into a big, odiferous pile ready for use the next night. During the war years we children slept in pyjamas that my ever-resourceful mother made out of flour bags.

But while the bedrooms were uncomfortable and untidy, the sitting room was sacrosanct. It was a space to be kept neat and clean where the family could gather and where we could entertain guests and friends.

My mother was uncompromising on the need to keep it this way: clean and clear of clutter. It was the public face of the Asmal family.

We had a shower and basin in a very small room for the use of all of us, and once again there was an outside toilet at Colenbrander Street, but at least it was for use by our family alone. Though there was no view into the toilet from the road this time, the trip to the toilet, through the chickens and their mess, often in the dark, was never very pleasant. I hated those expeditions. I did have, though, some interesting conversations, full of expletives, with the night-soil removers who objected to my holding up their work by sitting on the toilet reading by candlelight. All this gave me an enduring appreciation of the dignity that is provided by decent sanitation.

My childhood was punctuated by debilitating attacks of asthma. When it got out of control and I began wheezing and straining and coughing for breath, my mother called Mr Bux, who would come with his medical kit and give me an ephedrine injection in the backside. I must have had hundreds over the years. He was not a doctor but provided medical assistance for a small fee. My mother tried everything to bring me relief. When the family fasted at Ramadan, only I was allowed to eat. When the children went to school, I remained at home. Sometimes I wondered if she'd prefer that I die rather than suffer so, day after day. We didn't know then that a bit of exercise is good for asthmatics, so I was kept in cotton wool, not allowed to strain or run or compete physically. When I reached eighteen years, one doctor recommended a daily dose of whiskey mixed with the yellow of an egg and some nutmeg. And while the liquor is not exactly a mainstream curative, it has given me a solace that I have enjoyed, in greater or lesser amounts, to this day. I don't know what whiskey I drank then, but in Dublin I was introduced to Irish whiskey, which remains my favourite.

A second positive outcome of my asthmatic condition was that I became involved in cricket. I couldn't play the game, unlike my brother Dawood, who played for a team of South African 'Non-Europeans' in Kenya in 1958 under the captaincy of Basil D'Oliveira. Nevertheless, there was often a need for an umpire and I enjoyed being part of the action. From time to time I used to assist illiterate traders or shopkeepers to write or read letters they wanted to send or understand, and so, when the position of club secretary of the local Muslim cricket club, the

Commercial Cricket Club of Stanger, became vacant, I was asked to step in, even though I was only thirteen at the time. One of my first acts as club secretary was to introduce a motion to open the club to everyone, regardless of race or religion. This was duly passed. It was my first small taste of idealism in politics.

I retain some recollection of what was happening politically in 1940s South Africa, though this information swirled around in my head without purpose or clarity at the time. I had vaguely heard of the 'Africans' Claims' document adopted in December 1943 by the African National Congress (ANC). The document sought to take up the promise of greater participation in government for all oppressed peoples offered by Churchill and Roosevelt in the 1941 Atlantic Charter. It even contained a comprehensive bill of rights. The document was rejected by the Prime Minister, Jan Smuts, which led me to the realisation that Smuts was both a political charlatan and a racist. I remember, too, the famous 'Three Doctors' Pact' signed in 1947 by Drs A.B. Xuma of the ANC, Yusuf Dadoo of the Transvaal Indian Congress and Monty Naicker of the Natal Indian Congress, after a series of clashes between Indians and Africans in Durban. This again set out ordinary South Africans' demands for basic rights such as universal suffrage and freedom of movement. I was proud that this document was the first such agreement between a 'majority' and a 'minority' about the future of their country.

For me as a boy in Stanger, the 'Three Doctors' Pact' was a milestone on the path of non-racialism, giving me a clear sense of what it was to be South African. But the Pact also provided me with a sense of the international scope of the struggle for human rights. The declaration concluded by urging that 'a vigorous campaign be immediately launched and that every effort be made to compel the Union Government to implement the United Nations' decisions and to treat the Non-European peoples in South Africa in conformity with the principles of the United Nations Charter'. The struggle for human rights, I saw, was both non-racial in principle and international in scope.

I remember meeting that extraordinary leader Yusuf Dadoo when I was still young. He had been banned by the apartheid government and was not supposed to travel. But he came to Stanger, illegally, to encourage the collection of ideas and petitions that would lead to the formulation in 1955 of the Freedom Charter, one of South Africa's most important struggle documents. The Charter was a widely consulted, visionary declaration of rights and is the foundation for our country's present democratic Constitution.

I can also recall the sense of siege we felt when the National Party took power in 1948 and began to tighten the screws on 'non-white' lives. I am reminded even now of how my black compatriots felt about apartheid: apprehension, fear, mistrust, pessimism.

But these are youthful recollections and are frosted by the passage of time. It was only a few years later when I got to know Chief Albert Luthuli that my thoughts and understandings started to develop into a more concrete perspective on the world.

With my father's ruin and departure in search of temporary work, it was left to my mother to hold the family together. This was especially tough through the long, late-war years of the mid-1940s. With income from my father and from the two eldest brothers who lived with us, it was she who ensured there was food on the table, shirts on our backs and shoes polished for school. Though her diabetes caused her to suffer a great deal, this did not affect her infinite capacity to rear and care for us. In a male-dominated and heavily patriarchal society, mothers were usually relegated to the background, but in our case my mother was the anchor who provided stability and guidance in our lives.

I don't think my mother ever went to school. It was inconceivable then for a Muslim girl, and it had not changed much by my childhood. My very bright sister Khatija was forced to leave school at the age of twelve because of pressure from local Muslims, who told my parents that they would no longer frequent the shop if she was allowed to continue to secondary school. She has been angry about this ever since, and from her I take my enthusiasm for women's education.

With no formal education, my mother ran a household of ten virtually single-handed. She instilled in us the absolute need to live within our means. Some sacrifices had to be made, and it was painful for all of us, and especially for her, that the brightest of the Asmals, the second-born son, Mohammed (whom we called Nullabhai), had to leave at the end of primary school in order to augment the meagre family income.

My mother was illiterate in the precise sense of the world. But her inability to read and write did not preclude her from holding deep feelings for education, which she nurtured among the male children in particular. Ours was a close-knit family and she encouraged those who had to leave school early for work in order to assist those who were still at school or who hoped to enter higher education. She didn't understand our homework, but she insisted that we did it. We were too poor to give *zakāt* – a tithe for charity paid by those who could afford it – but my mother's approach was one of solidarity rather than of charity.

My mother raised no obstacle to my political awakening, even when later, as a school teacher, I supported the boycott of schools and brought the iconic Albert Luthuli, president of the African National Congress, to our home, an unheard of experience for most Indian families. All my mother wanted was that I should explain what I was doing. Too many books, she used to tease me, too many ideas, for a small head!

Small-town politics and narrow parochialism passed her by. She lived for her family though she did not entirely subscribe to the sentiment that 'every beetle is a gazelle in the eyes of a mother', because she could be critical of wrong turns and misbehaviour. There were many pressures exerted on her to conform to the mores of a small country town. She defended all of us from the outrageous demands and the sly hints of narrow-minded bigots. I recall one such incident when some neighbours complained to her that I was setting a bad example as I was too obsessed with books, listened to 'Western' music and did not show the appropriate degree of religious piety. I was a *moffie*, they declared – a terrible insult at the time. I recall my mother's anger at what she considered to be abuse of her son.

If she chastised us for our behaviour it was with words, never with her hand. In a society where corporal punishment was *de rigueur* in homes, schools and prisons, this discipline of hers set a remarkable example for me and nurtured a lifelong opposition to corporal punishment. I made a small salute in her direction when I successfully defended the abolition of such violence against children before the Constitutional Court during my tenure as Minister of Education.

Ours was a very argumentative family, with debate and loud conversations among the siblings: this in a traditional society where silence before elders was considered to be the only form of respect. Not once did our mother show the slightest inclination to silence us. We loved her because of her tolerance, her gentleness and understanding, values which were not entirely common currency among our relatives in Stanger.

She had little to laugh about, what with the demands made on her, an absent husband and, before long, two married sons under the same roof. She made time for all of us and attended to our needs. In my case, she had to respond to my constant attacks of asthma from the age of three onwards. Quite why asthmatics required special treatment is not clear to me now, but I was not about to oppose the special care and attention I received from my mother. She accepted an Asmal solution for the fast during Ramadan by appointing me official taster of the food for the family. This I had to do standing up in the pantry in the dark, to ensure that I did not enjoy the breach of the requirement to fast during daylight hours.

Although she had a central role in the family, I was strongly attached to my father. He always said he couldn't help me with my intellectual endeavours, but if I ever needed a shoulder to cry on, he was available. He used to tap his shoulder when he would tell me this. After he retired, I went with him to mosque every Friday, and I imagine he enjoyed hearing his friends pointing out his devout son. The day he died in 1958, I gave up going to mosque. I had been reading Bertrand Russell's *Why I Am Not a Christian*. My mother was upset and could not understand why a book on Christianity could influence Muslim beliefs.

At the time I was growing up, Stanger was a very colonial and racist town. When the white magistrate walked in the Main Street, as he did every evening, you went to the other side of the pavement if you weren't a white person. You never crossed his path. I became acutely aware of racism when I was chased away from a 'white' shop where I had gone to buy a newspaper. The experience stung a great deal.

As children we were not only argumentative, we were inquisitive, and we started asking questions: 'Why can't this happen? Why can't I go to a white school? Why do I have to go an Indian school?' Of course, asking those questions created fears and anxiety in the family. In such a small town, everyone was terrified of politics. Talk was dangerous.

The school I went to was by law an all-Indian one. Many of the kids used to walk eight or nine kilometres to school, without the benefit of breakfast. They were the children of Indian labourers, grandchildren of Indian indentured workers who had been brought to South Africa to work on the sugar-cane plantations in the middle of the nineteenth century. There was only one high school for Indians in the Lower Tugela area, a magisterial district that stretched from Groutville up to Maphumulo. At least a school meal was provided, usually sugar beans and rice, even if it did contain maggots and insects. For many children, it was the only daily meal they ate. There was enormous poverty everywhere. I'll never forget the ubiquitous sight of my fellow classmates with sores around their eyes, a classic and vivid sign of true poverty.

I was one of the lucky ones. We had to walk only a couple of kilometres to the Stanger Indian Secondary School. One had to cross the river to get to it, as there was no bridge. The best place to cross was near the police station, but if it had been raining and the water was too high, we had to turn back and go home. I had one jacket, one pair of grey trousers and one pair of shoes. These would grow more and more threadbare until enough money could be found to replace them. My shoes became so worn-down that on one occasion a rusty nail went straight through the sole and into my foot.

If there was a big contrast between the white part of town and the Indian section, comparing the white area to the black township of Shakaville was on another scale altogether. The deprivation was astonishing, even to the eyes of a child. There were no tarred roads, no shops, no recreational facilities, no trees or even any pavements. Houses were lean-to, fragile affairs hardly strong enough to keep the draught out, let alone the driving subtropical rain. We weren't allowed to go to Shakaville. I tried once to chair a debate at a school there, but we were not allowed to enter the township.

Almost all the teachers at the secondary school I went to weren't qualified, so many of my contemporaries missed out on opportunities because their curiosity wasn't whetted or their talents drawn out. There were two teachers who were graduates and, though they tried their best to encourage students in their areas of expertise, for the most part we were left to the mercies of the ignorant and the vicious. I don't have any false nostalgia about my school because it was an appalling place. All we had in the way of teaching aids was the 'spit factor', putting spit on our fingers to turn the pages of our textbooks.

There was one teacher, though, a Mr Keerath, who had a genuine love for literature and language. Although he was very strict and distanced himself from his pupils, he inspired an interest in me in books, dictionaries, and the discovery of language. He encouraged me to learn ten new words every day. But even the influence of a good teacher was limited in that educational system, as the school was a closed institution with a highly authoritarian administration.

Because the teachers were unqualified, they felt uncomfortable, and some of them resorted to physical violence in order to control the children. One of the worst used to take a ruler with a steel end and hit us on the knuckles with it until we bled. Indian children at that time were a pretty docile lot really, but corporal punishment was pervasive. So too was the rote learning and cramming that were forced upon us. These two dimensions of the education system, corporal punishment and rote learning, were issues I would come to tackle later when I became Minister of Education.

The teachers also gave no consideration to the impact of poverty on performance. The poor kids, the ones who walked kilometres and kilometres to school with no shoes, who had no place to bath or do homework, who were exhausted and hungry, were the ones who got beaten the most. They were beaten for their inattention, for their backwardness and for their smell. They were beaten because their parents worked in the sugar fields all day long and had no energy or time to pay them any heed. They were beaten because there would never be an enraged father marching through the school gates nor a tearful mother upbraiding the principal. They were beaten because when you are hungry, it's hard to learn and remember.

In spite of the obstacles and hardships, my family placed its trust in education. My father used to say, 'If you come first you get half-a-crown, if you come second you get two shillings, if you come third you get a kick in the backside.' But we never got a kick as he also disapproved of corporal punishment. We were the only household that I knew of like that in Stanger. Our respect for our parents developed through our close relationship, not because of the threat of violence. So I grew up in the absence of physical coercion and in a very inquiring household.

We didn't have a car and holidays were unheard of. My father was absent, more often than not. But there was no disgruntlement among us, no demands for better things in a society where wealth was a powerful index of status. Ours was a poor but happy, boisterous, loud family.

Every night, with Mr Keerath's encouragement in my head, I tried to learn ten new words, together with their etymology. I used to practise my new words at mealtimes and it would drive my family round the bend. 'Don't be so punctilious,' I might say to brother Sonny. 'Don't start with that nonsense, Kader,' he might reply, supported by a chorus of good-humoured family agreement. As mealtimes were so noisy, sometimes I would quietly practise the new words to myself. 'Are you mad, Kader?' Nullabhai used to ask.

With my father usually absent and my eldest brother often quiet, the loudest voices invariably belonged to Nullabhai, Sonny and me. We produced a great cacophony of noise. We would shout and gesticulate and eat and argue all at the same time. My mother would happily take in the growing crescendo of conversation; her brood enjoying each other, life, constant debate, ideas and arguments. Our meals were so noisy at times that the neighbours would ask if we were fighting.

Meanwhile, my father was packing tins and shelves in some faraway shop in a small town out there on the road, perhaps in the Midlands or somewhere along the Dolphin Coast. He was probably just starting out on a ten- or twelve-hour shift, getting the shop ready for the morning. He would be living at the back of the shop, probably sleeping on a mattress on the floor, wondering, perhaps, from time to time when he would be home and where he might find me a book.

Of my five brothers, the one I was closest to during my childhood was Nullabhai. He was about five years older than I was and was the cleverest of all the brothers. With sufficient resources, he could have gone on to do anything. I admired him greatly. He took me, Sonny and Abubaker under his wing. He pushed us really hard on our schoolwork, in part because he knew how important it was and in part to make up for his own lack of education after it was cut short. He and my eldest brother, Ebrahim, whom we called Mota, had gone to work in a garage owned by an uncle. Nullabhai was only twelve at the time, but the money they brought home was essential for the survival of the rest of the family.

Nullabhai retained great interest in and enthusiasm for academic work and went on to be a respected bookkeeper. He was really more like a chartered accountant, which I'm sure he would have been had the opportunity been available. He took great pride in seeing his younger brother go on to get his degree in medicine, from a major international university. Nullabhai was a real go-getter. He had enormous energy and was quite obsessed with learning.

In the claustrophobic society of the 1950s, with police informers and the passage of savage laws by the apartheid regime, it would have been easy for me to have retreated into a selfish, private world. But this was the period of my political education. In 1952 the Defiance Campaign broke out in South Africa. Based on Gandhi's notion of *satyagraha* – non-violent protest and resistance – thousands of South Africans of all races joined together to oppose the newly elected National Party's first initiatives to clothe racial separation in the armour of the state.

Several of the Natal Indian Congress's leaders, including Monty Naicker and J.N. Singh, were arrested in the campaign and sentenced to terms of imprisonment. They were marched daily in their prison uniforms right down Stanger's dusty main street. I'll never forget seeing them in their khaki short pants and red shirts, in the middle of winter. They seemed impervious to their situation, heroic.

The seeds of my own political consciousness began to germinate that winter. I undertook there and then to lead my school's stay-at-home campaign in solidarity. It was during the Defiance Campaign that I engaged for the first time in organised political action.

Of course in those days, Indians couldn't join the ANC, so that wasn't an option open to me. I didn't like the idea of organisations that were limited by race and so didn't feel inclined to join the Natal Indian Congress, as closely linked as it was at the time to the ANC. In any case it was a rule of engagement that teachers could not join political parties on pain of dismissal. Instead, I became involved politically on a more local level. I was asked as a young man to become the secretary of the local ratepayers' association, though I was not a ratepayer. Perhaps the shopkeepers, traders and garage owners who urged me to help them were impressed by my depth of experience as secretary of the local cricket club! Anyway, I agreed.

Before long, an important issue surfaced that forced the members of the ratepayers' association to engage more directly with political matters. As secretary, I was pitched head first into the morass of South Africa's burgeoning system of apartheid. Unsurprisingly, the big question concerned race: who should be allowed to live in certain areas and who should not. The infamous Group Areas Act was passed by Parliament in 1950 and, as a result, the government delineated particular suburbs and residential areas for habitation by one or other race group. Ordinarily the nice, central urban areas were demarcated for white use and the more remote, poorly equipped areas were set aside for coloured or Indian people, while Africans were shunted off to special townships miles away from the centre of towns. This demarcation was carried out by a panel known as the Group Areas Board, which heard submissions from interested parties and then made its recommendations to government for implementation. Throughout the country, in nearly every *dorp* and town, Africans, coloureds and Indians were uprooted from the centre of town and sent by state diktat to outlying areas. What would the Board decide to do in Stanger?

At the time the Natal Indian Congress was leading a campaign to boycott the Board's hearings, arguing that the proceedings were merely the pretext for a racist extravaganza, but local businesspeople were undecided or unsure about what to do. Many felt they should at least make representations to the Board to declare their preferences and interests. Their rationale was that they should collaborate with the Board to save their shops. Stanger was unusual in that it was the only town in South Africa where the majority of the inhabitants were Indian. Africans in Stanger had been corralled into a distant township, as they were everywhere else in South Africa, while the whites lived in a small enclave off the Durban Road. The effects remain today.

As the Board hearing date approached, my mother's brother Goolam, who led the ratepayers' association, let me know in no uncertain terms that I should keep my mouth shut. Goolam was a powerful and influential businessman in Stanger. He also employed two of my brothers. Goolam was the driving force behind the group who wanted to make submissions. He wanted to present Indian plans to the Board and make proposals. I told Goolam that I would refrain from speaking on condition that none of these alternative plans were presented to the

Board. I even promised my mother I wouldn't speak though I told her, 'We can't do this. We can't do this.'

The day of the Board hearings arrived. The small Stanger hall was packed with people, perhaps as many as a thousand. I sat right at the back and listened to events as they began to unfold. Before long, sure enough, Goolam stood up and announced that he had a set of proposals he had developed that would assist the Board in their deliberations. I then walked to the stage and stood ready to address the community. It was my first time in the bright light of public scrutiny and I was terrified. But I felt strongly about the issue, passionately. I agreed with the Indian Congress that people should not dignify the deliberations of this Board with alternative plans. The Board had an ardently and deliberately racist agenda and had been established to execute nothing less than the systematic racial division of our country and our community.

'We are Muslims, Hindus, Christians, merchants, workers, poor and rich,' I told the assembled citizenry of Stanger. 'But we are also South Africans and we all belong to this country.' South Africans of all races should live together, I cried, not be divided by bureaucrats. 'I grew up next to poor whites and Africans. And when we had fights we didn't fight as Indians or whites or Africans, we fought each other as kids.' How could we suggest, as Goolam was proposing, that poor people or whites live somewhere else? That condoned the very division and racism that the government and the Board were planning.

There was uproar in the hall, but the sentiment had swung away from Goolam and behind me. Overwhelmingly, the Indian community of Stanger decided not to collaborate with the Group Areas Board or to consent to alternative plans to help the Board carry out its work.

The next day, as I walked down Cooper Street, Stanger's main thoroughfare, illiterate Tamil trolley traders – called ghalloowallahs – came up to me. 'Am I also a South African?' they asked me. It was very touching. For the first time, they thought of themselves as belonging to more than just an ethnic or religious or racial group. They were part of a bigger thing, a nation, made up of all the shades and varieties and values that give true diversity such power.

I had always wanted to go to university. But by the time I matriculated in 1952, the family couldn't afford it. The second best option was for me to become a teacher. In order to raise the funds for teacher training college, my father and I went to friends, associates and wealthy members of the Indian community to borrow money. It was one of the most humiliating experiences of my life: seeing my father, hands clasped behind his back, asking for help on my behalf. It was excruciating. When you go as a beggar, nobody asks you to sit down and make yourself comfortable. You are made to stand and wait; passive, humble, desperate. I vowed never to do that to anyone, never to keep anyone standing for hours just for a moment of my time.

I learnt then about the insolence of wealth and power. My father and I went to these people, mainly wealthy Indians in Durban, and we asked for money. We got three pounds here and four pounds there and eventually we had enough. I was then able to enrol at the Springfield Teachers' Training College in Durban. The next phase of my life had begun.

I left Stanger in 1952 a very young and fairly immature man. Durban was a revelation. Springfield College was an all-Indian institution but for the first time I had decent teachers. At the beginning there were one or two Indian teachers, and most of the others were white, but collectively they were quality educators and I learnt a great deal about teaching, life and literature. One teacher introduced me to Shakespeare and made an enormous impact on me. I have loved Shakespeare ever since. The principal of the college, Alex Levine, was a very senior member of the South African Board of Deputies, an important body within the country's influential Jewish community. Israel had only just been established in the late 1940s following the UN partition plan, and Levine was passionate about Israel's place in the world. Though he was intensely religious, he was also a fierce believer in the necessity for Jews and Muslims to acknowledge their similarities and start getting along. He called me to his office one day to ask why I wasn't going to mosque on Fridays any more. He didn't ask me to sit down. He just blurted it out: 'Why don't you go to mosque? You have to go,' he told me. 'Jews and Muslims – we are Semites, monotheists, and we must stick together. Against the pantheists.' I laughed. It's funny how the closer you are, the more bitter the fight. But my faith was ebbing away, and I found the appalling conditions in which many South Africans lived, coupled with the increasing burden of apartheid, of more concern than otherworldly matters.

I stayed in a flat in the centre of Durban with a cousin. We had barely any money left after paying for our fees, books and clothing. All the same we had the time of our young lives. For the first time, I met Hindus and Tamils and Christians whom I could relate to. My best friends were no longer only Muslims. I also greatly enjoyed the repartee and discussions at the college. We talked about liberation and war, about literature and history. We thought, we debated, we argued, we met new people, we engaged our peers as our equals, we asked questions and we demanded answers. All this was soon under attack as the iron fist of apartheid crushed intellectual curiosity and stripped educational institutions of the capacity to stimulate and inspire.

I enjoyed English and history, did pretty well at biology and struggled in maths. I never seriously got to grips with what maths was all about. But English really captured my attention and imagination. I loved studying the English language and, with decent teachers, it became a lifelong passion.

I stretched my finances to buy cigarettes and we had to keep whiskey in the flat, for medicinal purposes of course! I read left-wing papers like the *Guardian* and *New Age*, both of which were later banned, and even helped to sell the *Guardian* at the Victoria Bus Station in Durban, where passers-by sometimes objected vociferously.

Two happy years at Springfield instilled in me a great passion for teaching. I could think of no better way of making one's way through life than by helping and nurturing young minds. I was ready to go out in the world to unleash the enthusiasm I had developed for educating young people.

In 1954 the Natal Provincial Administration, which had its headquarters in a big building in Pietermaritzburg, assigned me my first job as a teacher. I was 'deployed' to a school in Darnall, a small country town about fifteen kilometres from Stanger. Darnall is what Americans might call a company town. The sugar mill was the only show in town and all activities, enterprises and employment radiated from the sugar silos like a cobweb from a spider. I could not say that I was looking forward to teaching at an Indian school. I wanted to teach at a school without any qualifying adjective.

South Africa in the mid- to late 1950s was a country whose illness of racial bigotry had begun to take command of its body. The National Party had swept to power, taking all by surprise, and immediately set about implementing a radical plan of social engineering called apartheid. Stanger, like all the rest of South Africa, became a frightening place. All around us signs were erected barring non-white people from making use of public facilities such as swimming pools, libraries and train station platforms. Africans were declared non-permanent visitors to urban areas and were required, under pain of large fines or instant imprisonment, to carry passes authorising their presence in the cities.

The factories, mills and mines of South Africa had long been subject to racial barriers and the separation of the workforce. And the exploitative practices that companies had been using for years were now reinforced by the new Afrikaner-centred white political elite. So it was typical of the day for the white overseers and managers to live in the fancy part of Darnall and for the Africans and Indians to live cheek-by-jowl in the mill compound. All the Africans were in bachelor barracks, their families having been exiled to the rural areas of their birth. The Indians were at least allowed to live together as families, but each family usually occupied only one small room.

I was excited to be starting teaching. On the first day of my first job, I arrived at Darnall in a new suit, and feeling nervous but excited. My expectations were sadly lowered though when I was greeted by the principal and the first thing he did was hand me a cane. 'Here is your teaching aid,' he told me. 'Hit boys on the backside and girls on the hand. Off you go.' I never did hit any children, just as I had never been hit at home myself.

Darnall was a terrible place, especially on winter mornings when it was still dark as the bus arrived in the village. The school was situated up a steep hill beside the sugar mill. It was a treacherous climb when the winter rains turned the road into slippery mush. A teaching post in this godforsaken town was a bit of a come-down in the view of some of my wealthier relations, though not for my immediate family. I was one of the first Muslim teachers in Stanger and certainly the first teacher from my *kutum* or clan. It was a very big *kutum* and, while doctors, lawyers or shopkeepers were highly regarded, teachers did not enjoy much social prestige even then.

25

An Indian teacher was then paid about two-thirds of a white teacher's salary, but I was happy enough to be earning for the first time in my life. On getting my salary, I immediately paid a portion over to my mother. This left me with a few pounds on which to survive for the month. My father, who had retired when I began to teach, would never accept money from me or from anyone else for that matter. He hated the idea of depending on charity during his retirement. So I used to put some cigarettes aside for him, and we left it at that.

In spite of the overwhelming poverty, suffering and hardship which people in Darnall endured day in and day out, I was constantly amazed at their incredible hospitality and generosity. Even the poorest gave what they could to help the school. As the community had raised the money and built the school itself, it meant a lot to them. It was a way of trying to ensure that the new generation had opportunities and options the older one had missed. I used to get to Darnall very early in the morning and was always offered a cup of tea and a slice of bread. Initially, I had all the lower-middle-class prejudices about drinking from somebody else's cracked cup (in case I got some terrible disease), but I was soon overcome by the people's hospitality. It was very illuminating.

There was an extraordinarily free atmosphere in the mill compound which I passed every day. It was the first time I had encountered Africans who were not servants or night-soil workers. There were of course the usual arguments, but everybody got on with their lives and helped each other where they could. I was only just over twenty and didn't have much experience, but the situation helped to develop my sense of non-racialism and in a small way gave me an idea of what might be possible in South Africa.

The notion of staying in touch with ordinary people, of 'connecting' in the sense depicted by E.M. Forster, has been a passion, not a duty, throughout my life. We were not born to be racists. I have never lost my commitment to connecting with people. It has been like a contract for me, forged by the humble generosity and companionship of the mill compound and nurtured by decades of appreciation for the innate wisdom that people of all backgrounds possess.

While teaching at Darnall, I registered to do a bachelor's degree in English, history and politics, by correspondence, with the University of South Africa (Unisa). There were no local libraries that I was able to use and no Unisa advice centres then. I had to travel to find books. I also had to get special permission to read the 'banned' books that were on my reading list. This only added to the allure of the treasured texts. One of these books was James Joyce's *Ulysses*. I loved that book, and still do. Molly's soliloquy was the most moving thing I had ever read. It was a clarion call to my awakening consciousness. And yet, it was hardly explicit. That is one of the joys of the English language. It can be evocative without being crass or obvious. Joyce's words sang in my heart. The Irish writers and poets had begun their assault on me.

From Darnall I was promoted to my old secondary school in Stanger, in the middle of my studies. As a result I no longer had to get up so early. Still, it took me three hard years of intellectual isolation to complete my degree. Those who have done it will know that studying while working full-time is a lonely pastime. If you didn't understand something, you just had to shrug your shoulders and carry on. I wondered why there were strong inquisitions in Portugal and Spain, but not in Italy. I thought it interesting that Protestantism seemed so popular in cold countries. But there was nobody to ask and my questions remained unanswered.

Even though it wasn't quite the same as going to a real university, the books I began to read opened my eyes and my political views hardened. My mother used to say that books are dangerous. In my case, it was certainly true. Books were very dangerous. I started to understand what Marxism was all about. In South Africa at that time, Marxism was vilified, the Communist Party was banned and the ANC was labelled a communist conspiracy. The Suppression of Communism Act of 1950 was one of the most vicious pieces of legislation ever passed by the apartheid state. It enabled the state to shut down any party or organisation espousing dangerous anti-apartheid notions and ban individuals. I felt I had to find out about these dangerous ideas.

As the first stirrings of socialism took place in my mind, I realised intellectually that South Africa's most important task was to combat poverty. While apartheid was rapidly being embedded in the broader society, in Darnall fighting poverty seemed more pressing and immediate than the struggle against racism. Soon I discovered that I was wrong. Only with political equality could a free people tackle the burdens of poverty in our society.

Soon enough, apartheid came knocking at the door of my school.

The Bantu Education Act was introduced by the government in 1953. It was an iniquitous piece of legislation that prescribed a separate syllabus for African pupils, who were to be taught only the bare bones of literacy and numeracy, just enough to serve their white masters through their labour. In effect, history, science and the arts had been excised from the education of millions of young children. The Minister of Native Affairs at the time, and later Prime Minister, Hendrik Verwoerd, famously announced that Africans should not be taught to aspire to the greener pastures of their white compatriots and there was no need for them as 'hewers of wood and drawers of water' to gain knowledge they could never use. The effects of such a catastrophically inhuman attitude are still being felt in South Africa today, as underskilled teachers in formerly African schools struggle to teach a more ethical set of ideas and values. At the time I felt I simply could not go into school each day and teach the children in my care the disgraceful new curriculum called Christian National Education, a bigoted set of chauvinistic precepts if ever there was one.

As I studied for my degree and read articles and books full of ideas not generally encountered in a small town, I began to nurture the dream that I would one day be a lawyer and that I would study at a world-famous university like the London School of Economics and Political Science. I had set my heart on the LSE. It was a radical place, full of socialist ideas, unlike Oxford and Cambridge, which I was told were built on the blood of the slave trade. LSE had an altogether different pedigree. There was also a brilliant political scientist teaching there by the name of Harold Laski. I remember reading his book *A Grammar of Politics* for the political science course at Unisa, and admiring him greatly.

It was my brother Nullabhai who turned my dream of going to LSE into something tangible. He made it seem possible, and insisted on providing a financial contribution. 'You've always wanted to go to LSE,' he told me. 'Why don't you go?' Soon, I decided to go and applied for a passport.

By 1958 I'd finished my degree and was awaiting the outcome of my passport application. I had for a little while been the secretary of the Stanger Literary and Debating Society. The society was really a front for political discussions, though we did discuss literary things from time to time. A hot topic was the division between India and Pakistan, which still gripped our discussions ten years after partition. Tension between Muslims and Hindus was always there, but we used to joke about it to each other.

The debating society was my political home as teachers were not permitted to join political parties. In any case, membership of the ANC was closed to non-Africans even though I felt emotionally that the ANC was my political home. I saw no need to deepen my Indian affiliations. In truth, for a short while, I was embarrassed by them. As an eighteen-year-old I was ashamed of my father's beard and his red fez. I wondered why my father wasn't more like a white man, the apogee of value at that time. But while the embarrassment at my Indianness lasted only a few months in my teens, I was not inspired to embrace an Indians-only political organisation. It was Steve Biko, the Black Consciousness leader who came to the fore in the 1970s, who taught that acknowledging one's own identity did not necessarily mean excluding everyone else's. My preferred identity, even then, was South African, my awareness and appreciation of which were nurtured and inspired over these formative years by the powerful example of Chief Luthuli.

With the quashing of the Defiance Campaign and the growing strength of the apartheid state, the regime felt confident enough to lift its banning order on Chief Luthuli in 1955. As secretary of the Stanger Literary and Debating Society, I could think of no better person to address the community on the important issues of the day. I had met Luthuli on a number of occasions as he had been banned to the area of Groutville, just down the road from Stanger. I invited him to be the guest speaker at the next debating society meeting, scheduled to take place in the *Madrassa* hall in Stanger a week or two later. To my excitement he agreed. As many of my peers and even members of the community had not heard of Luthuli, the event at first attracted no particular interest.

But by the day of the debate, a very real atmosphere of expectation and anticipation had developed. Several hours before Luthuli was due to make his appearance, the hall was surrounded by police officers and the Special Branch. The chairman of the debating society took fright. 'This is your man, so you must chair the meeting,' he told me. I was nervous about being in the limelight and the possibility of a confrontation with the Special Branch, particularly as I was waiting to hear about my passport. This was then considered, for 'non-whites', a privilege rather than a right. But I agreed to chair the meeting and spent some time beforehand briefing the Chief.

Luthuli spoke for one and a half hours and held the packed hall in the palm of his hand. His mellifluous tones and stark common sense pierced many veils of ignorance. He spoke of the notion of a South African identity, of the challenge posed by the Nationalist government and its policies, and of the mounting non-racial campaign of resistance. He spoke so movingly in our small country town that I could literally see eyes being opened as he talked. I was twenty-four years old and very proud.

At last, I received my South African passport. In late 1958 I resigned from my job in Stanger and drew the little bit of pension money that I had saved over my four years of employment. Together with some help from my brothers I used the money to pay for a one-way ticket to Southampton on the transatlantic passenger liner the *Edinburgh Castle*.

A few months before I set sail for England, my father died. He was an extraordinarily generous man, to the point of exasperating my mother. I remember him returning home from one of his working trips, bearing a tray of ripe peaches and pocketfuls of sweets, which he distributed to the children of the neighbourhood. He loved children. When he died he was only sixty-five, but life had exacted a heavy toll on him and he looked much older than his years.

According to the lights of the world, my father was not a success. He had lost his business. He had been forced to spend years away from his family. He owned nothing, had saved nothing. But to me he was a magnificent, proud, kind, courageous failure whom I loved and admired greatly.

I left all my memories behind in Stanger as I departed for London in the hope of returning four years later as a qualified lawyer. But fate plays tricks, and in my case it was by the bucketful.

2

Exile and England

As the *Edinburgh Castle* sailed out of Cape Town harbour in the southern hemisphere summer of 1958 and I watched Table Mountain recede slowly into the horizon, it never occurred to me I might not be able to return to the land of my birth. I was going off to study law in England and afterwards return home to take on human rights cases. It was only much later that I viewed myself as an exile, after my marriage to Louise, who is white or, as E.M. Forster would have it, 'pinko-grey'. This meant I would fall foul of the Mixed Marriages Act and, worse still, the Immorality Act.

When I arrived in London, there were very few South African exiles, though of course after the crackdown on the liberation movements in 1960 many more were to find their way to England. Some fled to avoid long prison sentences, some left on exit permits, but all were affected to some degree by having been uprooted from their home. In most cases, exile is something that creeps up on people, who deal with it rather like bereavement: day by day, minute by minute. At times, the pain is so fierce, it is almost unbearable. At other times, exile throbs within you like a long-suffered, partially healed wound.

Part of the torture of exile is the unknowing, and in this I certainly shared. From exile you can only imagine the birth of a nephew or niece, the illness of a parent or child, the loss of a loved person or place. These things wash around within you, pricking your conscience, fraying your memories and serving as a constant reminder of your 'otherness' in this new place in which you live but which will never truly be home. All we had to cling to were the memories of the landscape; the sights, sounds and smells of home.

For some, such as my gifted countryman Can Themba, the isolating, bewildering pressures of exile were fatal. He threw himself off a skyscraper in Manhattan. Others coped or didn't cope, cried, died, bled or mourned. After England I moved to Ireland. Ireland's history is full of the songs and tears of exile. Perhaps that is why I ended up there. I was enfolded in its arms. In its compassion and empathy Ireland gave me, my wife Louise, and later our two boys succour and hope. I was fortunate too that Louise provided the security, love and support that meant that all our enterprises were joint ones.

But on the *Edinburgh Castle*, that warm summer's day right at the end of 1958, this all lay too far ahead to imagine. I was too excited to worry about loss and too young to think about exile, permanence and the march of decades. I left my country, moreover, at a time of growing hope. The National Party had been in power for ten years and many of us believed it was soon to falter. In the extremism of its programme and in the growing tide of resistance to its intentions, one felt that change for the good was in the air. Little did we know that the growing intransigence and belligerence of the apartheid regime would soon usher in almost three decades of darkness. Just around the corner, the Sharpeville massacre of March 1960 would change everything.

I sailed into Southampton on 9 January 1959, the very day that Fidel Castro marched triumphantly into Havana, Cuba. Almost immediately, my lessons began in the *realpolitik* of British prejudice. There on the dockside was a huge sign saying 'Stop Coloured Immigration'. Clearly, South Africa was not the only country in the world to be wrestling with issues of race and exclusion. In Britain, the arrival of immigrants from the Caribbean and South Asia brought racist antipathies to the surface, not just among workers fearful of losing their jobs, but in the middle class too. By 1959, when I arrived, immigration was a controversial issue, one on which discussion was frowned upon. It remains so even today in England, as in other European countries. Ironically, Britain's growing consciousness of race in the 1950s and 1960s spawned an environment in which efforts to mobilise support for an anti-racist crusade about a far-flung corner of Africa proved surprisingly fruitful. London was a centre of anti-colonialism and within a year of my arrival, there would be a great surge of freedom in Africa.

After stepping off the boat, I immediately set about trying to raise some funds. The university term at the London School of Economics (LSE) began only in October and it was then January, so I had more than eight months to earn some money to supplement what my family was to send me, and get settled before classes began. As a qualified teacher I imagined I might be able to get some teaching work and consequently I headed off to the London County Council to see what was available. The newly established comprehensive schools were always needing teachers, particularly schools in the poorer areas. I overheard the director of education offering my services to a local school principal on the phone. 'What's his English like?' was the only question posed by the head teacher, a Mrs Chetwynd, who, upon being told it was adequate, was more than happy to take me on. My plan was to assume a full-time teaching job and then resign in August or September, a month or two before I was due to start at the LSE. This would give me seven months' salary and enough resources to survive for a while. It would also provide me with a crash course in the complex class and religious politics of the English education system.

Within a week of arriving in England, I was teaching at Woodberry Down School in north-east London. It was exhilarating but difficult. Most of the children there were originally destined for the secondary modern school, given the prevailing English class distinction between the children of workers and the children of the middle class. The latter went to grammar schools. Almost immediately, I came up against the religious intolerance that was a hallmark of many inner-city schools at that time. 'I don't see you at assembly,' the same Mrs Chetwynd asked soon after I had joined the staff. In those days, assemblies were orthodox Church of England affairs featuring the Lord's Prayer and hymns about Jerusalem. 'Are you a Hindu? Or a Zoroastrian? A Buddhist perhaps? Are you a Jew?' I was asked, being proffered a spiritual menu from which I was invited to select something appropriate. When I replied that I was none of these, I could see the disapproval on her face. Her whole attitude changed. She would have accepted anything, but not nothing. Disbelief was intolerable. I don't think I was missed come October, at least not by her.

One teacher at Woodberry Down School did make me feel at home right away. He was Sam Fisher, an old communist who taught history. We were kindred spirits and my arrival in London was made all the more comfortable and enjoyable for his presence and support. Not all the teachers were as welcoming. Nor was I the only one who felt out of place at school in this largely working-class part of London. Hard on the heels of the Caribbean and Asian immigration wave of the late 1950s was the movement of these communities' children into the local schools. The 1958/59 school year was the first in which black children started attending the comprehensive schools in Britain in any significant numbers. The group of black children at Woodberry Down had a difficult time adapting to the hierarchies and prejudices of the British educational system.

In the beginning I too had a tough time. I was used to the relatively docile, obedient children of the Indian schools in which I had taught. Now I was faced with noisy, irreverent and occasionally even obstreperous kids. When the school's science teacher ran away with the gym instructor, I was asked to fill in for the former. On one occasion, which I still blush to recall, all the girls in the class pulled up their skirts above their knees when I entered the science laboratory. 'Please behave yourselves,' I pleaded in embarrassment, and was met by giggles. Eventually they did pull their skirts down.

At the end of the summer term, I handed in my statutory three months' notice to the London County Council, and in September I became a student once more, starting on my law degree at the LSE. While my family was puzzled that I had rejected the offer of a place at Cambridge University in favour of the LSE, it had long been my dream to go there and sit at the feet of such luminaries as Harold Laski.

In those early months in London, I was forced to overhaul piece by piece my entire perspective on what being British entailed. Throughout my teenage years and into my early twenties I had been an avid follower of the major political events of the day. I collected newspaper cuttings about every important development. I was also something of an authority on Church of England clerics and their sex lives – the result of having been recommended in South Africa to read the *News of the World* – though this paper also gave me access to insights and analyses provided by brilliant commentators and columnists of the day.

I was still at that stage a colonialist and an anglophile. Indeed, when the British royal family came to visit South Africa in 1947, I was chosen from among the Indian children in the old Natal to present a bouquet to Princess Margaret Rose. I couldn't have been prouder, even though, when the crucial moment arrived, I curtsied instead of bowing. I was a royalist to the core. Back at home, I even got beaten up for my sympathies when I raised the Union Jack in our garden after Archbishop Makarios was exiled by the British forces in Cyprus. Ten years later, when I read about the independence celebrations in Ghana, the first African country to throw off its colonial yoke, and about the liberation war in Kenya, my imagination was fired and I became caught up in the current of anti-colonialism.

Gradually in my twenties, the gloss of all things British and colonial began to wear off. I read *Brideshead Revisited* and developed a dislike for the British upper class. I couldn't transfer my loyalty to those people because I didn't have the belief that they were worth embracing. Instead I appreciated the strength and determination of the coalminers, the workers, the Irish. I appreciated the great English tradition of Nonconformism. And I enjoyed reading the outstanding commentators of the day like Michael Foot and Aneurin Bevan. Hearing about Ghana's independence under its first president, Kwame Nkrumah, and Kenya's liberation war made me realise that for all that was admirable in its history, Britain nursed a legacy of oppression, exploitation and racism. I was determined to learn more, and went to every left-wing lecture and debate that I could find. At that time the Movement for Colonial Freedom, with roots in the British labour movement, was campaigning for independence for Britain's African colonies; Christian Action, headed by John Collins, Canon of St Paul's Cathedral, was raising funds for anti-apartheid leaders on trial in South Africa; and the Committee of African Organisations, consisting mainly of African students living in London, provided a platform to exiled politicians from all over English-speaking Africa. I joined the activities of all these bodies.

In London, I met up with other South African exiles. There was Abdul Minty, later a key player in the international anti-apartheid movement, who had been in England barely a year when I turned up. The Pahad brothers, Essop and Aziz, arrived too; both went on to become ministers in the post-apartheid South African government. There was Tennyson Makiwane, a former Treason trialist and ANC youth leader, who had left South Africa in January 1959 and never returned home; and Mac Maharaj, Steve Naidoo and Tony Seedat, who at various times shared a flat with me. Steve Naidoo was in fact the person who had induced me to give up teaching in South Africa and study law.

We young South Africans gravitated around the home of Patsy and Vella Pillay, which was in the north of the city; they had been married in South Africa just before marriage across the colour bar was outlawed. Slowly our numbers expanded. Many of these young South Africans would become leading players in the international Anti-Apartheid Movement, bringing an energy and commitment that would sustain the early campaigns to enforce economic sanctions against South Africa.

In England, the idea of a consumer boycott of South African goods began to gain in popularity towards the end of the 1950s. Already when I arrived, exiles had begun picketing shops to dissuade consumers from buying South African goods. On 26 June 1959, a few months after my arrival, I was one of some five hundred people who gathered in Holborn Hall to launch a boycott of South African fruit and other products. Among the speakers at the meeting, which was hosted by the Committee of African Organisations, was Julius Nyerere, as well as Tennyson Makiwane and Vella Pillay, who spoke on behalf of the ANC and the South African Indian Congress respectively. The Holborn meeting was held to coincide with the launch back in South Africa of the ANC's campaign to boycott goods produced by firms known to support the ruling National Party.

If any one event galvanised the Boycott Movement into action it was Chief Albert Luthuli's plea for sanctions that he issued as president-general of the ANC in July 1959. 'I appeal', he said, on behalf of the people of South Africa, 'to all governments throughout the world, to people everywhere, to all organisations and institutions in every land and at every level to act now to impose such sanctions on South Africa that will bring about the vital necessary change and avert what can become the greatest African tragedy of our time.' In the longer term Luthuli's appeal was looked upon by the Anti-Apartheid Movement as its founding statement. In the shorter term it gave fresh impetus to the boycott campaign, which activists saw as the main weapon for exercising pressure on the apartheid regime to implement fundamental change. Over the decades this would mushroom into UN resolutions, comprehensive sanctions, arms embargoes and increasing restrictions on apartheid South Africa's access to the world.

The Boycott Movement – and subsequently the Anti-Apartheid Movement – was very clear that its policies must be in line with the broad liberation movement in South Africa. While it developed a special relationship with the ANC, the Anti-Apartheid Movement was a British organisation and not an exclusively ANC support group, though in the course of events it took its inspiration and ideas for action from that body. This apparent contradiction, of a movement which had at its heart a relationship with the ANC but which did not perceive this as an exclusive relationship, was to produce tensions, but at the same time it was essential to its success.

My own affiliation to the ANC can be dated to the months soon after my arrival. Until its conference at Morogoro in Tanzania in 1969, a decade later, only Africans could become members of the ANC. While the party believed in non-racialism, it also thought for some time that the political goals of the struggle were best served in race-specific political bodies like the South African Indian Congress and the (white) Congress of Democrats. In this way it would be easier to organise and less likely to attract police attention. This all changed at Morogoro. I had never joined the Indian Congress back home because I was not allowed to do so as a teacher, but now, in London, I eagerly joined the ANC. Even though formal membership was not open to me, I felt I had at last found a political home in which I was comfortable and welcome. There was no need to join formally; I simply became part of the organisation and worked as an active member of it.

A little later in the same year, I also joined the underground South African Communist Party (SACP). Many of the young, progressive exiled South Africans with whom I worked and campaigned in London were Party members, and it was almost natural that I would sign up too. A number of us were involved in a small clandestine group led by Vella Pillay. To say I was plunged in at the deep end is an exaggeration, but it is true that the first request we received was that we arrange the distribution of the first issue of the *African Communist* – and all the subsequent issues – not only in Britain but in South Africa. This journal was a new venture by the SACP. We met in a house in North London on Tuesday nights to put the magazine in envelopes, under conditions of extreme secrecy. A little later, after Louise and I were married, she never questioned where I went every Tuesday evening – a sign of the trust that we held in each other. I just used to say that I was off to a meeting, and as I was in demand as a speaker this did not seem strange.

Apart from the need for secrecy, we had to ensure that the South African Special Branch did not get wind of our operations. We used to buy fancy wrapping paper from Harvey Nicols, Marks & Spencer or Sainsbury's in which to roll up the journal, and then take small parcels of them to different post offices around London. I don't think we missed a single edition, though the load was very heavy, shared between only five or eight of us – Vella was a hard taskmaster. No one could deny how much the *African Communist* was appreciated in South Africa, as we learnt from new exiles.

Given the anti-communist fervour of the time, in Britain as much as in South Africa, we had to maintain in public the separation between the Anti-Apartheid Movement and the SACP, even though many of us served in both. For us working in the underground struggle, we didn't make any specific differentiation between the ANC and the SACP. But as this was a time of virulent anti-communism, outside the ANC we had to make the distinction quite clear.

Though there may have been a period when leading members of the SACP in the ANC tended to reflect much more the position of the Party, on the whole this was done with subtlety and care. Some ANC leaders never mentioned the SACP or its policies in their public addresses. I can't recall, for instance, the young Thabo Mbeki in exile ever pushing the party line when head of publications and then of the International Secretariat of the ANC. I shared platforms with him, and in the speeches I heard him give I don't ever remember that he reflected a particular SACP position that was not shared by the ANC, even though he was a member of the Party's Politburo. I also don't think it's correct to say that the SACP dominated or ran the ANC.

For almost three decades I remained a member of the SACP, and a disciplined member at that. But when I returned to South Africa in 1990 I said to myself, 'Now that I'm home I'm a member of the ANC only.'

After the sporadic protests of the 1950s, what raised international opposition against apartheid to a whole new level was the events in the

South African township of Sharpeville on 21 March 1960. For many then and now, including the Truth and Reconciliation Commission, this was the day the liberation struggle truly began. In this dusty township close to Vereeniging police fired on a peaceful protest against the pass laws that had been organised by the Pan Africanist Congress (PAC), a breakaway from the ANC, and killed sixty-nine township residents and injured many more. As a result of the massacre, South Africa's official ideology of racial discrimination was catapulted to the top of the global political agenda.

Very soon after we got news of Sharpeville, some of us put up a notice at LSE announcing a demonstration outside South Africa House, the High Commission located off Trafalgar Square. The bill was torn down and an official Students Union notice was put up by the Union president, who was a Tory. Some fifteen hundred students then gathered in the Old Theatre, many of them wearing the distinctive black, purple and yellow scarves of the LSE. Though we weren't permitted to carry banners or posters as the planned demonstration would be taking place within one mile of the Houses of Parliament, where such a demonstration was illegal, we set off in any case and joined many thousands of others who were marching down The Strand and gathering outside South Africa House to protest against the killings.

During the protest, two of my English friends were arrested. The only relevant telephone number I had was for the National Council for Civil Liberties (NCCL). (Like many British organisations, the NCCL then and the AAM in the future felt no need to describe themselves as British, which was a source of some irritation to the non-English or non-British elements.) The Council was very under-resourced and apparently had only two men, a woman and a dog working for it. I got through, thankfully, to the woman, who listened carefully to my story before bursting into an embarrassed giggle. 'There is nothing we can do,' she told me sympathetically. 'I'm afraid we can't give you free legal advice. We just don't have the funds.' The woman's name was Louise Parkinson and I would soon be bumping into her again.

As I rushed around trying to get my friends out of the cells and save their nascent legal careers, I learnt much about the British legal system. One of my law professors advised that the two should plead guilty to malicious damage to property (a matchbox was found on one of them), pay three or four pounds and be done with it. I was horrified, but it seemed the only thing to do. If they had not pleaded guilty and had been convicted in a higher court, with all the attendant publicity, it would have meant an end to any hope of a legal career.

The protests outside South Africa House went on for almost a week and culminated in a march from Hyde Park to Trafalgar Square, organised by the Boycott Movement and attended by thousands of people. Never before had the consequences of apartheid been so evident as in the blood that stained the streets of Sharpeville. Here was evidence for all to see of state-sanctioned prejudice and criminality, sheathed in an iron fist.

At home in South Africa, the regime moved quickly to still dissent and disable the black opposition. A State of Emergency was declared and both the ANC and the PAC were banned. Thousands of activists were arrested. Heavy penalties were imposed for membership or support of banned parties, running from long terms of imprisonment all the way to the death penalty. Newspapers could no longer quote or present the opinions of banned parties or their leaders. The state's heavy-handed actions led to the departure and exile of dozens of anti-apartheid activists, who had no choice but to continue the fight beyond the regime's reach. Some of these new exiles, like the ANC president Oliver Tambo and the Indian Congress and Communist Party leader Yusuf Dadoo, brought with them immense administrative and leadership capacity. This naturally gave new impetus to the internationalisation of the struggle against apartheid.

In London, Tambo established a proper ANC office. Although under-resourced, it began to exert a very direct influence on the growing Anti-Apartheid Movement. In fact, we in the Anti-Apartheid Movement always took our leadership from the ANC. This was not always a popular position, particularly after the formation of the ANC's armed wing in 1961 and the turn to military and guerrilla activities. I remember arguing with fellow exiles about the decision, as at that stage I was not in favour of the resort to violence. More pertinent, however, for the group of exiles and their friends and supporters in London was a statement issued by the ANC calling on the UN to impose 'full economic sanctions against the Union of South Africa'.

True to our Congress affiliations, we as the initiators of the British boycott moved to translate the ANC's call into an international campaign. On 20 April 1960, a meeting of the Boycott Committee members, for the first time calling itself the Anti-Apartheid Movement (AAM), agreed to hold a discussion on wider economic sanctions. Some recall that I was the one who suggested the name of the Anti-Apartheid Movement, but I don't remember this and it's not really important. What does matter is that the establishment of the AAM was largely an initiative by South Africans living in London at that time.

Although the impetus for the formation of the movement came from South Africans, we all knew that it would not achieve much unless it became a British movement and became engaged in British political life. In the early years this was not always easy, especially at the height of the Cold War. Thanks to politicians such as Barbara Castle, David Steel, Martin Ennals, Jeremy Thorpe and Joan Lestor, who became AAM office-bearers in the 1960s and early 1970s, the movement was able to put down firm roots in British society.

In social terms, the Anti-Apartheid Movement was exceptional in bringing black and white people together in Britain. Often, this was fuelled by the sheer calibre of persons involved in it. They were always passionate, empathetic and energetic, and this rubbed off on anyone who came into contact with them. There was, for instance, a remarkable Ghanaian called Dennis Phombeah, head of the Committee of African Organisations, who drew people toward him like moths to a flame. The AAM was a kind of melting pot of opposition to apartheid.

Just as it was South Africans who'd been at the heart of the Boycott Movement, so it was South Africans associated with the ANC or SACP who formed the core of the first executive committee of the AAM. Among them were Tennyson Makiwane, Vella Pillay, Abdul Minty and Rosalynde Ainslie. Ros Ainslie, who came from Cape Town, was appointed the AAM's honorary secretary. As Ros de Lanerolle, she later headed up the famous feminist publishing house in London called the Women's Press. Loved by all, she was a woman of extraordinary integrity, very open-minded, whose advice was sought by all of us regardless of our political affiliations. Ros was succeeded in 1962 as secretary of the AAM by Abdul Minty, who acted in this capacity until the dissolution of the movement in the early 1990s.

I was in effect the first treasurer of the AAM and, to start with, it was all a bit amateurish. In the very beginning the AAM didn't have a bank account, so for a brief period it was all paid in and out of my account. On one occasion, I recall travelling across London with someone's baby carrier full of cash. This was the proceeds of a 'Freedom Day' function on 26 June 1962 organised by the AAM, in which the famous actor Peter O'Toole had been persuaded to take part and deliver an oration. Having just broken his arm, he came full of anti-pain injections, and with his arm in a sling, but he gave the oration, written by Ronald Segal, in splendid style. The cash poured in. Louise and I carried the money on the Underground to Tufnell Park and then walked to our flat. There we spread the notes on the table, and took great pleasure in counting it all out. 'Look! Here's a £50 note,' we called as the larger denominations were picked out of the pile. In the end, we had almost £900, which was a lot of money in 1962. We kept the cash in small bags for the whole weekend before depositing it, with great pleasure, on the Monday morning. I served as the treasurer of the AAM for a year before moving to Dublin.

At the AAM's very first meeting, the idea to develop the call for sanctions was endorsed by Yusuf Dadoo, who was present. He suggested future action should include a UN call for economic sanctions and a request to the trade union movement and to African states not to handle oil destined for South Africa. Vella Pillay then drafted a Programme of Action, calling publicly for sanctions, a move that was to have profound implications for the future of the anti-apartheid struggle because it was the first of its kind.

The AAM's call for a boycott of South African goods was soon supported by the Labour and Liberal parties of Britain, by the influential Trade Union Council (TUC) and by several co-operative societies. On the back of this burgeoning support and interest, new anti-apartheid organisations sprang up in other countries, especially in the West, and the boycott spread.

In 1959 and for the first few years of the 1960s, I travelled all over London for the Boycott and Anti-Apartheid movements, taking part in pickets, boycotts and protests, and speaking at meetings. I also travelled further afield to talk to concerned groups, such as in Wales, where I once stayed overnight at the home of S.O. Davies, the renowned MP for Merthyr Tydfil and representative of the South Wales Miners'

Federation. S.O. kindly asked me how long I had been in England, and though it was only a few months he insisted that I should ring up home at once. I was a little nervous in case the South African Special Branch came to know about my political activities, but nevertheless I really appreciated the kindness. We may have been sworn at by passers-by objecting to our pickets, but these infrequent unpleasantnesses were more than compensated for by acts of kindness such as Davies's.

For me, London in the early 1960s was an extraordinary experience. When I first arrived, I felt like a Caliban from the colonies. I was always nervous of speaking, even though I didn't feel this anywhere else. That's the thing about the colonised. But I was amazed by the vibrancy, by the industry and by the creativity of London. I loved to walk the city streets, especially the bridges, pubs and cobbled alleys of Charles Dickens's London. The city incubated in me what was to become a lifelong love for the theatre and the cinema. The West End at the time was humming with the bold rebellion of John Osborne and his angry young peers. Tennessee Williams and Samuel Beckett tore at the edifice of the complacent West with their fingernails. Laurence Olivier held court in epic Shakespearian dramas at the Old Vic.

I still know London better than Dublin though I lived in Dublin for almost thirty years. I loved London for its history and for its political debates, its theatre and cinema. I saw all the Buñuel films and the Russian and Japanese classics. When I moved to Dublin, I had to dispose of a small suitcaseful of theatre programmes. One which I ought to have kept was of a performance of Shaw's *Major Barbara* in which the legendary Irish actor Siobhán McKenna took the lead role. Hers was a memorable performance. After many curtain calls, she raised her hand for silence and called out to the audience: 'You are wonderful in England. But you can be even better if your soldiers would leave Ireland.' The reaction was predictable. McKenna was denounced by the right-wing press as contributing to the IRA border campaign. I was delighted when she later became a sponsor of the Irish Anti-Apartheid Movement.

I watched all the Charlie Chaplin films and the Ingmar Bergman ones too. I immersed myself in the cultural life, and indeed in the counter-cultural life, of one of the world's greatest cities. I read all the books I couldn't get hold of in South Africa and my knowledge deepened by the day. Even before I got to London, I'd always had an affinity with England. My political development had taken place through my knowledge of English politics and history. Two books in particular had been hugely influential: E.P. Thompson's *The Making of the English Working Class* and K.W. Wedderburn's *The Worker and the Law*.

However, there wasn't much time in London for reading as I was running around for the Boycott Movement and doing my work for university. It was difficult to combine the different roles I played. Often I would sit up until three in the morning reading, voraciously, everything I could get my hands on, from Joyce's *Portrait of the Artist as a Young Man* and *Finnegan's Wake* to the West Indian writer George Lamming, whom I met through Ethel de Keyser, one of the leading figures in the AAM.

I learnt a great deal in the short time I spent in London, not only about the theatre, literature and the law, but about life, the struggle for freedom and justice. I met all the great liberation fighters in London, many of them from Africa. This gave me enormous insight into how to strengthen our freedom, and how not to repeat the sins, crimes and betrayals (of what they stood for) of many of the liberation movements. I could see how the needs of the people were betrayed too easily through self-aggrandisement and corruption. I understood that the values for which a struggle took place should not be compromised, that the means never justified the ends when it came to morality. I learnt that you can't force people to believe in you and that you also can't force people to reconcile with or understand each other if they don't want to.

In 1960 I was invited to attend an AAM fundraising party at a house in Hampstead. By then I had a big black beard and lots of hair. I could appear very dramatic but, in truth, was a shy person especially when it came to women. I was introduced by our hostess to Louise Parkinson, the same woman who had laughed at me when I called the National Council for Civil Liberties only a few weeks previously, and was told we should start dancing.

It was clear from the start that I couldn't dance, and frankly neither could Louise. In fact we had both gone to the party in order to meet Michael Harmel, a prominent activist who had just arrived from South Africa. But I have no recollection of what he spoke about. Rather, I remember asking Louise if she would like to come with me to the London première of the South African musical *King Kong*. With music by Todd Matshikiza, *King Kong* told a classic South African tale of boxers, gangsters and democrats set to the jazz and bluesy rhythms of the township. The musical took the West End by storm and was the perfect first date for a relationship that would grow from strength to strength. After the show we went to a party and met with members of the cast, including the renowned South African trombonist Jonas Gwangwa. It was a great evening. A few months later Louise proposed to me.

As was usual in the ANC at the time, I consulted the leadership about my intention to marry. This was in the aftermath of Sharpeville and things were still very tight. Thousands of people had been arrested at home and the movement was in the throes of a major reorganisation. Was this the time to be worrying the great Oliver Tambo or Yusuf Dadoo about matters of the heart? I needn't have worried as both men had compassion in spades.

Tambo was very clear: an unhappy cadre was not a good activist. Follow your heart, he told me, which I did. Such generosity of spirit from a leader – who at the same time had to find cadres to return to South Africa to carry on the underground struggle – made an enormous impression on me. Yusuf Dadoo took a similar position. Generosity of spirit did not preclude toughness on the part of either man.

In fact, Tambo and Dadoo were more encouraging about the match than my own family. My brothers did not inform my mother of my marriage to Louise, because one or two of them disapproved of it. Many months later, when she learnt about it, my mother did not consult her sons but sent the only piece of jewellery she owned – her ring – to Louise. We value it as a memento of a remarkable woman who was progressive in a deeply conservative society and magnanimous when there was so much racial and personal meanness around. Louise and I were married on 30 December 1961 in a registry office presided over by a Mr Love. He did not really live up to his name, for when Louise went to see him to arrange the date, he asked whether I belonged to an obscure religion. Louise of course said no, I came from a Muslim background, and was then given a lecture on the possibility that I already had one or more wives back in South Africa. There was snow on the ground the day after the ceremony and we threw snowballs at each other on Hampstead Heath – with disastrous results: I got bronchitis and was confined to bed for a week.

There were a small number of South Africans at the London School of Economics at this time, and I think I lived with half of them. Home base was a house in Downhills Park Road, Tottenham, in North London. A sweet English couple lived downstairs and the South Africans occupied the flat upstairs. Our countrymen drifted in and out in a merry-go-round of exile. Many an activist slept on our couch or floor.

There were three bedrooms, of which mine was the smallest; it was barely a box. We had a small kitchen, a sitting room and the complete works of Karl Marx on the bookshelf. We pooled all our resources and shared the duties but, in the end, our experiment in socialism proved a failure. As I had a fetish about cleanliness, I ended up doing much of the cooking and cleaning. Everyone was so busy, it was almost impossible to call a meeting at which all would be present. This made managing our little commune difficult.

After Louise and I were married we moved to Tufnell Park and we set about our studies, work and Anti-Apartheid Movement (or, in Louise's case, the Campaign for Nuclear Disarmament) activities with ferocity. After my first set of exam results, I was made an LSE scholar. This meant my family could stop sending me money and I became financially secure, though not exactly wealthy. Louise kept the job at the National Council for Civil Liberties and brought in a useful £10 a month. I graduated from LSE in 1962 in spite of a solemn warning from one of my law professors that to get married in one's final year was a recipe for disaster. Next I began a master's degree.

With a view to becoming a barrister, I also joined Lincoln's Inn, which was the cheapest Inn to join and the closest to LSE. It was a strange experience going through the rituals and traditions of the Bar, from the sherries to the compulsory dinners, in the beautiful halls of Lincoln's Inn. When I went for dinner, I was placed at the far end from the bigwigs at High Table, usually seated next to three Muslim would-be barristers. This suited me as they didn't drink, which meant I could have their share of the bottle of rather good wine. It was always strange at the end of those evenings to hop on the bus to North London, back to South African exile chaos. I later completed the Bar exams.

Lawyers in most times and places tend towards conservatism and London in the early 1960s was no exception. One of my LSE professors told me I would do better to join the Society of Labour Lawyers and avoid the more left-leaning Haldane Society of Socialist Lawyers. 'Some of them are known communists, I believe,' he warned. I promptly joined the Haldane, eventually becoming one of its vice-presidents. It was and is a genuinely broad left group, strongly anti-colonialist and supportive of the Anti-Apartheid Movement.

I loved London, even though I knew by the early 1960s that I couldn't stay there. In an emotional way I didn't want to feel as if I was in exile. I wanted to retain my South Africanness without cutting myself off from contact with the milieu in which I was living my life. After marrying Louise, I knew we could not return to South Africa. It was illegal for couples of mixed race to marry or live together there. In any case, the political situation and my involvement with the ANC and the Anti-Apartheid Movement would almost certainly have led to my immediate, long-term incarceration. The South African Embassy in London had already refused to renew my passport.

Both Louise and I were keen to work in Africa and so when the opportunity arose I applied for a job at the University of Ghana in Legon. I was interviewed by Conor Cruise O'Brien, who was then its Vice-Chancellor, and was successful. Shortly after that, however, I discovered that I was unable to have children, and so we decided to stay in Europe, and put our names down with an adoption society in London. I turned down the Ghanaian job but soon afterwards was invited to apply for a junior lectureship in law at Trinity College Dublin. Dr O'Brien had recommended me when the law school had not found any suitable candidate.

When I mentioned these events to Tambo, he unhesitatingly told me that the ANC already had offices in a number of African countries, and my skills would be useful in countries which were either collaborating with apartheid or which might be persuaded to support the struggle. Though my heart really lay in Africa, Tambo encouraged me to take up the post in Dublin, which I duly did. We left London with mixed feelings, the comradeship of the movement being foremost in our minds, and headed off to Dublin with the idea of staying a year or two. In the end we would live in Ireland for twenty-seven years.

3

Ireland

When I was growing up, my father told me a lot about the Irish and their struggle. He was fervent about the fight against colonialism generally and spoke especially vividly about Irish efforts over the centuries to shrug off the yoke of English power. In time, I added to a basic grasp of Irish politics a lifelong love affair with Irish lyricism. Now, Brendan Behan and James Joyce, W.B. Yeats and Seamus Heaney are as much part of me as the blood in my veins.

My first visit to Ireland was a memorable if inelegant affair, a raw introduction to Irish congeniality. It was Christmas 1959, and I was travelling by ferry to Dun Laoghaire to meet some former students. The journey across the Irish Sea was bitterly cold. There was nowhere to sit, crammed as the ferry was with men and women returning home for Christmas. Tired, cold and a bit seasick, I sat on the floor and added grubbiness to my list of woes. 'So, why are you looking so miserable?' a fellow Irish traveller leaned over and asked. He handed me a bottle of Guinness, and then another. The witty exchanges and laughter grew apace; the Guinness flowed. Before I knew it I was staggering ashore and in love with Ireland and the Irish already. My former students looked at me in utter amazement. They knew me from South Africa as a neatly dressed man, particular about my language and appearance. Instead they found me happy and dishevelled. I stumbled off the ferry with my overcoat in my left hand, jacket in my right, tie askew and sober as a seaman on home leave. They were completely taken aback.

Ireland does that to you. It overwhelms you with its empathy and its generosity. It's a small country with less than three million inhabitants at the time of our arrival and yet the struggle against apartheid was never more passionately taken up than on Irish turf. In the 1960s, however, few Irish people had ever even heard of apartheid. It took the Rivonia Trial and the travails of Mandela to crystallise latent sympathy for the oppressed of South Africa into an active movement. By the 1980s, the Irish Anti-Apartheid Movement was in the vanguard of the international campaign. Our victory over apartheid was due in no small measure to the commitment and sacrifice of the Irish, given as copiously as that Guinness on the ferry to Dun Laoghaire.

In the 1960s Ireland was a country of large-scale unemployment, social division and, in Northern Ireland, looming political violence. Yet, regardless of their own problems and of the remoteness of Africa, the Irish reached out to the oppressed of southern Africa with great generosity. While the captains and the kings – as Brendan Behan would have called them – gave us public respectability, the real passion came from the ordinary people of Ireland. They were the ones who gave us both support and inspiration and who made our work such a success. But there was something different about the Irish. They had a history of struggle against their British colonial masters; and later on I was much struck by the fact that government ministers who were prepared to speak at anti-apartheid meetings were not afraid to talk of 'imperialists'. People seemed to care deeply for their fellow beings. They were not only capable of profound empathy; they were able to act upon it instinctively.

The strongest support we got in Ireland came from the Irish trade union movement. The relationship between the Anti-Apartheid Movement and the Irish trade unions was a remarkable axis of support and mobilisation for several decades. From Michael Mullen, general secretary of the Irish Transport and General Workers' Union, and Donal Nevin, general secretary of the Irish Congress of Trade Unions (with whom I developed particularly close links), to the thousands of shop stewards and ordinary members, something about the fight against apartheid stirred their hearts. It was the unions who got the boycott campaign in Ireland up and running; it was the unions who gave firepower to the application of the academic, sporting and cultural boycotts by threatening to withdraw their labour. At every turn, the unions were there to support us. They formed the backbone of the Anti-Apartheid Movement in Ireland and their material, financial and ideological support added enormous value to our struggle.

For my part, I did what I could to assist them. I spoke on hundreds of occasions at union meetings and rallies. I wrote the rule books and constitutions of a number of Irish unions. This process of codification became important after a series of court rulings in Ireland in which the unions were castigated from the bench for failing to follow the correct rules and procedures. To help the unions and their members understand their history and the law of the land, I started giving evening classes on these topics. Every Tuesday night I would set off in my little car, usually in the rain, to the Workers' College in Rathgar, Dublin.

I think those lectures made an impact on the people who attended them and on the unions who benefited from the new levels of knowledge in the movement. Some of my former students have gone on to high-powered positions in the civil service or have become leaders in the labour movement. I don't think any other university professor in Ireland at that time made any effort to help the trade unions. We were mutually supportive, the Anti-Apartheid Movement and the unions, and the benefits for both parties were substantial.

I was also an external examiner for the newly established Regional Technical Colleges for a number of years and this meant travelling from one end of the country to the other. Some were large, ugly institutions, not like the handsome, well-resourced universities. I had to work hard to make my teaching on the law relevant to the students. A student from Donegal might be more interested in hearing about the legal framework of the fishing industry than about more theoretical jurisprudential matters. I thought long and hard about what might drive students such as these and what it was that they should be learning. By travelling and teaching and speaking at dozens of union and community meetings, I was gradually absorbed into Irish life.

It is true that Ireland's history has many parallels with South Africa's. Ireland was of course a colony of Britain for hundreds of years, and the Penal Laws bore a number of similarities with apartheid laws. Irish people were even at one time labelled 'surplus population' and pushed westwards to the poor rural areas, just like the 'surplus people' endorsed out of the so-called white cities and towns in South Africa. One nineteenth-century British prime minister, Lord Salisbury, cheerfully lumped together the Irish and those he called Hottentots –

the Khoi herders of southern Africa – as being 'lesser races, unfit for self-government'.

What is more, the Freedom Charter, drawn up by the ANC in 1955, with its bold initial declaration that South Africa belongs to all who live in it, black and white, echoed Ireland's own Proclamation of Independence of 1916, which declared that all the children of the nation should be cherished equally. When Chief Luthuli called for a world-wide boycott of South African goods, that too struck a chord, for the word 'boycott' originated in Ireland, deriving from a Captain Boycott, agent for an absentee landlord, whose tenants refused to recognise him because of his violent and abusive behaviour.

I believe the enormous support from the Irish people for the Anti-Apartheid Movement was motivated at root by the anti-colonial instinct that has its roots in Irish history. The connection between South Africa and Ireland goes deep. Indeed, the Irish had supported the Boers during their war against the English in the Anglo-Boer War in 1899–1902. Irish support for South Africa has its origins in history and in the notion that the enemy of my enemy is my friend. I was lucky enough to meet some of the older people who had taken part in the Irish War of Independence. I remember particularly General Seán MacEoin, who was popularly known as the 'Blacksmith of Ballinalee' for his part in the Irish freedom struggle. He had supported the Boers' position against the British during the Anglo-Boer War, but went on to say, 'The Boers have turned against their own principles by exploiting the blacks.' So there was an extraordinary anti-colonial spirit in Ireland, which was transformed into anti-racist and anti-apartheid sentiment.

Of course Ireland has not been spared its own race and class issues, and I was confronted by some of these virtually from day one. Even though I had a decent job at the university, Louise and I struggled to find a flat. We looked at dozens of places and were told each time, 'Sorry, but it's taken.' The situation would probably not have been so bad had it not been for the fact that shortly before this a South African student had murdered his girlfriend, chopped her up and tried to get rid of the evidence in the furnace of the restaurant where he was working. Eventually, Louise had to go looking by herself. Of course, the name Asmal was hardly Irish, and when the inevitable question was asked, and she had to answer that her husband was from South Africa, the flat was suddenly no longer available.

On one occasion she went to view a small flat in a largely Protestant suburb, where she managed to persuade the little old lady who owned it that my job in the (Protestant) Trinity College overcame any consideration of my race. But then, 'Does he have a beard?' she enquired. 'Yes,' said Louise. So we lost that place too. Eventually, though, we did find a flat, where we stayed for five years until Louise's parents helped us buy a small house.

But Ireland was not all Guinness and sympathy. Around Christmas of 1965, I was asked to take part in a debate in Kilkenny on the topic of Rhodesia's unilateral declaration of independence (UDI). It was one of the most depressing events I ever went to in Ireland, though it was billed as 'Kilkenny's literary event of the year'. The pro-Rhodesian side of the debate had brought in Rhodesian expats from all over Ireland to support them, one of whom declared, quite seriously, 'If I saw an Indian and a cobra, I would shoot the Indian first.' I think the locals were rather angry that so many outsiders had been brought in, so we won the debate, by a small margin. Nonetheless, we all trooped off for drinks afterwards at the stately residence of Lady Bellew. As soon as I walked in, Lady Bellew ostentatiously offered me South African sherry. And as soon as her back was turned I poured it into the nearest flower pot. In this milieu the level of understanding about political developments in Africa generally and about UDI in particular was alarmingly superficial and was founded on a basic set of racist assumptions.

I contrast this with the warmth and jocularity of the Irish working class. To give one example, I was on the train one day, on a small subsidiary line. It was freezing cold and I was on my way to give a lecture in Tralee. We pulled into a station and I stood up to stretch my legs and have a smoke. Suddenly, there was banging on the window. Three big men stood outside peering in at me. I lowered the window. 'Are you that prick Kader Asmal?' one of them asked. I looked at them, apprehensive as to what was coming next. 'We're with you down the line, Kader,' they said, laughing.

Irish history predisposed the Irish people to sympathise with the cause of an oppressed people and to support their efforts to win their freedom. People from all walks of life and with widely divergent political views found they could identify with the anti-apartheid struggle and made their talents and energy available to us. This depth and variety were a real strength.

Prior to the establishment of the Irish Anti-Apartheid Movement (IAAM)* in 1964, anti-apartheid activity in Ireland took its cue from Chief Albert Luthuli's call in 1959 to boycott South African goods. The boycott was supported and promoted mainly by trade unionists and prominent members of the left political establishment. There were also a number of South African students studying in Dublin, mostly at the Royal College of Surgeons, who were active in the boycott campaign. However, the college was not keen on its students taking part in demonstrations, especially after some mild trouble during a pro-Lumumba march in 1960. Only a few continued actively, though a wider group calling itself the South Africa Circle met quietly once a month to discuss aspects of apartheid and to educate its members about the struggle.

Then, in 1963, the leaders of Umkhonto weSizwe, the ANC's newly established armed wing, were arrested at Liliesleaf farm in Rivonia near Johannesburg. It was widely expected that the accused would be found guilty and sentenced to death. The high-profile raid and subsequent trial drew attention to the plight of political prisoners in apartheid's jails and led to the British Anti-Apartheid Movement setting up the World Campaign for the Release of South African Political Prisoners.

At that stage there was no formal Irish organisation to promote these campaigns though students were becoming aware of them. In November 1963 a packed meeting took place in Trinity College's

---

* The story of the IAAM told in this book is necessarily brief. I should like to pay tribute to the members, particularly of the executive committee, who gave so generously of their time and skills. Mention must be made of Fr Austin Flannery, president of the IAAM; his successor as president, the Rev. Terence McCaughey, a Trinity College academic and Presbyterian minister; Tony Ffrench, who played a large role in our anti-South African immigration campaign; Rafique Mottiar, our treasurer for many years; Garry Kilgallen; Barry Desmond; Noel Harris; and Joan Burton, who acted as honorary secretary. The list is too long to complete.

Graduate Memorial Building. The meeting, which I had organised with other Irish well-wishers, was addressed by Arthur Goldreich, a South African communist who was among those arrested following the Rivonia raid. He and Harold Wolpe had recently escaped from South Africa to Swaziland dressed as Catholic priests, eventually finding their way to London. This unusual means of escape, combined with Arthur Goldreich's dashing and romantic air (he was later a tank commander in the Israeli army), caught the public imagination.

After the meeting, an elderly but very friendly academic took me aside and told me, after he had learnt of my involvement in the event: 'Never shit on your doorstep.' (I have to say this sounds more elegant in Irish.) But I disappointed my friend, as in my working hours Trinity College was to become the centre of my activities – apart from my academic life – focusing on civil liberties and apartheid.

In the wake of the meeting at Trinity College we decided to go ahead and set up the Irish Anti-Apartheid Movement. It took a few months to find sponsors, but soon enough people rallied to the call. Once we had some funds and growing public support, we thought a major event should be hosted that would really push the new movement into the spotlight. The Mansion House, the Lord Mayor's residence, is a famous place in Ireland and any number of historic events and meetings have taken place there over the years. So the Mansion House was redolent with history and perfect for the official launch of the IAAM. However, we were a little nervous that, with its seating capacity of nine hundred people, a small turnout at the venue would be humiliating and damaging. As it happened, we needn't have worried. It was packed with friends and supporters. The meeting led to the formal establishment of the IAAM, of which I was elected vice-chair and Louise honorary administrative secretary. We were up and running.

Speakers at the meeting in April 1964 came from different Irish political parties and included Michael Harmel, a South African of Irish extraction, who had fled the country the previous year while awaiting trial for contravening his banning orders. He was a prominent member of the Congress of Democrats and secretary of the South African Communist Party. Harmel completely bowled the audience over.

Speaker after speaker warned of the inevitability of armed conflict if the apartheid regime persisted with its policies, and called on the

Irish government to support the anti-apartheid struggle. The variety of speakers at that meeting, representing all political parties in the Dáil (the lower house of the Irish Parliament), set the pattern for the IAAM in years to come. It was remarkable that in the atmosphere of the times, in the continuing Cold War, an audience liberally sprinkled with nuns could applaud the secretary of the Communist Party. Irish anti-imperialist sentiments were stronger than anti-communist feelings. This was also demonstrated by the impressive list of sponsors who later appeared on the IAAM letterhead. They included Mary Robinson, later the first woman President of the country; Garret FitzGerald, later Foreign Minister and then Taoiseach (Prime Minister); and three existing or future Nobel Prize winners: John Hume, Seán MacBride and Seamus Heaney. In all, over thirty leading Irish men and women – professionals, artists and dramatists, academics, senators and politicians – agreed over time to act as sponsors. Their names on the IAAM letterhead were a powerful means of confirming the basic legitimacy of the struggle against apartheid and building public support for the movement.

It is remarkable how the IAAM succeeded in capturing the public imagination in a small country such as Ireland. But capture the public imagination we did. For over thirty years, the IAAM kept alive the torch of solidarity with the peoples of southern Africa. The movement was the instrument through which the voice of the Irish people was heard. Thousands of members and supporters – well-known names, ordinary people – marched, picketed, raised their political voices, and gave of their time and money. Legions of Irish women and men committed themselves to working in the cause of freedom and justice for all South Africans. Particular tribute must be paid to the executive committee members of the IAAM, many of whom were involved from the very beginning and who carried on even when times were depressing and political activity was at a low ebb in apartheid South Africa. They came from the churches, from political parties, academic life, student organisations and trade unions, or from no organisation at all; all were passionate about the anti-apartheid cause.

The movement was careful to keep its focus very clear. Apartheid was not just an evil in itself, but a threat to the peace of southern Africa and hence to the world. It was, as the United Nations was eventually to declare, a crime against humanity. The belief that one set of people was inferior to another purely on the basis of skin colour was an insult to black people everywhere, and an encouragement to all racists. Though the IAAM often came under pressure to take up other causes, including the issue of discrimination in Northern Ireland, it maintained steadfastly that apartheid was a unique evil which required a unique response. Many of its members were active in other political causes and social movements, but those causes were not allowed to impinge on the IAAM's work.

At the time of its foundation, as for most of its existence, the IAAM was run entirely by volunteers and was largely financed by the subscriptions of its members and affiliated organisations. Twice a month on Monday nights, volunteers met, at first in the small flat Louise and I had moved into and, later, in our house. Our home became the centre of many of our anti-apartheid activities, with Louise shouldering a huge amount of the administration, for which she was never paid. Whereas I was often the public face of our work, Louise – known for her meticulous eye for detail – was the person behind the scenes, quietly making the arrangements.

From early on the IAAM produced a monthly newsletter, *Amandla*, which members were entitled to receive free of charge. *Amandla* was an invaluable instrument for promoting the IAAM campaigns and the struggle against racism and colonialism. It appeared regularly throughout the movement's existence. It was first produced on an ancient duplicating machine housed in a cold, dark garage. A number of committee members would staple and fold the pages mostly while sitting on the floor in our or someone else's home while others wrote out the addresses of the members and stamped the envelopes. It was convivial if undemanding work, and gave a chance for lively discussion of events. Tea and even, occasionally, whiskey were provided at the end of the work-party. In later years the technology improved and the work was not so laborious, but the comradeship persisted. It would be years before the IAAM could afford paid secretarial assistance, and the movement only occupied a tiny office at the end of its existence, from 1991 to 1994, operating for the rest of the time from our home in Dublin.

Right after its establishment, the IAAM joined the international campaign to save the lives of the accused in the Rivonia Trial, who included Nelson Mandela and Walter Sisulu. Its first activity was to collect signatures for an international petition as part of the World Campaign for the Release of South African Political Prisoners. Many thousands of Irish men and women signed the petition, including half of the members of the Irish Parliament. The trial remained the focus of international anti-apartheid efforts until sentence was handed down in June. When Nelson Mandela and his co-accused were sentenced to life imprisonment in June 1964, world outrage was ignited, and the cause of the struggle against apartheid captured the public imagination. Importantly, the campaign to save the lives of the accused and the protests that followed their conviction were not directed merely at the Rivonia Trial. The trial became a metonym for the regime's racism and oppression, and protests pointedly criticised the South African government, its apartheid policies and the white supremacist assumptions on which these were founded.

From its inception, the thrust of the IAAM's work was to isolate South Africa, economically, culturally, in sport and in diplomatic relations. These objectives accorded with the strategy of the anti-apartheid movement worldwide, and demonstrated a sharp appreciation of the tactical possibilities of increasing international interdependence. In this strategy, sanctions, boycotts and embargoes were the principal weapons.

A significant early success for the academic and cultural boycott was the campaign to persuade Irish playwrights to refuse to allow their plays to be performed in South Africa before segregated audiences. In September 1964, twenty-nine leading Irish playwrights joined the campaign, among them Samuel Beckett and Seán O'Casey. Growing support, if not in the Irish government itself, at least in the hearts and minds of Irish people, was demonstrated two years later when a hundred and fifty Irish academics undertook not to take up posts in South Africa as long as apartheid lasted. These included leading scientists, historians, lawyers and administrators in Irish universities. The list of names was a roll call of Irish academics, many of whom broke their previous contacts with South Africa as a result.

The second half of the 1960s proved to be more challenging for the IAAM as the situation in South Africa changed. With the major black political organisations now banned and all their leaders either in jail or in exile, South Africa – at least for whites – entered a kind of Indian summer as the economy grew at a rate only second in the world to Japan's. For us in the IAAM this was a very difficult time. Membership numbers were low and turnout at our meetings was poor. Out of eighteen members only five or six would turn up. In those dark days much of our work receded and we struggled to keep it alive. Publicly we said that you couldn't put a timetable to ending apartheid, and indeed not until the mid-1980s did we feel that there was an imminent prospect of going home.

At that time I thought that I'd never return to South Africa. It was very tempting then to consider assimilating completely into Irish society. Some of my friends and associates encouraged me to think about becoming a member of a political party in Ireland and then going on to stand for the Senate. I should have liked to do so and thought hard about it. I was even told at one point after I joined the South African Cabinet in 1994 that the Irish Prime Minister had once commented that I was number twenty-seven in his Cabinet of twenty-six members. My own empathy with the political struggle of the Irish people inevitably led to my involvement in the politics of that country, and probably launched my lifelong legal interest in the question of people's right to self-determination. In 1976, when the British government announced that it was seeking to extend the period that detainees could be held without trial, I helped found the Irish Council for Civil Liberties and remained chairperson of that organisation until my return to South Africa. I also helped the Social Democratic and Labour Party of Northern Ireland write its constitution.

In the mid-1980s my identification with the Irish struggle led to my readily agreeing to lead an international lawyers' inquiry into the lethal use of firearms by the security forces in Northern Ireland. This came after a particularly severe spate of killings by soldiers and policemen of unarmed civilians in which the perpetrators were officially freed and even vindicated. With my close friend Richard Harvey of the Haldane Society of Socialist Lawyers and other members of the commission, we visited Derry, Armagh and Belfast, taking statements and hearing evidence. I still recall with some amusement my shock at one of these hearings when a witness launched a vehement attack on 'those black bastards'. It must have been the obvious surprise on my face that prompted Richard to rapidly explain that 'black bastards' was the term commonly used to describe the security forces in their black uniforms. The report we published, *Shoot to Kill? International Lawyers' Inquiry into the Lethal Use of Firearms by the Security Forces in Northern Ireland*, released in 1985, was so damning that I like to think it had some impact on forcing the British government's decision soon after to conduct its own inquiries.

In 1989 I gave the annual D.N. Pritt Memorial Lecture for the Haldane Society, entitling it 'If Law Is the Enemy', in which I charged my audience of socialist lawyers with knowing more about human rights in South Africa and doing too little about abuses of human rights in Northern Ireland, for which their own government was responsible. I argued that repression is not the answer to politically inspired violence, that the partition of Ireland was wrong and that the people of the whole island of Ireland had the right to self-determination. To say the least, these were not universally popular themes at the time. But after the lecture, a group of non-lawyers asked me if I thought there was scope for an NGO in Britain to focus on those human rights abuses. I said I would support them in this, and thus was born one of the most effective NGOs to arise out of the conflict, British Irish Rights Watch (BIRW), under its tireless director, Jane Winter. I readily agreed to be one of its three sponsors, together with Helena Kennedy QC and Michael Mansfield QC.

It wasn't only the politics of Ireland that concerned me. I was honoured to work with Princeton University's Professor Richard Falk on the International Commission to Enquire into Reported Violations of International Law by Israel during its invasion of Lebanon. As my interest in the recognition of the national right to self-determination grew and led to involvement in international legal issues, Unesco honoured me in 1983 by awarding me the Prix Unesco for the Advancement of Human Rights. But all of that came much later. Despite my strong commitment to the Irish struggle for self-determination and my growing involvement in international movements for human rights, I knew my deeper involvement in Ireland and international politics would have meant cutting my connections to South Africa. Thankfully, my wife Louise is pretty tough and, after talking it through, we agreed to remain resolute in our commitment to the struggle in South Africa while continuing our interest in civil liberties in the whole of Ireland.

This is not all I owe to Louise. The quiet force behind the IAAM office in our home, she was also a quiet – and sometimes not so quiet – force behind all the decisions in my life, large and small. It is still rare that I don't consult her, even if I may then fail to act on her advice. Her strength, courage and wisdom permeated our homes and our lives. It is unlikely that I could have done what I have achieved in my life – and not only personally but, above all, politically – without her. Every tribute with which I have been honoured for my efforts in the struggle against apartheid and for human rights anywhere and everywhere in the world I consider an award that I owe at least in part to Louise and share with her.

After the lean years at the end of the 1960s, things slowly began to look up for the Anti-Apartheid Movement. The new decade started off particularly well with the successful enforcement of a boycott of the Springbok rugby tour in the winter of 1969/70. Prior to their arrival in Ireland in January 1970, the Springbok team had already suffered substantial disruption in the UK at the hands of protesters led by the South African-born Peter Hain. During the previous December opposition to the Irish visit began to gather momentum, with the IAAM winning support from the Irish Congress of Trade Unions and the Labour Party in its call for protest. The Irish Transport and General Workers' Union asked its members to refuse to cater for the touring South Africans, and for a while it seemed that the team would be unable to find transport or hotel accommodation. Neither President Eamon de Valera nor any Cabinet minister attended the test match, as was customary; and some fifty prominent figures signed a manifesto that they would also boycott the match. Though the game went ahead at the rugby ground in Lansdowne Road, it was played behind barbed wire, erected to prevent protesters from disturbing the game, and in front of a small group of spectators, while outside the rugby ground crowds picketed the match. The publicity generated by the Springbok tour of 1970 provided a huge boost to the IAAM's campaigns.

I have always had a great passion for sport, particularly cricket, which may be why I found myself getting very involved in the campaign to isolate South African sport. In about 1972 I met up with Sam Ramsamy, newly arrived in exile in Britain, and a driving force behind the sports boycott. Sam later become the executive chairman of the South African Non-Racial Olympic Committee (Sanroc), which had been formed in South Africa in 1962 but had been driven underground by the banning of its leaders and had reconstituted itself in the UK and the US in 1966.

As I was a member of Sanroc, Sam drew on my legal expertise and I increasingly found myself playing the role of its unofficial legal adviser. I assisted Ramsamy in drawing up legal memoranda and sometimes accompanied him as he travelled around the world, persuading international sporting bodies of the importance of isolating South African sportsmen and -women. In 1970 the International Olympic Committee banned South Africa from its ranks. We also had a lot of support from sporting bodies in African countries that were gaining independence at the time and later from the International Campaign Against Apartheid Sport (ICAAS) and the International Association of Athletics Federations (IAAF). As a result, by the mid-1970s the international isolation of South African sport was virtually complete for all major sports codes, with the exception of hockey. Given that in South Africa sport has always had the status of something like a religion, the sports boycott hit hard. As Ramsamy has said, 'the first chinks in the armour of apartheid legislation' appeared as a result of the government's efforts to promote its beloved sporting programme in the context of increasing international isolation.

The success of the sports boycott, starting with the Springbok tour of 1969/70, kickstarted a period of accelerated growth for the IAAM and brought a dramatic increase in membership. This growth continued as more and more local and national organisations, student and trade unions, and other public and private bodies became affiliates of the IAAM, a development crucial to building a broad-based public consensus on opposition to apartheid. By the mid-1970s the IAAM could claim the broadest coalition of national organisations in Ireland's history, including, somewhat controversially, Sinn Féin.

But it was the Soweto student uprising of June 1976 that really transformed the outlook and fortunes of the IAAM, as it did for South

Africa. The bravery of the schoolchildren who marched against the imposition of Afrikaans, and the appalling massacre of hundreds of them, had an electrifying effect around the world. Within three or four months the revolt had spread from one end of the country to the other. For the first time since the National Party took power in 1948, a revolt on a mass scale took place. It was, as the state immediately feared, a harbinger of things to come.

Initially, the dramatic expansion of international interest in southern Africa following the Soweto uprising placed great pressure on the IAAM. As the only Irish organisation dealing solely with southern African issues, the IAAM was increasingly called upon to provide information and assistance. It responded by co-operating still more closely with solidarity movements in countries like Britain, the Netherlands, Australia, New Zealand, the United States and Japan as well as with international organisations and institutions working to combat apartheid. Of these, the International Defence and Aid Fund (Idaf) and the UN's Special Committee Against Apartheid were the most central to the IAAM's work. The UN committee assisted especially during International Anti-Apartheid Year in 1978, when Irish participation in the international solidarity movement really surged ahead.

In these years the IAAM also became more directly involved with the liberation movements of southern Africa. Among them, the ANC remained the IAAM's greatest inspiration and the movement took its cue from Oliver Tambo's leadership. But we worked too with Swapo of South West Africa/Namibia, Frelimo of Mozambique and, initially, Zapu of Rhodesia/Zimbabwe. We also supported the African Party for the Independence of Cape Verde and Guinea (PAIGC). Amilcar Cabral, the leader of the PAIGC, inspired us with his speeches and his writings. He combined the virtues of an intellectual and the strength of a guerrilla. In 1971 he came to speak at a big gathering in Dublin, at which he famously compared the Irish solidarity movement to the white foam on top of a glass of black Guinness. I had originally met him at the first conference on the liberation of southern Africa held in Khartoum in 1965. It was very moving for me to be there and rub shoulders with the leading figures of the liberation movements. Indeed, it was his accessibility and approachability in Khartoum – I remember engaging him in conversation on a bus – that enabled us to invite him to Dublin a few years later. The three days I spent with Cabral during his visit fortified my feelings about liberation as a catalyst for the full development of the oppressed.

One of the highlights of our deepening engagement with the liberation movements of southern Africa took place in 1975 when Louise and I were invited to attend the independence celebrations of Mozambique. It was our first joint visit to southern Africa and was especially poignant as the father of Mozambique's freedom, Eduardo Mondlane, with whom I had numerous discussions in Khartoum in 1965, had been killed earlier. As we were about to land in Maputo, the steward on our aeroplane asked for our attention and said: 'Ladies and gentlemen, in a few moments we shall be entering the Portuguese colony of Mozambique, which in a day's time will be the People's Republic of Mozambique. In greeting the people of Mozambique, I hope that they will forgive us for five hundred years of colonial exploitation.' I have always wondered what happened to the brave steward.

As for the actual independence celebrations, what struck me most was the humility of Agostinho Neto, the leader of the struggle in Angola, who, like us, was a guest. Poet, theoretician and guerrilla leader, he was most unassuming. When we were held up in a traffic jam on the way to the stadium where the 'handover' celebrations were due to take place, Neto got out of his car and strolled around without any regard for his personal security. Our car was just behind his modest Volkswagen. Though he was to become the first President of an independent Angola later in the same year, Angola's travails would only end when South African forces were forced to withdraw from the country after their defeat at Cuito Cuanavale more than a decade later.

For the IAAM in the 1970s and 1980s, conferences and international seminars were a vital plank in the international effort to foster solidarity and mobilise for action. These meetings provided forums where representatives of anti-apartheid movements, liberation movements, NGOs and solidarity groups from different parts of the world could come together to share perspectives, debate strategy and plan future campaigns. Perhaps the most decisive conference of all in determining the future campaign against apartheid was that on European Economic Community (EEC) relations with South Africa, organised and hosted by the IAAM in January 1979. The timing of the conference was significant: in July, Ireland would be assuming the chair of the Council of Ministers of the EEC.

The Soweto uprising of 1976 had stoked the sanctions debate with pressing questions about the extent of international complicity with apartheid. In Western Europe, such probing questions increasingly turned the spotlight of anti-apartheid activism onto the EEC. In the late 1970s, EEC countries were among South Africa's main trading partners. At the same time, EEC countries were South Africa's largest investors, accounting for sixty-four per cent of total foreign investment. Arguably more significant than trade relations was the EEC's facilitation of financial loans to the South African government.

As a general policy the EEC favoured trade with South Africa, with the result that the more progressive policy positions of smaller member countries, such as Denmark, Sweden, the Netherlands and Ireland, were toned down. Not only did these governments retreat from their earlier stances, but increasingly activists were met with the stock response that member governments must first secure the support of the whole EEC before they could act against apartheid South Africa.

In the light of these developments, the IAAM organised in 1979 the first international conference on EEC links with apartheid. Held at the end of January, it attracted a wide range of delegates and representatives of organisations, including the Irish, British, Scottish and Dutch Anti-Apartheid Movements, the UN's Special Committee Against Apartheid, the ANC as well as the EEC.

The conference was opened by Michael O'Kennedy, Irish Minister of Foreign Affairs. The main address was given by Oliver Tambo, who famously declared, 'The EEC is the lifeblood of apartheid,' and focused the following two days' discussions firmly on Western governments' collaboration with the apartheid regime. In the event Tambo's speech condemning EEC trade with South Africa proved the vital spark that set in motion co-ordinated initiatives across the EEC for opposing apartheid. No longer was the focus of our campaigns limited to national work but it took on a collective European perspective. At the same time the conference gave new impetus to the various sanctions and boycott campaigns organised by the Anti-Apartheid Movement during the 1980s, and set the stage for the final push against the embattled apartheid state.

The 1980s opened with a spectacular *coup de main* against one of South Africa's most strategic installations. Although the IAAM as an organisation had no part in it, the attack did involve an Irish connection, a fact that till now has not been public knowledge.

To tell what happened, I need to go back a little in time. In the late 1970s, I was asked if it was possible to arrange military training for some MK combatants. I wanted very much to undertake this task, but it was a delicate one because it would of necessity involve the IRA. None of us wished to place the ANC office in London in any jeopardy nor fuel the allegations of connivance between the ANC and IRA.

I went to see the general secretary of the Communist Party of Ireland, Michael O'Riordan, who was a man of great integrity and whom I trusted to keep secret the information at his disposal. He in turn contacted Gerry Adams of Sinn Féin, and it was arranged that two military experts would come to Dublin to meet two MK personnel and take them to a safe place for two weeks of intensive training. On the date arranged I was to be away, so I instructed Louise as to what she was to say when the MK men rang. In standard secret-service style, nothing was to be written down, and everything had to be remembered. Whether through my inadequate instruction, or Louise's utter terror and fear of somehow betraying the operation, the wrong answer was given and the two MK men went back to London without meeting their contacts. Later, however, we did arrange a successful meeting, the training was conducted, and I believe the expertise the MK cadres obtained was duly imparted to others in the ANC camps in Angola.

Then, on 1 June 1980, South Africa was shocked by one of the most daring and audacious acts of military insurgency in the struggle against apartheid. On that day the country's major oil refinery plant in the town of Sasolburg was bombed by explosives. Black smoke billowed over the Highveld. Every newspaper and television station carried pictures, footage and stories of the attack. And, while the damage to the refinery was, according to the apartheid regime, relatively superficial, the propaganda value and its effect on the morale of the liberation movement were inestimable.

Yet only Louise and I knew that the attack on Sasolburg was the result of reconnaissance carried out by members of the IRA. I had again been approached by the MK High Command, who wanted us to find two people to conduct a reconnaissance operation and report back on the feasibility of attacking Sasol, South Africa's major oil refinery, vital to the maintenance of the apartheid state. Located on the Vaal River, Sasol was a perfect target. It was highly strategic but relatively undefended. There were also few people wandering about the plant at night, so the chances of inflicting civilian casualties were small.

I undertook this task quite separately from the IAAM. This was partly to protect the organisation and partly for reasons of security. We knew too that right-wing British intelligence services and right-wing British media would use the information to undermine the ANC and the broad Anti-Apartheid Movement. Once again I arranged the task with Gerry Adams of Sinn Féin, through the intermediation of Michael O'Riordan. Though I no longer recall the names of the persons who volunteered, if indeed I ever knew them, they laid the ground for one of the most dramatic operations carried out by MK personnel.

Some months after we'd set arrangements in place, Louise rang me at work to say that I must come home immediately. Not knowing what to expect, I excused myself from an important academic meeting at Trinity College and drove as fast as I could in the Dublin traffic. Unlike today with satellite television, there were no news channels as such, and I had to wait a while before the news came round again. There on the television was the extraordinary spectacle of Sasol in flames, lighting up the sky for miles around. We cheered and felt we had made a major contribution to the struggle. It was a huge morale booster and must have been the same in South Africa, though the authorities did their best to minimise the impact of the attack.

In great excitement we phoned our fellow committee members of the IAAM, who came to gape and cheer with us at the spectacular explosion that had hit a vital South African installation. It was evident to all of us that the regime had suffered a demonstrable loss and embarrassment. Yet only Louise and I knew that the attack on Sasolburg was the result of reconnaissance carried out by members of the IRA. At the time the ANC accepted responsibility for the coup and much later the three active participants, all MK cadres, applied for and obtained amnesty from the Truth and Reconciliation Commission.

Over the years Louise and I had been requested by the ANC in London to help with a number of tasks, which we undertook quite separately from the IAAM. Indeed, not long after we settled in Dublin, I was asked by Joe Slovo to return to South Africa secretly. I had a British passport and there were some urgent messages he wanted carried home. I thought long and hard about the request. Of course it was total madness, suicide. The South African authorities knew well enough who I was by then. They would have picked me up the moment my foot first alighted on South African soil. But what was my moral duty? I had been requested to perform a task, a foolhardy task maybe, but an official ANC task nonetheless, and one for which there were at that stage few comrades available. Could I say no? In the end, I refused. I am not sure Joe ever forgave me completely.

At the time of the Sasolburg attack, I was very much in tune with Ireland and with Irish needs and aspirations. I was a strong believer in Irish independence and in a united Ireland. But I never supported the IRA. The attack on Sasolburg had nothing to do with the IAAM, and nobody knew about the story behind it except Louise and me. When the plant blew up, we were so excited, I suppose some of the other IAAM people must have wondered if we had any connection or involvement.

Incidentally, a few months after the attack, in January 1981, Sinn Féin – the IRA's political parent – applied to the IAAM for affiliation. This provoked intense discussions within the movement, not only in Ireland but in Britain and beyond. The position of the IAAM executive committee was that any organisation could affiliate on condition that it supported the three basic objectives of the international anti-apartheid movement: the isolation of South Africa, support for the liberation struggle (which after the Rivonia Trial meant support for the armed struggle) and the provision of humanitarian assistance. Sinn Féin supported all of these objectives and was duly affiliated. This caused some furore in the media. I was not at home when the press started calling and a weary Louise, still recovering from a bout of flu, had to field endless calls. Sinn Féin had no representation on the IAAM's executive committee and played no part in policy formulation. It was merely one of some ninety affiliates. Nevertheless, at the September 1984 annual general meeting, a motion was introduced for Sinn Féin's expulsion. The motion was withdrawn after it was agreed to refer the issue to a meeting of the executive, where the issue was subsequently discussed at length and Sinn Féin's affiliation was reaffirmed.

For me, the connection with Sinn Féin and the intensifying armed campaign in South Africa highlighted the whole question of the role of violence, and the morality of war, in the struggle for freedom. Of course there were people who declared that the ANC was a terrorist organisation. Our argument, on the contrary, was that the armed struggle was legitimate because we had no other recourse: every other opportunity for protest and opposition had been closed. This argument succeeded in Ireland. Whereas anti-apartheid movements in other countries may have downplayed the armed struggle, we never compromised our stance. Our consistent position was that the struggle to end apartheid was three-pronged and comprised the resistance of the South African people inside South Africa, international sanctions and boycott campaigns, and the armed struggle.

I myself struggled to accept the absolute prioritisation of violence in the struggle for which some of my colleagues in the movement were pushing. My own view, like Nelson Mandela's, was that South Africans are not by nature a violent people. We have a long history of non-violence which is deeply ingrained. It was crucial that we didn't turn the anti-apartheid struggle into a racial bloodbath. There would have been no recovery from that.

When Albert Luthuli, as president of the ANC, accepted the need for the formation of MK in 1960, he did so on condition that MK was kept separate from the ANC. This was enormously important, for since the 1920s the ANC had led the campaign for a rights-based approach to the struggle against apartheid. At the same time I acknowledge that symbolic military actions, such as the Sasolburg attack, were necessary.

The armed struggle – always under the control of the political forces – played a strategic part, but a distinctly unique part, in our drive for liberation.

The 1980s had opened with a spectacular blow against apartheid and continued with mounting success by the Anti-Apartheid Movement in turning the screws ever more tightly on the South African regime. One important aspect of this was the campaign for the cultural and academic boycott. This was distinct among the numerous IAAM campaigns in that there was not unanimous agreement within the movement about its strategic value. Some members advanced the view that within the framework of education and culture there should be free and regular contact, though isolation of the racist regime in all other spheres should be maintained. However, supporters of this view could not argue against the facts of disparity in the allocation of government funding for white and for black education, as in all other spheres of life. Though the debate would continue, eventually leading to a traumatic public falling out between the IAAM and Dr Conor Cruise O'Brien, the movement's former chairman, the IAAM's position on the need for cultural and academic boycotts would remain unchanged.

During the 1980s the UN Centre Against Apartheid proved an important ally in the IAAM's efforts to maintain and extend the boycott. Particularly powerful was the register of entertainers who performed in South Africa, published annually by the Centre. This register, styled after the register of sportsmen and -women who openly defied the sports boycott, attracted similar criticism. Following Paul Simon's listing for visiting South Africa during the production of his *Graceland* album, I was personally accused of supporting 'a pathetic, isolationist, misunderstanding of what Simon tried to do on his new music album'. I replied: 'Let's get one or two things quite clear ... However well intentioned a musician or entertainer may be, the demand of the trade unions and the liberation movements is not to have anything to do with South Africa.' On another occasion, I explained the principle: 'Neither Paul Simon nor any other musician, however well known, can interpret the demands of the people of South Africa

… These demands are quite clear: the total boycott of apartheid in all its manifestations.'

I must add that it was very difficult to explain this to some people because of their personal magnetism. I spent more than an hour with Eartha Kitt, sitting on the floor at her feet, trying to persuade her to give an undertaking not to perform in South Africa again. Faced by a choice between a picket and an undertaking, she agreed to the latter.

Over the years, the register included a very small number of Irish entertainers, among them Joe Dolan, Geraldine Branagan and the popular Irish singing duo, Foster and Allen. The IAAM was particularly incensed at Branagan, whose tour of South Africa in the mid-1980s included performances for South African troops. A report in the South African press that 'an Irish blonde bombshell' would be touring the country prompted Louise to quip, 'In the land of apartheid blonde is beautiful and it seems that to be a bombshell is the highest tribute that can be paid!'

Luke Kelly, of those great Irish singers the Dubliners, came to speak to me one day. They had been offered enormous benefits to perform in South Africa. They were wonderful artists and really could have done with the money. Luke said to me, 'Kader, what about all these things I hear about change in South Africa? The lavatories are non-racial now.' I said, 'You don't believe that, do you, Luke? The main thing is not that the lavatories are open to blacks. The main thing is that the whites need you to bolster their racist state because you belong to the world and they are isolated.' 'Alright,' he said, 'we're not going.' So apartheid South Africa got only third-rate artists; no first-class performers went.

In the mid-1980s Trinity College Dublin became the focus of an important debate about the academic boycott. The university had by and large supported the boycott and had consistently set benchmarks for institutions of higher education in Ireland, for example in 1971, when the university's Council resolved not to own shares in any company that traded or had a subsidiary that traded in South Africa. A decade later, the Council resolved that the university would not retain any formal or institutional links with academic or state institutions in South Africa. Then, in 1986, the Council resolved on principle that financial assistance or leave of absence sought by academic staff for purposes of visiting South Africa would be denied. The university effectively forbade its faculty staff to collaborate with South African scholars. University College adopted a similar position and soon enough the national Department of Education came out in support of 'the cessation of all academic, cultural, scientific and sports relations that would support the apartheid regime of South Africa'.

The year that Trinity moved to strengthen the academic boycott also saw the most public challenge to the academic boycott yet when the renowned scholar, journalist and former IAAM chairman, Dr Conor Cruise O'Brien, accepted an invitation to deliver a series of lectures at the University of Cape Town (UCT) in 1986. There was a public outcry at this extraordinary change of tune by O'Brien and I publicly expressed my sense of shame at his 'act of betrayal'. O'Brien's initial response was dismissive: 'Stuff them. I will not have my conscience run for me by Kader Asmal.' Two days later O'Brien lashed out at me personally, accusing me of running the IAAM 'as a branch of a disciplined international revolutionary movement, with no room for deviations of any kind or for the exercise of personal judgment or individual conscience. You are to toe the line or else.'

The fall-out between O'Brien and the IAAM provoked heated debate in the press. Despite the fact that O'Brien's criticism of the IAAM included a personal attack on me, I tried to avoid conspiratorial rhetoric. Instead, I noted that the IAAM's policies and principles were decided upon by democratic processes at the movement's annual general meetings and that their inspiration came not from 'a cabal of red-eyed revolutionaries but from the resolutions of the General Assembly of the United Nations'. I noted too that the academic boycott had been taken up by the IAAM in 1967, the year O'Brien became the movement's chairman.

Despite protests against his flouting of the principles he had previously held dear, O'Brien nevertheless accepted UCT's offer. However, in Cape Town he faced a barrage of criticism from student activists who mounted a vociferous campaign against him. In the face of growing criticism in South Africa and following the disruption of his lectures, O'Brien was forced to abandon his lecture series and return to Ireland, though still defiantly proclaiming his satisfaction at having broken the boycott and thereby, so he claimed, having provoked a discussion on academic freedom.

On his return O'Brien and I took part in a television debate on the most popular and longest-running programme in Ireland. Foolishly, I referred to him as Conor at the start and was slapped down for this familiarity on my part. The debate was very acrimonious. Towards the end, the presenter asked me: 'Come on, Kader, do you forgive Conor for going to South Africa?' I later understood from the grapevine that all pub conversations stopped at this question as the drinkers waited for my response. This was: 'It is not for me to do so; it is the prerogative of South Africans who asked for the cultural boycott and it is they who must decide.' I believe that the silence was broken by loud cheers.

Notwithstanding the O'Brien affair, the academic boycott became immensely successful both in Ireland and beyond. What surprised me was that conservative academics who had previously gone to South Africa now asked me what they could do concretely, apart from cutting their ties. My answer was that they should support scholarship funds set up for black South African students by the IAAM and Idaf. In time, as the cultural and academic boycotts intensified, South Africa became more and more isolated. It was a significant victory.

By the 1980s sanctions or the economic boycott had become the lynchpin of the international anti-apartheid movement's strategy. Economists argue over the extent to which sanctions damaged and distorted the South African economy and over how heavily economic difficulties weighed in President F.W. de Klerk's decision to meet his enemies at the negotiating table. However, that sanctions placed an impossible burden on the regime is beyond doubt, as Barend du Plessis, then Minister of Finance, acknowledged in 1990 when he declared that disinvestment was the dagger that finally immobilised apartheid.

In the Irish struggle against apartheid the Dunnes strike of 1984–5 was a watershed event. This industrial action was unique, not only for the length of time it was sustained, but also for its role in acting as a rallying point for the trade boycott and the larger sanctions debate. What is more, it forced the Irish government into adopting an unequivocal (though limited) policy on trade with South Africa.

Already in 1981, the Irish Congress of Trade Unions (ICTU) had adopted a series of resolutions appealing for support for the international campaign to end apartheid. Of these resolutions, the most far-reaching called for 'the ending of all collaboration ... with South Africa' and urged affiliated unions and their members to 'block the handling of South African goods at points of import, distribution and sale'. Adding its own voice to this union position, the Irish Distributive and Administrative Trade Union (Idatu), an ICTU affiliate, passed a resolution in 1984 calling for a boycott of all South African goods. And so when Karen Gearon, Idatu shop steward at Dunnes Stores in Dublin's Henry Street, received a union circular outlining the resolution, she called her members together. They supported it unanimously. The catalyst for the strike came on 17 July 1984 when Mary Manning, a cashier and Idatu member, refused to handle the purchase of two South African grapefruit, in accordance with the union resolutions.

Though the affected customer was sympathetic, management was not and Manning was suspended indefinitely until she agreed to handle all goods on sale in the shop. She refused to place her employer's instructions over her union's, and nine of her fellow union members went on strike in support. Two days later, Idatu gave official backing to the strike and ICTU granted permission to picket the shop.

Thus began the Dunnes strike. For the following two and a half years, ten young women workers and one young man would stand on the picket line day in and day out, in all kinds of weather. They were on occasion subjected to taunts and jeers, were called 'nigger-lovers', spat at and sometimes manhandled. Two strikers were visited by the Special Branch. Yet despite intimidation, the strikers' extraordinary display of solidarity drew widespread praise and support.

The day the strike officially began on 19 July, the IAAM put out a statement of support for the strikers. It also contributed funds and issued appeals for contributions to a strike fund established by Idatu. IAAM members and supporters were present as well on the picket lines. Marius Schoon, a South African anti-apartheid activist resident in Dublin since the murder of his wife and daughter by a South African security force bomb, was a frequent participant. I must confess that picketing in the winters imposed great strains on solidarity. The wetness of the Irish weather was persistent and adhesive. So it was a triumph for these young working-class protesters to get someone like me, who hardly ever went to my children's school events, to attend nearly every weekend during the strike.

Attempts to negotiate an end to the strike came to naught. When IDATU took the matter to the Labour Court, Dunnes refused to appear. The court released a report which endorsed the boycott of South African goods as a legitimate means of continuing the anti-apartheid struggle in the international arena. The court recommended that the Minister of Labour meet with all supermarket owners to discuss the implementation of the boycott and proposed that the minister explore the possibility of a code for conscientious objections to handling South African goods.

Before long, Dunnes Stores was being widely censured. The strike significantly heightened public consciousness of the boycott and became an inspiration to sympathisers and activists around the world, including Bishop Desmond Tutu, who travelled to Dublin to meet the strikers en route to Stockholm where he was to collect his Nobel Prize for Peace. After expressing his pride at the strikers' 'extraordinary actions,' he addressed a personal message to the store owner: 'Here are young people of whom you ought to be proud, because they are people of such tremendous integrity. You should be glad that you have people of such calibre working for you.'

The ongoing dispute not only prompted numerous gestures of solidarity and statements of support, but also produced very tangible advances in the Irish struggle against apartheid. Dublin dockworkers showed their solidarity by blacking all goods destined for Dunnes Stores, forcing Dunnes to transport their South African merchandise to Dublin via Belfast. Many shops also decided to remove South African goods from their shelves, including large department stores such as Clery's, Bests and Roches Stores. Motivated more out of prudence than solidarity, the voluntary removal of South African goods was nevertheless a significant victory.

In December 1986, following a government announcement that it was considering a ban on South African fruit and vegetables, the daily picket was called off. The difficulty faced by the government, a coalition of the Labour Party and Fianna Fáil, was that it sought a rules-based approach to banning trade with South Africa, even if only in fruit and vegetables. The solution came from Ruairi Quinn, the Minister for Labour and a long-standing IAAM supporter. Having been given the advice that any effort to ban South African produce was contrary to the terms of Ireland's EEC membership and the various obligations of the General Agreement on Tariffs and Trade (GATT), he discovered from examination of International Labour Organisation conventions that imported goods and services that were the product of forced or prison labour could be banned under international law. Having by chance secured evidence that some prisoners in South African jails were being hired out, at a pittance, to white farmers, he persuaded the government to introduce a suitably worded ban on the importation of South African produce which did not compromise the country's commitment to its international agreements. As Ruairi Quinn says, 'The announcement of the ban was a triumph, and the dispute ended with the eleven workers being feted nationally and internationally.'

The strike had an enormous impact on Irish and international support for the anti-apartheid struggle and was widely celebrated as a stunning example of the power of direct action. The strikers' principled stand against handling South African goods, eventually leading to a total ban on South African fruit and vegetables in Ireland, inspired activists and rank-and-file supporters of anti-apartheid organisations, not only in Ireland, but internationally too.

What is more, the Dunnes strike also occasioned a more general and sustained critique of the Irish government's posture regarding the international campaign for comprehensive sanctions against South Africa. Historically, though the Irish government's policy toward apartheid was more progressive than that of most other Western governments, its condemnations usually spoke more loudly than its actions. Its own preference for 'selective, graduated sanctions' fitted in with the framework of 'constructive engagement' advocated by its senior EEC partners, Britain and West Germany, and by the US. Still, the government stopped short of advocating dialogue with Pretoria, as implied by 'constructive engagement'.

That the government did not institute comprehensive sanctions remained a source of deep frustration for the IAAM. On the other hand, that the government did not entirely fall in with the major Western powers and continually had to defend its position on apartheid is testimony to the IAAM's success at elevating apartheid, an issue of seemingly little direct importance to Ireland, to the top of the national agenda.

I have already mentioned in passing the close relations that existed between the IAAM and the International Defence and Aid Fund for Southern Africa. Idaf was in essence an extraordinarily successful example of legitimate money laundering for a worthy cause. It was aimed at helping the families of jailed South African activists and providing legal defence for the series of trials of opponents of apartheid. The term 'money laundering' implies a certain criminality, of course, which is true if one considers that it was apartheid laws – described by the United Nations as a 'crime against humanity' – that we were circumventing. But, if we are to cast such an activity in moral terms, Idaf was a powerful force for good which alleviated suffering on a massive scale and saved many lives from the gallows. It did this by secrecy, volunteerism and a wickedly crafty scheme that the apartheid state never cracked. It didn't start that way, but that is how it developed. I am very proud to have been associated with it, being vice-president for fifteen years and serving it for even more. This is a story of international solidarity, of the awakening of a moral conscience and selflessness, without precedent. It is a story worth telling.

When in 1952 the ANC launched the Defiance Campaign against apartheid's unjust laws, the state reacted by arresting the protesters, thousands of them. This was difficult enough for the jailed, but it also placed huge pressure on the families they left behind. In the midst of this crisis, the indefatigable Anglican priest Trevor Huddleston wrote to John Collins, a canon of St Paul's Cathedral in London, to ask for help. Funds were needed, Huddleston wrote, to help tide the families over until their breadwinners could be returned to their homes. As a response to Huddleston's appeal, Collins established a small organisation called Christian Action. This was to become the parent of one of the biggest NGOs in Britain, Idaf, and was to have a profound impact on the struggle against apartheid and, in particular, on the lives of the activists and their families.

Having assisted with the Defiance Campaign in 1952, Christian Action was soon called on to help again when in December 1956, a hundred and fifty-six anti-apartheid leaders were arrested by the police in a series of dramatic pre-dawn raids and charged with high treason, a capital offence. In response to a request from the Bishop of Johannesburg, Ambrose Reeves, for help with legal representation for the accused and support for their families, most of whom had just lost their sole breadwinners, Collins wrote out a cheque there and then for £100. He also gave the assurance that Christian Action would look after the accused and, in the meantime, would care for their families. This was very much the way Collins operated. He would agree to pay and then find the money later.

On hearing the news of Collins's positive and immediate response, Reeves set up a corresponding Treason Trial Defence Fund to raise money from within South Africa and established a committee to administer the funds. The fund that Collins set up in London, combined with Reeves's, soon became known as the Defence and Aid Fund and later, and more colloquially, Idaf.

Collins was a rather extraordinary, strongly self-willed man. He had a big, booming voice that sounded like a lion roaring. He was profoundly charismatic. His presence dominated every meeting or conference he attended. He always stood on ceremony and he liked to be in total control. He spoke with a marked upper-class accent, which made his sudden turns to anger all the more surprising and impactful. At heart, though, Collins was quintessentially a peaceful, spiritual man. He spoke out against the Vietnam War and in favour of nuclear disarmament. After visiting South Africa briefly in 1950, he maintained a deeply empathetic connection to the continent. I got on well with him.

The activity around the Treason Trial set the pattern for Idaf when it came to the conduct of later trials. Collins insisted that the very best lawyers be employed in the defence of activists. Then, in consultation with the accused, indeed at their initiative and that of their organisations, a strategic approach was adopted to put the regime on trial, and every opportunity was taken through cross-examination and legal analysis to highlight the inequity and brutality of the apartheid system. Another device was the funding of an observer, an internationally recognised legal authority, to observe and report on trials. In 1963–4, it was Idaf that took up the defence of Nelson Mandela and the other Rivonia trialists, playing a considerable role in saving the movement's leadership from the gallows. Idaf also took up legal representation at scores of other trials, inquests and investigations.

But the Defence and Aid Fund's success posed a threat to the South African state. On 18 March 1966, no longer able to tolerate the fund, the government banned it under the Suppression of Communism Act. The immediate consequence of a banning under this Act was that it now became a criminal offence, punishable by long terms of imprisonment, for anyone in South Africa to receive funds or any kind of assistance from Idaf. In response, Idaf devised an elaborate and brilliant system to circumvent this restriction, in effect a form of money laundering that took place through a chain of legal firms. This made it almost impossible for the government to figure out who was actually footing the bills for the defence of activists on trial.

After the banning of the Defence and Aid Fund, Collins also had to devise a system whereby funds could be sent to the families of convicted political prisoners or those detained or awaiting trial, who were often in dire need. It was decided to recruit volunteers who would send postal orders to the families to cover minimal living expenses and often help with the education of children. If the prisoner was on Robben Island the money would also cover the cost of a correspondence course and the expense of a visit by the family.

Idaf's aid programme was to become legendary, a collective feat of subterfuge and concealment. A mailing list was developed and a roster of letter-writers drawn up in Britain, Sweden, Norway, Ireland and, later, Canada and Denmark. By the time Idaf closed in the 1990s, there was a worldwide army of correspondents, as they were called, numbering over seven hundred, many corresponding with as many as ten families, who sent an annual total of about £3 million to thousands of recipients in South Africa. Of this army, none but a tiny handful (of the early ones) knew they were working for Idaf. The system not only had a built-in security system that was virtually impregnable, but had an accounting system that was virtually perfect.

My work in fundraising on behalf of Idaf became a regular activity, and its campaign for the release of political prisoners became a central feature of my own political work in Ireland and elsewhere. In 1965, when the IAAM affiliated to Idaf, I attended Idaf's annual conference in London. The following year I became Idaf vice-president, a post I would hold until 1981. That I was at the same time vice-chairman of the IAAM helped to deepen relations between the two bodies. In 1975 the IAAM played host when Idaf held its conference in Dublin. Louise drove around the city looking for suitable hotel accommodation (not so available then) and came back with descriptions of rather dark, dismal conference rooms or, in one instance, a conference room cum ballroom, with pillars draped in red velvet. 'It sounds like a brothel,' I said. The previous year Canon Collins had been among the prominent speakers at IAAM's tenth anniversary meeting. Though the IAAM set up a local Idaf committee, the attempt to have two separate organisations was soon abandoned. This did not mean that support for the work of Idaf was lacking, rather the opposite; but Ireland is a small country and it seemed an unnecessary duplication of resources to be holding two meetings when one could cover both activities.

The history of Idaf's contribution to alleviating apartheid suffering was a mammoth effort in which we in Ireland played a small but significant role. We recruited some twenty-five correspondents to write letters and send money to the families of political prisoners in South Africa. Such was our obsession with security that we used a special typewriter for Idaf work only, kept our documents in a safe and didn't ever talk about our Idaf work on the telephone. Louise only ever took cash to the post office to buy postal orders for the correspondents. Often she carried thousands of pounds with her.

The way it worked was that Idaf headquarters in London would send instructions to Garry Kilgallen, a long-standing executive committee member of the IAAM and a bank official by profession. (At his prompting, the Central Bank of Ireland helped to conceal the source of Idaf funds by allowing the letter-writers to fill in the purpose of the monetary gifts as simply 'charitable donation'.) On receiving the instructions from Idaf London, Garry would in turn brief Louise. As the country co-ordinator for Ireland, she would collect the necessary cash for each correspondent and pass the money on, together with details of the recipients, to our volunteers. Most of these were women: working-class women, wives of academics, IAAM members, in fact anyone we knew who had a bit of time to spare. Every two months they would write innocuous letters to their families, enclosing £30 in postal orders for subsistence expenses. The enclosed letter would be full of pleasantries but would not incriminate the recipient. Recipients often did not know they were receiving money from Idaf and assumed they were getting a little help from well-wishers. There have been cases where the beneficiaries and the correspondents stayed in touch long after the fall of apartheid, have visited each other or have become friends. It was a very intricate system, but the apartheid state never broke it.

One of Louise's key assistants was her father, a major in the Second World War, who had been the first British officer to enter Belsen concentration camp after liberation. This was something he never spoke of, even though he knew of my great interest in the Nuremberg Trials. He never let me see his old papers, which he kept hidden in the attic. There was much about him that was surprising. On his first visit to Ireland to spend Christmas with us, this upright Englishman, the very essence of propriety, ended up poaching for wild trout with the local postman. He couldn't understand a word of the postman's Kerry accent, but they just seemed to hit it off. One day when we were talking about Idaf, he offered to help. He not only sent money regularly, but also recruited almost a dozen correspondents from among his own circle and from the West Indian community in the Midlands of England. The anti-apartheid struggle always was efficient at unearthing people of distinction who were moved to help, sometimes from the most unlikely and unexpected quarters.

The success of Idaf over the years generated a great deal of money to support its activities and work. In fact, the organisation sent something like £90 million to South Africa during Idaf's life. During that time we supported many thousands of people, including Winnie Mandela and the current President of South Africa, Jacob Zuma, who I recall had a lady from the English Midlands send him money every month. Idaf's most dramatic work, though, was in the defence of people charged in South Africa with political offences.

It is ironic that I ended up in 2005 as president of the Financial Action Task Force, based in Paris, which deals with the prevention of money laundering. But at least when we engaged in this activity, it was for a legitimate and just cause and against an illegitimate and unjust regime.

That Idaf made a difference, there is no question at all. It provided counsel for hundreds of trials and dozens of inquests and commissions of inquiry. There were showcase trials and modest individual trials. In every one, the apartheid state was unveiled in all its ugliness and brutality. This, in turn, fuelled international antipathy to apartheid and generated both support and funding for Idaf's work and for the anti-apartheid movement as a whole.

Idaf was one of the great examples of international human solidarity. Its information pamphlets were an invaluable aid and were circulated and sold by us in the IAAM and by solidarity movements all over the world. Idaf provides yet further evidence of the success of the anti-apartheid movement in awakening the conscience of the world about apartheid South Africa.

In late 1989 F.W. de Klerk, a former Minister of Education, replaced P.W. Botha as leader of the National Party and as State President of South Africa. He aroused enormous expectations when he announced the release of all the Rivonia trialists. The world was certain Mandela could not be long following, as indeed was Mandela himself. That momentous event happened on 11 February 1990, not a week after De Klerk used his address at the opening of South Africa's Parliament on 2 February to lift bans on the African National Congress, the South African Communist Party, the Pan Africanist Congress and other organisations and to announce the release of many (but not all) political prisoners.

Louise recalls representing the IAAM at a meeting of the Release Mandela Campaign in London, and being summoned to a room full of journalists and television cameras. The atmosphere was tense with expectation, yet when one journalist listening to the radio announced that Mandela was to be released, there was utter silence. After nearly thirty years of campaigning for this outcome, it was hard to believe it had happened. Only when the same announcement appeared on television, did cheers and ANC salutes erupt. I myself was interviewed by the well-known presenter on Irish radio, Gay Byrne, about Mandela's release and was told: 'Now you can go home, Kader.'

Back in Dublin, plans were put in place to celebrate the occasion. Yet amid the excitement at Mandela's release and the unbanning of the ANC, the IAAM was acutely aware of new dangers. The legislative framework of apartheid remained in place; thousands of political prisoners remained in prison; and troops still occupied the townships. The facts were simple: apartheid was far from abolished, though the regime was substantially weakened. The struggle therefore not only had to continue, but had to be intensified.

What was required of the apartheid regime was 'profound and irreversible change' as a precondition for the lifting of sanctions. The debate about the sufficiency of De Klerk's actions turned on this point. Thus, a major part of the IAAM's work during this period involved convincing the Irish government to leave sanctions against South Africa in place and to use its influence in the EEC to prevent a softening of its position. In this effort, the figure of Nelson Mandela would loom large.

Over the years one of our projects at the IAAM was a campaign to persuade the Dublin City Council to grant Nelson Mandela the freedom of the city. For some time this was unsuccessful, as councillors were afraid that to support the former leader of the ANC's armed wing in this way would be to encourage demands that IRA prisoners in Northern Ireland be granted the same honour. In July 1988, however, Dublin became the first capital city to declare Nelson Mandela a freeman of the city. Among other privileges, this granted him the right to drive his herd of cattle through town.

When Nelson Mandela emerged from nearly three decades of incarceration on 11 February 1990 there was rapturous celebration throughout South Africa and around the world. Ireland shared in the global rejoicing. In Dublin, the ANC flag flew from public buildings, including the historic Mansion House, and 'Mandela Free' was illuminated in huge letters on Liberty Hall, the home of the Irish Transport and General Workers' Union. Parties were held spontaneously and our home became the centre of day-long celebrations with neighbours and well-wishers delivering flowers and greeting cards. On the day of his release the whole house was crowded with people, peering at the television set in expectation. Finally, after some hours' delay, Nelson Mandela emerged from the jail, and the cheers erupted and the champagne corks popped. It was a great day of celebration, not only in Dublin, but also in other parts of Ireland. An IAAM statement celebrated Mandela's release, but at the same time pressed for the release of all political prisoners and called for renewed pressure on the regime to end apartheid.

However, the crowds celebrating Nelson Mandela's release were nothing compared to the thousands who welcomed him during his visit to Dublin in early July 1990. Mandela arrived at Dublin International Airport a few hours ahead of the Irish national soccer team who were returning from the soccer World Cup. One of the first black professional footballers to have been selected for Ireland was Paul McGrath, and though he played for English clubs, he was enormously popular in Ireland. As Mandela's motorcade travelled from the airport, there were shouts of 'Ooh ah, ooh ah, Paul McGrath's Da!' from the affectionate Dublin working-class fans who lined the route into the city.

Following a private lunch with trade union leaders and members of the IAAM at the Mansion House, Mandela finally received the freedom of the city that had been conferred on him in 1988. Speaking to the crowds, he told them: 'We have come here to invite you to walk with us on the last mile of our protracted struggle. We have come here to thank you for not forgetting us. We have come here to encourage you to hold steadfast.' The following day, Mandela addressed the Irish Parliament, a rare honour for a private citizen, and in the evening a dinner was hosted by the Taoiseach in his honour. It was unprecedented for a person who was not a head of state or government to meet the President of Ireland and be given a dinner by the Prime Minister. Such was the esteem in which Mandela was held that all the rules and protocols went by the board.

Although Mandela cautioned in his address to the Parliament that 'We should not mistake the promise of change for change itself' and asserted that the struggle against apartheid must continue, the effect of President De Klerk's actions on the issue of international sanctions against South Africa was electric. Those who had never really supported sanctions now saw the opportunity to release South Africa from their 'burden'. The IAAM denounced such attempts to integrate South Africa into the international community of nations, not only because they were premature, but also because the regime had not undertaken to move in an irreversible manner towards the elimination of apartheid and meeting the core demands of the Harare Declaration – the ANC's position on the basic conditions to be met before negotiations could begin. From this moment on, the IAAM had to double its efforts to ensure that diplomatic and economic pressure from Ireland was maintained on De Klerk's government. It was only when Mandela urged the UN in late 1993 to lift all remaining sanctions and, finally, when in April 1994 South Africans went to the polls in the country's first democratic elections, that the movement felt it could step back and consider its work as at an end.

Shortly thereafter, the last general meeting of the IAAM took place at the Mansion House on 28 May 1994. It had been thirty years and a month since the founding of the IAAM at a similarly well-attended meeting at the same venue. In 1964 the Rivonia Trial was just beginning and the IAAM began its illustrious history by campaigning for the release of Mandela and his co-accused who were facing the death penalty. Now, three decades later, apartheid was defeated and Mandela was President of a free South Africa.

Tribute was paid to the Irish people for their support and faithful companionship in the struggle against apartheid. Then, after the meeting concluded and the IAAM was officially disbanded, members adjourned to a party in the Mansion House. It was a wonderfully happy and joyous celebration. South Africa had at last reached the long-awaited goal of democracy for which so many brave people had struggled and died.

In 1990 I resigned as chairman of the IAAM and, shortly after Mandela's visit to Dublin, returned to South Africa, leaving Ireland behind. For almost thirty years Ireland gave me refuge in exile, a livelihood in law, and much personal enrichment over nearly three decades. My life revolved around the university, where I taught law – human rights law, labour law and international law – and where I eventually became the Dean of the Faculty of Arts. Soon after joining I recall Conor Cruise O'Brien telling me that TCD (as Trinity College Dublin is colloquially known) had the best law school in the world. He was not to know that at that time there were only two full-time staff members in the school.

For me, TCD embodied the very best of liberal values, placing great emphasis on academic freedom and freedom of expression. What gave me much pleasure was the real collegial atmosphere, which made for a rich and stimulating academic life. I enjoyed teaching right in the heart of the city where every facility could be found, including, I dare say, almost thirty pubs.

My academic career also took me as a visiting academic to Christ's College, Cambridge, and later to Warwick University for short spells in the mid-1970s. In 1987 I was overjoyed to take up a post during the summer semester as the inaugural Nelson Mandela Professor at Rutgers, living with friends in the vibrant community of Harlem, New York. I also gave occasional lectures at Princeton.

Our life in Ireland was centred not only on the university but also on Dublin, where we met poets and artists, politicians and activists, who made the city an exciting and energising place. In that context, I learnt the importance of poetic creativity and artistic expression in affirming our fundamental humanity. My friend Seamus Heaney has observed that our best poetry merges the timeless and the timely, the eternal and the ordinary. So does our best in law, our best in politics. In Dublin, meeting and becoming friends with extraordinary Irish artists, I was profoundly influenced by a poetry that translated the highest aspirations of our struggle for human rights and political liberation.

On the occasion of my seventy-fifth birthday in 2010 I was reminded of my lifelong attachment to Ireland, my second home. Among the warm wishes I received were many from Ireland, including one from the Irish President, Mary McAleese, a former student of mine at Trinity College, and an especially generous message from the Irish Minister for Foreign Affairs, Micheál Martin, in which he thanked me for my efforts to raise 'public awareness in Ireland of the evils of apartheid' during my years as the IAAM chairman. He then went on to say, "The Government and People of Ireland are enormously indebted to you for your contribution to public life in Ireland ... You played a highly valuable role in the development of the appreciation of the importance of human rights law in both parts of Ireland.'

Such acknowledgement is very kind, and demonstrates the extent to which Louise and I became deeply involved emotionally in Irish life. This small country will always be my second home. On the occasions

I have returned to Ireland since leaving, I have been treated with great fondness and respect. I feel as if I am one of their own. It is very moving. After almost twenty years' absence, one might expect them to have forgotten about me and about our struggle, but the Irish still have that interest, still have that feeling of compassion, still care about what's happening six thousand miles away in distant South Africa.

4

Law in the Service of Humanity

When I was a law student in London, I was fascinated by the way in which law seemed to be developing. It was no longer limited to the nation-state system but encompassed new entities. It was exciting to be part of this new development as a result of which individuals were no longer objects of the law but had become its subjects. We in the Third World would contribute substantially to this development.

International law has proven to be one of the most effective instruments of liberation available and it played a critical role in the demise of apartheid. In 1960 the insightful Algerian jurist Mohammed Bedjaoui (later, president of the International Court of Justice) wrote of how international law had become an agent of hegemony, aggression, colonisation, racism and the abuse of peoples. As I told him when I met him in the 1960s, his task was to invent the rules of international law. My task, on the other hand, was to attempt to apply them to apartheid South Africa.

I believe the harnessing of international law and the liberation of its transformative potency have arisen in large measure as a result of the various strategies conceived and implemented in the struggle against colonialism and the campaign to liberate South Africa from apartheid. In our struggle, we used international law as it had never been used before. We pursued every avenue we could, in my case especially through writing papers and articles on the subject. Years later I was thrilled to meet young militants from Umkhonto weSizwe (MK), who told me that they had read my legal papers while in the ANC camps in southern

Africa. Little by little, the law changed and with it the ability of arrogant rogue states to stubbornly resist the demands of justice and democracy.

Historically, international law was concerned with relations between states; individuals were of concern only in national or domestic law, and a state could treat its subjects or citizens as it desired. The evolution of international law as a means of protecting individuals reached its first high point with the Nuremberg Trials after the Second World War. They proved a powerful catalyst for change within both international and human rights law. What made the Nuremberg Trials so important was that they enforced the distinction between a country's right to engage in a war and the manner in which that war was conducted. The context, in other words, forced the law to shift. A state could no longer plead that individuals were not the business of international law.

There had been three Geneva Conventions drawn up in the late nineteenth and early twentieth century, though comprehensive rules for the conduct of war were laid down only in 1949 in the wake of the horrors of the Second World War. These determined how civilians were to be treated and created a category of person known as the 'prisoner of war' (POW). Of course this category and these Conventions concerned the conduct of individuals in a formal warfare situation, such as that between antagonistic countries. However, the important point was the distinction between combatants and non-combatants, the latter receiving special treatment for the first time.

National liberation wars are rarely as formal. More often than not, they are guerrilla wars waged in an internecine fashion and in situations where the legitimacy of power itself has been challenged. How could we apply the Geneva Convention to the informal, guerrilla wars of liberation as well as the orthodox cases of inter-state hostility? This was a critical question for those, including me, who spent considerable time promoting the legitimacy and therefore the legal status of liberation movements.

As a law student at the London School of Economics in the early 1960s, I started to develop my lifelong interest in the impact of legal rules on the process of national liberation and on liberation movements. I soon began to grapple with South Africa's unique circumstances and with the truly revolutionary legal concepts of self-determination, the criminality of colonialism, the right of national liberation movements to legal protection and the right to rebel against oppression and injustice. I was curious about the legal evolution of these rules and devoted much of my academic career to identifying the sources of these changes and considering how the transformation of law could be brought about through the collective role of the United Nations (UN) 'family' – the General Assembly, the Security Council, the International Court of Justice and other organs.

How did international law become a tool not only in the liberation of peoples but in the entrenchment and sustenance of fundamental human rights? There were many facets to this development. The emphasis on human rights in the UN Charter, the galvanising force of the Universal Declaration of Human Rights, the change in membership of the UN, the different values that prevailed in international debates, all contributed. The admission of over fifty free and independent countries from Africa and Asia provided for a critical mass in the General Assembly and other organs of the UN in support of these developments. As regards South Africa in particular, the newly independent countries were no longer prepared to tolerate the existence of a state and system that rejected *their* right to existence: apartheid was considered by them, rightly, as a direct assault on their humanity. As a result of all these developments, the nature of the international legal order changed and a new emphasis came to be given to the principle of self-determination of peoples as the foundation of sovereignty. Powerful states, especially colonial powers, may have resisted this development; and some liberal academics may have dismissed the new obligations as part of the 'soft law' of the UN. But they could not deny that the world would never be the same again because these rules legitimated the struggle for freedom and provided the basis for concrete assistance to liberation movements.

The first dent on the idea that what a state does to its 'own' population was a matter of domestic jurisdiction was in fact provided by the response to the apartheid question. The orthodox and conservative approach to law-making conferred on states the exclusive capacity to make rules, especially taking into account that only states were persons in international law. But the UN systems and the UN Charter have played an important role in ensuring that international law is not solely concerned with states but that individuals and other entities can also be the bearers of rights and responsibilities. In 1970 the International

Court of Justice – the highest judicial organ in the world – noted that the old view, that states owe duties only to other states and that these duties can arise only out of specific bilateral obligations, was no longer valid.

During the decades of the anti-apartheid struggle, international jurisprudence developed to the point that states lost their monopoly over law creation where matters at the fundamental core of international legal principle are involved. Racial discrimination as state policy was not only declared a violation of international law but was considered to be in violation of *jus cogens*, part of a higher variety of laws which states could not amend and with which they could not conflict. This restricted the capacity of states to enter into bilateral relations that did not take into account such matters as the prohibition of the illegal use of force, crimes against humanity, war crimes and, of course, apartheid.

Under the auspices of the UN – which became the juridical conscience of humanity – it was possible for the anti-apartheid solidarity movement to obtain assistance from the global mobilisation against apartheid. Less obviously, the movement also contributed to the international community by supplying an abundance of theoretical and practical arguments against blind deference to domestic political tyranny. Indeed, the anti-apartheid movement was instrumental in changing the face of international law itself by giving impetus to the international legal norm of non-discrimination and to the clear-cut acceptance of the principle of self-determination as a rule of international law.

The story of the international community's collective involvement in combating apartheid rested on the establishment of an initial linkage and then the piece-by-piece construction of a brightly lit, multi-structured legal edifice that towered over apartheid's dark and inhuman secrets. It was a strategy based on the very logic of law itself: find a point of agreement and then build an iron-clad argument with each agreed point founded irresistibly and indisputably on the last. The first link was the one between racial equality and decolonisation. Once that was established, a number of consensual principles were added which hardened into UN resolutions and which then became entrenched in international law. These principles were that resistance to colonial, racist and alien regimes was legitimate, that liberation movements in these circumstances were entitled to use all necessary means, that all states should provide moral and material assistance to these movements, that representatives of these liberation movements should find a place in the UN and, finally, that the protection of the Geneva Convention should be extended to national liberation movements and their members. Once this edifice was in place, sanctions, boycotts and embargoes followed, underpinned by the collective opprobrium of the nations of the world.

My personal involvement in the utilisation of international law, beyond the early musings of a student and the scholarly writings of an academic, took place following the establishment of the Special Committee on Apartheid (later renamed the Special Committee Against Apartheid) in 1963. Created by the UN General Assembly, the Special Committee would become a prodigious force at the UN, earning the respect and admiration of member states, with the obvious exceptions of apartheid South Africa and Portugal prior to the overthrow of the Salazar regime in 1974, as well as those countries antagonistic to sanctions.

The Committee's driving force was the Indian-born Enuga S. Reddy, initially as its principal secretary from 1963 and later as the director of the Centre Against Apartheid and assistant General Secretary of the UN until his retirement in 1984. A UN official since 1949, Reddy knew well the limitations and possibilities of UN bureaucracy and power, and under his guidance the Special Committee became a real ally and influential champion of the anti-apartheid struggle.

Following two successful international seminars on apartheid, in October 1967 the Special Committee submitted an important report to the General Assembly and the Security Council. It proposed a detailed campaign for the international isolation of South Africa based on strengthened relations with and between international organisations, states and NGOs; and it recommended that steps be taken to publicise efforts in this regard. Reddy's proposals were well received and the General Assembly authorised the campaign in December 1967. This campaign, the first of its kind by a UN body, formed the basis for a sustained collaboration between the international collective of national anti-apartheid movements and the UN, a partnership (as Reddy described it) without precedent in relations between the UN and NGOs.

A special relationship developed between the Irish Anti-Apartheid

Movement (IAAM), chaired by me, and the Special Committee headed by Reddy. Even before the campaign, the Special Committee had established close links with the IAAM, and supplied it with bulk copies of pamphlets and literature about various aspects of apartheid. The IAAM reported breaches of UN sanctions to the Special Committee and, as an IAAM representative, I attended the Special Committee hearings in London in 1968. The Committee also assisted when Louise and I compiled annual reports on the Irish government's voting record at the UN – a unique exercise. Our relations with the UN were stepped up in the 1970s with ever greater volumes of material being exchanged. Growing public awareness of the IAAM's work meant we received more reports of sanctions violations, and these were duly passed on to the Special Committee.

In 1973 apartheid was formally recognised as a crime against humanity when the General Assembly adopted the International Convention on the Suppression and Punishment of the Crime of Apartheid, which, like the Genocide Convention, imposes individual responsibility for such a crime. At the same time the General Assembly declared that the apartheid regime was illegitimate and had no right to represent the people of South Africa. Associated with this was the reaffirmation of the 'legitimacy of the struggle of the oppressed people of South Africa and their liberation movements, by all possible means, for the seizure of power by the people and the exercise of their inalienable rights to self-determination', and the further and important acknowledgement of the national liberation movements recognised by the Organisation of African Unity as the 'authentic representatives of the overwhelming majority of the South African people'.

The Soweto uprising beginning in June 1976 gave new impetus to the international struggle against apartheid. World outrage at the South African regime's response to the uprising was unambiguous. Nothing could mitigate the sheer brutality and naked racism of white policemen firing on unarmed black schoolchildren. The Soweto uprising put apartheid squarely in the international spotlight and emphasised anew South Africa's pariah status in the international community. Public opinion demanded that it be completely isolated. The sanctions regime had to be intensified and the sports, cultural and academic boycotts imposed without exception.

Not three days after 16 June 1976, the Security Council passed a resolution 'strongly condemning the South African Government for its resort to massive violence against and killing of the African people'. The resolution further called on the regime to 'eliminate apartheid,' the strongest Security Council statement yet and a strong signal to the regime that the period of unqualified support from the major Western powers was ending. This point was driven home in July 1976 when the International Convention on the Suppression and Punishment of the Crime of Apartheid, adopted by the General Assembly in 1973, came into force, earlier than expected, as countries showed their anger by speedily ratifying the Convention.

In October, when the first of South Africa's bantustans was declared 'independent', the UN General Assembly rejected the declaration of independence and called upon all governments to deny recognition to the so-called Republic of Transkei. In November, the General Assembly adopted a comprehensive Programme of Action against apartheid and established an ad hoc committee to prepare an international convention against apartheid in sport, proclaimed the following December. Then, in November 1977, the Security Council unanimously adopted Resolution 418, imposing an arms embargo against South Africa. The embargo was a significant advance for anti-apartheid forces.

Members of the Irish Anti-Apartheid Movement had played an important role in the Lagos World Conference for Action Against Apartheid from which the demand for an arms embargo had emerged. I was one of the rapporteurs at the conference. The embargo did not directly affect Ireland, which was not an arms manufacturer, but because the embargo was mandatory it brought the prospect of other sanctions nearer. The UN then declared 1978 International Anti-Apartheid Year and initiated a number of activities, including the World Conference to Combat Racism and Racial Discrimination in Geneva.

Not since Sharpeville had South Africa received such extensive international attention or been the focus of such vehement international condemnation, if not by the governments of the major Western powers, then certainly by public opinion throughout the world.

In 1977 the UN began negotiations over the terms of Protocol I and Protocol II of the Geneva Convention. For the first time, liberation movements such as the ANC were invited to Geneva to participate as observers. The ANC called on its 'back-room boys' to assist in its preparations, and I was one of those who helped. One of the Conventions dealt with movements fighting against racism, colonialism and foreign occupancy, a trilogy of factors that qualified a body to be called a liberation movement. Together with other movements mainly from the Third World, the ANC pushed hard for the acceptance of this Convention. It opened the way for liberation movements to make a declaration that they would respect the Geneva Convention and treat captured belligerents as POWs. This, in turn, might persuade the states subject to wars of liberation to similarly observe the Geneva Convention when it came to the treatment of liberation fighters. Clearly, much was at stake for these movements and for their personnel.

On 6 April 1979 Solomon Mahlangu was hanged in Pretoria Central Prison. Mahlangu was a combatant of the ANC's military wing, Umkhonto weSizwe, who had been arrested (and subsequently tortured) following a shoot-out with the police. His death gave new impetus to our desire to protect our members. We had long contended that the struggle against apartheid was not simply a civil war, a domestic matter in which the international community could not interfere, but a war for national liberation, legitimated by international law. Consequently, combatants of the ANC should be treated as POWs. The regime, on the other hand, would not budge from its position that 'terrorists' should be given no quarter.

At my suggestion, the ANC agreed that we should focus on the way the two Protocols adopted under the Geneva Convention in 1977 recognised that the concept of international armed conflict extended to cover wars of national liberation. Tambo agreed that we should investigate how the status of the ANC would be enhanced by making a declaration under Protocol I of 1977 that spelt out this development. He thought it sounded like a good idea, but believed it should also involve the South West Africa People's Organisation (Swapo), neighbouring Namibia's liberation movement. As Namibia was essentially a South African colony at this time, the ANC's relations with Swapo were close and fraternal. Swapo had also made its own indelible impression on international law.

Swapo was established in 1960 and began its armed struggle following a disgraceful judgment by the International Court of Justice in 1966. Three years later, the General Assembly recognised Swapo as the sole and authentic representative of the Namibian people, supported its armed struggle for self-determination, freedom and national independence, and invited member states to provide assistance for this struggle. Significantly, the Assembly invited Swapo to participate as an observer in the work and sessions of the General Assembly and in conferences convened under the auspices of the Assembly (later to include all UN bodies). Swapo had, as a result, enjoyed special status and was considered the organ for self-determination for Namibia. I myself had close relations with Swapo as an honorary legal adviser. In fact, I was to participate in the only bilateral negotiations between Swapo and the apartheid regime in 1980. However, after being approached Swapo didn't reply to the invitation to participate in a Protocol I declaration, in all likelihood because its administration could not cope with all the demands made on it.

At the time I was a member of the International Commission of Inquiry into the Crimes of the Apartheid Regime. When my intentions to assist in formalising the legal status of the ANC as an armed liberation movement became known among my peers in Dublin, I started to come under some pressure. Colleagues suggested that my engagement with this aspect of the law might compromise my prospects for career advancement. The parallels with Ireland's own struggles and the possibilities for the IRA to consider a similar declaration were clearly a worrying factor. I paid little heed to such concerns, as I did not consider the IRA to be a liberation movement.

After some time, I wrote to Tambo and told him that I had received no reply from Swapo. When he urged me to go ahead, I did, beginning at first with a round of negotiations with the Swiss government, the principal keeper of the Geneva Convention. The Swiss responded by saying that for complex legal reasons they weren't interested in supporting or accepting such a declaration. In my view, the Swiss were wrong.

We could have made this non-recognition into an international issue, which would have frittered away a great deal of time and energy. Instead, another avenue occurred to me, which I thought might accomplish a similar outcome. If the Swiss government couldn't accept a declaration under Protocol I, perhaps another venerable Swiss institution, the

International Committee of the Red Cross (ICRC), might do so.

With Tambo's support, I contacted the ICRC, which is housed in a stunningly beautiful building in Geneva. I met with the ICRC's smart legal team and they were very positive about the idea of the ANC presenting the ICRC with a declaration, which they would then endorse. In November 1980 a high-powered delegation from the ANC, including Tambo and its treasurer, Thomas Nkobi, travelled from Lusaka to the ICRC's headquarters.

The signing of the declaration was a grand but humbling event, not least owing to Tambo's statesman-like qualities. Having greeted the president of the ICRC, the leader of the ANC rose to the occasion in sublime fashion. 'We have always defined the enemy in terms of a system of domination and not of a people or a race,' he said, 'our values being fundamentally different in contrast to the apartheid regime', which had 'displayed a shameless and ruthless disregard for all the norms of humanity'. We were all spellbound. Here was our leader, the representative of our liberation movement, who was giving voice to the historic nature of his movement's commitment to humane values in the conduct of war and who in the process moved the staid representatives of the ICRC to loud applause.

The effects of the ANC declaration were felt very quickly in South Africa. Within a short time, lawyers who had defended Swapo guerrillas in the apartheid courts and who had invoked the 'new' humanitarian law, felt that earlier inhibitions about claiming a similar status for ANC trialists had now evaporated in the light of the ANC's declaration. So, in a nutshell, lawyers were able to refer back to international law to validate the legitimacy of liberation movements. As a result of this declaration some South African lawyers refused to continue with the usual demonisation of the ANC in the courts. There were also ripples of surprise and support among some Afrikaners.

Tambo, who always respected lawyers as he felt the ANC lawyers were agents of change, had triumphed. The decision to make the declaration was a collective National Executive Committee decision of the ANC, but it was the quality of presentation by an individual that made the impact. We were not the only ones who admired Tambo; he evoked this emotion even from unsympathetic sources. He was the liberation movement's most consummate diplomat. Tambo spent thirty years of his life in exile pursuing the task of initiating and cementing international solidarity. 'No other post-World War Two struggle for decolonisation has been so fully globalised; no other has magnetised so many people across such national divides, or imbued them with such a resilient sense of common cause,' according to one assessment cited by his biographer Luli Callinicos. 'This outstanding phenomenon owed the major part of its success to Tambo's *indima* diplomacy, laid down step by step, acre by acre, in the long hard years of struggle.'

The signing of the declaration in November 1980 and its lodging with the ICRC formed a great moment in the history of our struggle. It also made a substantial impact at the UN. In particular, the ANC's status was affirmed, and this opened doors to participation in all kinds of forums and also to much greater levels of support from the international community in general and from the UN in particular. No longer were liberation movements assumed to be a bunch of thugs and murderers, but instead they came to be treated as organisations with legitimate grievances against despotic states.

I felt triumphant about the achievement. Here was a document that established the moral basis of our struggle. It demanded, in so far as was possible, that our combatants should be treated as POWs. While this was hardly always the case, the declaration set up a standard of care that made it very clear when the apartheid regime was falling foul of international law and when it was acting within it. At home in South Africa, the declaration became a useful tool in the defence of activists on trial for treason and subversion.

The signing of the declaration received little if any coverage in the South African media. This was in part because Tambo and the ANC leadership were all banned persons and couldn't be quoted in the South African press. It was also another illustration of the cravenness of the South African media; they didn't consider such a development important enough to send a reporter. Other international media did attend, thankfully, so articles and material came to circulate in the public domain. Louise and I were both proud to be associated with the organisation of the visit by the ANC and the preparation of Oliver Tambo's speech.

The UN acted as an invaluable instrument to promote concerted action against the apartheid regime. Initially the world organisation had responded to the campaign begun by the newly independent African states, at the request of the liberation movements, for sanctions against South Africa after Sharpeville. The UN Special Committee Against Apartheid later played a central role in promoting an oil embargo and other measures by governments; it helped establish funds for assistance to South African political prisoners and their families, and refugees; and it encouraged boycotts and other action by the public. There is no question that the crisis in South Africa in the mid-1980s together with sanctions, withdrawal of investments and loans, boycotts and public opinion heralded change and the eventual end of apartheid.

Today, the right to self-determination of colonial peoples is an incontestable legal principle. This right formed part and parcel of the International Convention on the Elimination of All Forms of Racial Discrimination, adopted by the General Assembly in 1965, which is also the most highly ratified convention. International law, as Enuga Reddy once said, did not free any colony, nor did political declarations by the UN (such as the declaration on decolonisation). But it did help in the process. Albie Sachs's words also ring true: 'while one should always be sceptical about the law's pretensions, one should never be cynical about the law's possibilities.'

The anti-apartheid struggle was a critical factor in the mobilisation of international law. International law, in turn, became a vital weapon in the armoury of universal human rights and in the authority and capacity of the collective international community to intervene on behalf of the oppressed. The war against apartheid became far more than the oppressed people of a single nation fighting with their friends to oppose it. It became a world war for justice and human rights in which the combined efforts of the citizens of the globe served to pull down the tyrants. As Enuga Reddy recalls: 'I can think of no other coalition of this scope, of no other campaign that was carried on so long with persistence, and no other cause for which so many people in so many countries made sacrifices.'

The process of defining, year by year, a new code of human rights remains an unfinished journey. And that is why, practically but also philosophically, we must now more fully elaborate – and agree – on the implementation of a new framework for individual rights that recognises the right of different ethnic and social groups to hold diverse values, religions and world-views. This is a central issue of our time and is based on central truths.

Globalisation, while no doubt an ugly word, has shaped this new terrain enormously. Pressures of globalisation have given many communities, individuals and cultures a feeling of threat and marginalisation. We need to define, just as we have in terms of individual rights, a balancing new concept of cultural diversity, liberty and rights. We need to do this not only because of corrosive risks – from xenophobic opposition to radically new patterns of international migration, for example – but because 'identity' politics is one of the most dangerous forces now at play. In Europe, in particular, this involves an intense exercise to identify so-called 'core values' threatened by 'alien forces'. Issues of 'us' and 'them' remain a razor-sharp division embedded, all too often, in the landscape of nations and the wider international community.

We must confront these risks by asserting the central truth that each person has multiple identities: among the most obvious are class, religion, gender, sexual orientation, citizenship, political affiliations. All require respect. When they become issues of cultural division in any society, they also need an approach of wisdom, tolerance and understanding. In some areas, we have made much progress: in the rights of women, for example, although this progress is still uneven and far too limited.

Identities obviously overlap, but the starting point for new definitions of the rights of national identity and of cultural liberty is respect for each set of identities. They also need to be anchored in the way the state treats social groups. This means promoting participation, not just condemning exclusion; equality of respect in all its dimensions as well as, more formally, legal equality of rights. It means, in the vivid language of Albie Sachs, the right to be the same and the right to be different.

So, cultural accommodation is not the enemy of a cohesive society or of the state. The very opposite in fact: it is the best way of strengthening society and the bonds that link its different elements. Human rights and national identity are not in tension. South Africa now has universal standards of rights – as reflected in the Constitution – that must be enlarged in an agenda of action to accommodate cultural diversity – as a right as well as a necessity.

The central issue, therefore, remains tolerance, pluralism, the concept of cultural rights – within states as well as between states – as core dimensions of the agenda and universal discourse of human rights. This has practical dimensions: cultural property; balancing the 'customary rights' of groups with wider law; issues of language; symbols of religion; and equal rights of social groups to a full share in economic and social life. And it means, in the era of globalisation, paying special attention to the rights of the poor, indigenous peoples, cultural goods, the rights of migrants and so on.

This is what the Unesco Convention of 2005 on the Protection and Promotion of the Diversity of Cultural Expressions attempts to do. The Convention describes cultural diversity as a 'common heritage' and its defence as an 'ethical imperative inseparable from respect for human dignity'. I was honoured to be chosen by the participating states to chair the conference, which adopted this Convention in the space of two years. Some of the states may have regretted my appointment when their chairperson drove the discussion to a conclusion that was not to their liking. I had gone round lobbying states for their support and, when it was not forthcoming, I asked if they had a mandate from home not to support the Convention. The outcome was overwhelming support, with the main opposition coming from Israel and the US. The French conferred the Légion d'honneur on me because of this success and because of my record on human rights.

We in South Africa have our own proud record: the 1943 bill of rights in the 'Africans' Claims' document, demanding collective and individual rights for all South Africans; the Women's Charter of 1954, which includes the remarkable statement 'the level of civilisation which any society has reached can be measured by the degree of freedom that its members enjoy'; and, of course, the jewel of our 1996 Constitution with its core values of freedom, equality, social justice and dignity. South Africa's Constitutional Court is the ultimate guardian of the claim inscribed in our coat of arms: 'out of diversity comes unity'.

We need, in short, to build social models around the core truth expressed by Kant: 'nothing straight can be made from the crooked timber of humanity'. Complexity is the basis of all social, political and economic life.

5

Constitution Writing

From the mid-1980s, pressure mounted on the ANC to put forward concrete proposals for a post-apartheid constitutional order. As the situation at home became increasingly repressive and resistance increasingly determined, the world wanted to know what the ANC's vision was for a new South Africa and what constitutional arrangements the ANC envisaged to redress the crime of apartheid. These requests did not come from our friends, although they too were waiting to see what kind of South Africa we contemplated.

At this time an astonishing array of constitutional proposals for South Africa were being put forward and debated by a spectrum of organisations, academics, activists and think-tanks, both at home and internationally, often by people who saw themselves as strongly anti-apartheid. However, the centrepiece of all these proposals – including consociationalism and federalism – was the protection of the rights of minorities and the provision of mechanisms to ensure adequate representation of minority groups in government. In some cases, veto powers or special representation on executives was advocated.

Jurisprudence in minority rights has a long and proud history. However, in South Africa, the argument that whites should be accorded some or other version of these was based on an inversion and perversion of this legal-philosophical tradition. Minorities are usually protected to enable them to overcome an imposed disadvantage. But in South Africa it was the majority that had been denied and excluded and must overcome disadvantage, while it was the minority that enjoyed privilege. The minority rights argument was being used in an attempt to protect minority privileges and to frustrate majority rule. It was a ploy by whites which implied that they shared a common cause with Indian and coloured communities in fearing democratic majority rule. Of course, the corollary was that whites feared being treated as they had treated blacks.

I have always felt there is a fundamental and demonstrable rift between liberal notions of rights and my own (and the ANC's) version. It was the arch-liberal Karl Popper who argued that freedom is inconsistent with equality, that there is a tension between first-generation rights, which restrain the state, and second-generation rights, which outline the state's obligations. For me, rights are naturally critically important, but if you have a deeply unequal society and an overburdensome load of state obligations, these rights will never be adequately protected or commonly enjoyed. If there is unemployment, people need benefits; if they are sick, they need to be cared for; if injured, they must be provided for. These are the essential and first obligations of the democratic state. I imagine a democratic state as a ship. Below the waterline are the fundamental first-generation political and civil 'blue rights' and, above, the second-generation economic 'red rights'. (Third-generation rights, like the right to a clean environment, in other words 'green or environmental rights', are also reflected in our Constitution.) If you remove or compromise the second, the boat sinks. Liberals would rather have a perfect democracy that sinks and we would rather have an imperfect democracy that floats: that is the difference between us. Where the liberals make a mistake is in trying to pretend that the first-generation rights do not have any impact on or any major conflict with the second-generation rights. This is untrue if one considers that the right to vote, for example, requires the state to spend tremendous amounts of money to ensure that voting is fair and free.

In the mid-1980s we were acutely aware of the increasing political pressure on the ANC to respond to the speculation and increasing expectation that the regime was willing to negotiate. Around the time we began thinking about constitutional guidelines, an initiative was started in Durban that would be touted as just such a 'solution', made the more virtuous because it had supposedly come about through honest dialogue between white and black South Africans engaged in a sincere attempt to find an equitable alternative to apartheid. The KwaZulu-Natal Indaba was an ongoing conference held between April and November 1986, as an initiative of Chief Mangosuthu Buthelezi of the Inkatha Freedom Party (IFP). Since the 1970s, according to some commentators, Pretoria had been grooming Buthelezi as a credible alternative to the ANC.

The Indaba was presented as an exercise in constitutional reform that would demonstrate how a lasting political settlement of the national conflict might be achieved. It claimed it would show how apartheid could be peacefully dismantled and the different race groups reconciled. The Indaba was indeed celebrated by local (white) commentators and analysts as a shining example of what could be achieved through dialogue rather than violence, sanctions and disinvestment. However, its proposed bill of rights was anything but progressive. In effect, the bill of rights shifted the responsibility to promote and protect human rights from the public to the private realm. For example, the right to associate freely was strongly promoted as a private, voluntary action and, if people wanted to live together as whites, their right to do so would be protected by private law and the state would not be able to intervene. I coined the phrase 'privatising apartheid' to describe the main thrust of the Indaba's human rights proposals, though I subsequently forgot the term until a good friend and later Constitutional Court judge, Albie Sachs, used it extensively in his writings and, upon my congratulating him on a clever turn of phrase, he reminded me that I was its author.

For the regime, the Indaba was a public relations coup because it gave the impression that the National Party was willing to reform apartheid. For Buthelezi, the Indaba promoted him as a moderate, black leader. Internationally, the proposals won support from the Reagan and Thatcher administrations.

Oliver Tambo was a gifted leader and strategist who was loved and admired within the ANC and among its allies. His nightmare at that time was that the National Party would call a conference to write a new constitution for South Africa, and the ANC would be caught unawares. With his remarkable tactical insight he 'woke' from this nightmare knowing that the time had come for the ANC to draw up its own constitutional options, and he resolved in mid-1985 to establish a Constitutional Committee. A Legal Committee was already in existence by then, which dealt with everything from meetings with international lawyers to signing leases for ANC houses and marrying ANC cadres. Four members of the Legal Committee were made permanent members of the new Constitutional Committee.

Oliver Tambo had an intuitive grasp of how best to transform principles into strategic action, without compromising the former, to better effect the latter. He recognised that, from a strategic perspective, it was crucial that the ANC not appear hesitant or wavering in the face of proposals for a post-apartheid constitutional order and not find itself in the position of responding to others. If there was to be a serious debate on this most fundamental of questions, the ANC had to position itself as a lead agent. It therefore had to state its principled critique of the various proposals being circulated and debated with great fanfare and enthusiasm, not only to rebut the enemy's claims that the ANC had none and was nothing more than an organisation of communists and terrorists, but also to recognise and respond to the many participants in this burgeoning debate who identified with the struggle against apartheid. These participants sincerely thought of themselves as being anti-apartheid and were honestly looking for a way forward, even if their proposals left much to be desired. Thus, while the enemy would be resolutely refuted and dismissed, where the proposals of friends and allies erred their errors in thinking would be gently but firmly pointed out. With these tactical considerations in mind, Tambo established the ANC's Constitutional Committee to direct its attention towards crafting a post-apartheid constitution. I was called in from Dublin to become part of it.

The first meeting of the Constitutional Committee lasted for five days and took place at the ANC's headquarters in Lusaka, Zambia. It opened on 8 January 1986, the seventy-fourth anniversary of the founding of the ANC. The meeting was chaired by Jack Simons, a senior scholar, ANC cadre and communist who had gone into exile after being told he couldn't lecture any more in South Africa and that his books had been banned. Apart from possessing a beautiful library and being known for working by candlelight, he was the most terrifying driver you can imagine. He used to fly around Lusaka in his little car at the most extraordinary speed and with scant concern for other road users. He chaired the ANC's Constitutional Committee for four years and was instrumental in guiding its work and in coaxing out the vital papers and documents that were to become the foundation of the ANC's constitutional position.

In his opening address at the inaugural meeting of the ANC's Constitutional Committee, Tambo laid out our broad task. Outlining the growing demand from people around the world, including our supporters, for our vision for a new South Africa, he explained that while the Freedom Charter clearly set out the ANC's visions and principles, what was now needed was a blueprint from the ANC for its proposed structures of government, voting and electoral system, the judiciary, and so on. It fell to us to investigate constitutional proposals and draw up a constitutional framework for a post-apartheid South Africa. No time frame was adopted. This would be a unique exercise, unprecedented in the history of the movement.

Most of the discussion on 8 and 9 January expanded on the challenging task ahead. We began by noting that our constitution would have to state boldly some basic aims, including equality, majority rule and national unity in the sense of one people corresponding to one country. These aims, drawn from the 'Africans' Claims' document of 1943 and reflective of the vision of the Freedom Charter, were nothing new and were entirely compatible with the basic objective of the anti-apartheid struggle. More than aims, they were principles that should of necessity constitute the premises of our new constitution and conclusively repudiate the white supremacist vision of racially differentiated groups with their own segregated government structures and territories. At the same time, our constitution would recognise, accommodate and even celebrate South Africa's diversity and the multiculturalism of our society. The belief that a unitary state could accommodate South Africa's plurality would become increasingly important over the next two or three years when we would deny alternative constitutional models, put forward by friends and foes alike, that emphasised South Africa's heterogeneity. Even some anti-apartheid activists found it very difficult to imagine how a society as divided and fraught with tensions as South Africa could exist in unity and peace.

Although there was no precedent in the ANC's long history for drafting substantive constitutional proposals, we had available to us a long tradition of resistance against oppression during which the principles of our struggle were developed organically and democratically and set down in such important documents as the 'Africans' Claims', the Women's Charter and the Freedom Charter. 'Africans' Claims in South Africa', adopted at the December 1943 ANC annual conference, became the ANC's first guiding document. At its heart was a bill of rights, based on one drawn up by the ANC founder Pixley ka Isaka Seme back in 1926, that demanded for the people of South Africa the same rights and freedoms as those of the Atlantic Charter, which had been signed by the Allied powers in 1941. In fact it can be said that it went further than current international principles by asserting human rights, including women's rights, land rights, socio-economic rights and the rights to health, education, welfare and employment, which would advance dignity and equality of opportunity for all South Africans. This early guiding document was written in the newly assertive language of the more radical ANC Youth League. It set the tone for the Women's Charter, adopted by the ANC's Federation of South African Women more than a decade later in 1954. Itself a far-sighted document, the Women's Charter took the radical step for the time of claiming women's rights as human rights.

So when the committee began its work, it was building on half a century of campaigning for human rights and emphasising the Freedom Charter. Certainly its vision of a just and equitable South Africa guided us through many dark years of struggle and remained a beacon, but it was not in itself a constitution, nor did it provide constitutional guidelines. The task at hand was for the committee to enlarge the significance of the Charter by transforming it from a programme for the future into the centrepiece of a new constitution.

In addition to these historical documents, which were in themselves human rights landmarks, we also had available to us the deliberations and resolutions of the two crucial ANC national consultative conferences held in exile: the Morogoro Conference held in Tanzania in 1969 and the Kabwe Conference held in Zambia in 1985. Still, the task would prove deeply challenging. Though the principles of our struggle were beyond reproach, we now had to apply them honestly and strategically to realise the Freedom Charter's vision and to displace proposals that would maintain white privilege and the status quo under the guise of minority rights.

Among the issues we debated during that first meeting of the Constitutional Committee was what kind of parliamentary system and voting system would best suit South Africa. Would our new constitution entrench a bill of rights and, if so, how would it be enforced and its provisions protected? Would it include minority rights? Particularly important was the question whether we wanted a unitary or federal state. The ANC had previously expressed itself against federalism for a number of reasons. For one thing, federalism weakens central government. If we wanted to address apartheid's injustices, we would need a strong central government. Moreover, if South Africa was a federal state, it would open the door to white minority rule and would preserve the whites' economic power base. We would also have to give careful consideration to the various possible geographical configurations that would result from the reincorporation of the bantustans or 'independent homelands'. Finally we would have to take into account right-wing Afrikaner leaders and their plans to 'preserve' the former Boer republics of the Orange Free State and Transvaal.

The group then considered how to proceed. We needed to study the constitutions of democracies, including the United States, Portugal, Canada, Australia and the Federal Republic of Germany. We agreed that I would collect various precedents and constitutional materials and make these available to the group. The group was not aiming to arrive at an agreed constitution. Rather, our task was to clarify concepts, put options to the National Executive Committee (NEC) of the ANC and lay down certain constitutional precepts. We noted that we were obligated to nobody, but were responding to the interests, problems and struggles of our people. The remainder of the week the committee spent going through the Freedom Charter clause by clause, identifying those areas where the Charter did not give direction and discussing our preferred solutions. Not for the first time discussion went in the direction of a bill of rights and, with Albie Sachs, I was mandated to work on a first draft.

Following our first meeting, the committee produced a report for the NEC on our discussions as well as reflections and recommendations on some of these difficult questions, particularly those issues on which the Freedom Charter gave no direction. The report was sent to the ANC's National Working Committee (NWC) for consideration and three weeks later Jack Simons received a reply from Ruth Mompati on behalf of the NWC. She noted that 'this is the first occasion on which the ANC has even attempted to give constitutional expression to its programmatic demands' and commended us on 'a difficult job well done'. However, the NWC's response was also very critical. In particular, it asked that we direct ourselves to three key questions. Firstly, did we contemplate a transitional constitution? Secondly, were our proposals primarily meant to be a mobilising instrument, or were they intended as a tactical tool 'in the event that negotiations are forced upon us'? And lastly, how would our constitution translate the slogan 'Power to the People' into a framework that ensured that government was always subject to the people?

Our reply to the first question was that our proposals, although provisional, embodied propositions, principles and concepts that were permanent and would feature in every constitution we proposed. To the second question, we argued that placing the Freedom Charter at the centre of our proposals was both strategic, because it unequivocally itemised the objectives of the struggle, and tactical, because it indicated procedures to be followed to meet these objectives. On the third question, we admitted that the issue of how to ensure people participated in decision-making and the processes of government, beyond merely exercising their right to vote, was a grey area in our report. However, we agreed that it was essential that people became involved, through local community organisations, trade unions, churches and other channels, and generally participated in raising the level of political understanding.

The questions identified by the NWC's critique were part of a larger collection of difficult questions that frustrated our efforts to begin drafting a constitution. For one thing, there were so many unknowns. The situation in South Africa was simply too unpredictable and so much depended on how the Pretoria regime would be removed from power. Would it be by insurrection, a popular uprising, or the ballot box? In every one of these scenarios, we would still need a constitution, but each would require a very different kind of document. In the event of a violent overthrow or popular insurrection, the constitution would be imposed on the victor's terms, as had happened in Japan following its defeat by the United States at the end of the Second World War. If, however, the constitution came about through negotiation, then it would obviously reflect the give-and-take and principled compromises that are part and parcel of negotiations. The committee felt strongly that we could not pre-empt history with a document that might look completely out of date in a few years, depending on the nature of the change.

There was a second difficulty, and one that was more deeply felt in that it stemmed from the movement's basic principles. It was related to that third deeply troubling question posed by the NWC. At a profound level, a constitution is the embodiment of the will of the nation; if it is to enjoy legitimacy, it must come from the people. In other words, the authors of a constitution must have a mandate from the people. This is why the Freedom Charter was so important. The Freedom Charter, drafted on the basis of the popular claims and aspirations brought to Kliptown from across South Africa, embodied the genuine will of the people. But the Congress of the People back in the 1950s was also the last time the movement had been assembled and able to grant a mandate to its leaders. To produce a constitution now would therefore be highly problematic; it would presuppose that a group of experts could draft the document and then present it to the people with attendant arguments as to why it served their best interests. Such an approach reversed the correct order because the constitution would come from leaders and technical experts, such as our committee, but not from the people. Therefore, to proceed with drafting a constitution at that time would undermine the nature of true constitutionalism in our country just at the moment that a free and democratic constitutional order was being seriously contemplated for the first time in South Africa's traumatic history.

For these two reasons we opted for a different approach based on that proposed in Nicaragua following the defeat of the Somoza dynasty. A number of armed groups participated in that revolutionary struggle and, even before Somoza's defeat in 1979, agreed between them on a number of constitutional principles. Albie Sachs had visited Nicaragua and saw how the principles they agreed on became a beacon of hope and a source of unity among the different parties to the conflict. He thought that something similar might offer us a useful way forward. Therefore, instead of authoring a draft constitution, we resolved to draw up a set of guidelines to inform the ANC's approach to a post-apartheid constitutional order. All the same, we were still beset by the difficulties of working in a rapidly changing political environment marked by escalating conflict.

At the time there was an ongoing flurry of constitutional proposals and meetings between white South Africans, particularly Afrikaners, and the ANC, most famously in Dakar, in Senegal, in June 1987. As the ANC's Constitutional Committee, we were acutely aware that our guidelines would have to systematically refute the many proposals, like those of the Indaba and others, that sought to privatise rather than abolish apartheid, retain racial identity as an organising feature of the electoral and parliamentary system, and preserve white minority rule. In this way, these alternative proposals actually stimulated our work on the constitutional guidelines.

The other event that guided us in our task of developing guidelines was Oliver Tambo's annual statement delivered on the ANC's anniversary in 1987. On 8 January the ANC celebrated seventy-five years of activism, resistance and struggle, and the organisation committed itself to multi-party democracy and state governance centred on an entrenched bill of rights. This was a significant moment, coming as it did amid increasing expectations about the possibility of finding a negotiated solution to one of the century's most intractable conflicts. It was also very significant because of what it rejected. In the event of a revolutionary overthrow of the Pretoria regime or popular insurrection against its illegitimate authority, there would probably have been calls to consolidate popular power in the form of direct popular representation, or a people's power constitution, as we termed it in our discussions. But this was not the same as a people-oriented constitution, which is more socially responsive and progressive in the way it structures the distribution and use of power. A people-oriented constitution was also substantially closer to the demands of the Freedom Charter.

Given the increasingly belligerent and violent background, the ANC leadership might have been expected to accede to a variant of people's power constitutionalism. This was not the case, however. Not only did Tambo's statement in January 1987 reject a people's power constitution, but the call was never seriously made, debated or theorised. Later, the constitutional guidelines would be critiqued from a people's power perspective by Joe Slovo and Pallo Jordan, among others, but such a critique was part of the ANC's tradition of open debate and consensual decision-making and was intended to focus critical reflection on whether the guidelines were people-oriented enough. That critique was certainly not a call to supplant the people-oriented vision of the Freedom Charter with a people's power constitution that would consolidate the gains of the revolution at the expense of certain basic rights.

If anything, Tambo's statement made it clear that the progression from political struggle to democratic order had to be via a constitution that guaranteed individual and equal rights, including second-generation rights. Crucial to this democratic vision was the transformation of the economy so that all South Africans, not only whites privileged by apartheid, could share in the wealth of our country. The ANC's vision of a post-apartheid South Africa, therefore, was of a multi-party project to transform our fragmented country into a society committed to justice and freedom for all. In other words, our people-oriented constitution would be founded on an entrenched bill of rights, responsive to the urgency of transformation and its realisation.

From the perspective of the Constitutional Committee, our task was now clear. Benefiting from our analysis of the KwaZulu-Natal Indaba – Pretoria's opening gambit – and the guidance and commitment of Tambo and the ANC leadership, we were in a position to draft constitutional guidelines.

We completed our draft constitutional guidelines document in the course of 1987 and submitted it to the National Executive Committee for review. The NEC approved them and they were then presented for debate and approval to the ANC in March 1988 at a conference hosted at the University of Zambia in Lusaka. By this time Nelson Mandela had begun his careful interaction with the regime from within prison. The NEC, through various channels, kept in touch with Mandela and soon embarked on a remarkable campaign, led by the ANC president, Oliver Tambo, to delineate precisely the conditions that were necessary for full negotiations to commence with the apartheid government over South Africa's democratic future.

The constitutional guidelines set down twenty-five principles for a future constitution based on the vision of an independent, unitary, democratic, non-racial South Africa. There would be a single legislature (unlike the racially segregated tricameral system which the government had introduced as a positive 'reform' in 1983 and which continued to exclude black South Africans from government in the land of their birth) and, along with the executive and judiciary, would be representative of the people of South Africa. Sovereignty would therefore reside with the people and would be exercised through the three branches of government. Everyone would have the right to vote and to stand for election.

On the question of national identity, it would be state policy to promote a single national identity, inclusive of all South Africans, but respectful of cultural and linguistic diversity. This issue of national identity generated much discussion within the ANC and was eventually dropped when it came to finalising the national constitution. There were just too many questions created by entrenching a single national identity. Who decides what this national identity is? Would it be obligatory to subscribe to it? You can only genuinely impose a single national identity by force of arms, and we certainly didn't want to have to do that. I recalled later a conversation I had with a visiting French admiral at his embassy in Cape Town. He told me that the French unitary state – of which most French are proud – was the result of conquest and the triumph of state power. He should know, as he came from Brittany where the Breton language was banned until the 1960s. To avoid inviting civil war, we dropped the clause about national identity from the draft constitution. As it turned out, there was no need for it in any case. A major national survey conducted by the Human Sciences Research Council ten years after the introduction of democracy found that almost ninety per cent of South Africans were proud of their membership of the South African nation.

The ANC's guidelines set out that the constitution would include a bill of rights based on the Freedom Charter, in terms of which basic freedoms would be constitutionally protected, including freedom of association, expression, thought, worship and the press. The state and all social institutions would be constitutionally bound to eradicate racism and hatred. The bill of rights would also oblige the state and society to uproot the social and economic inequalities created by decades of apartheid and centuries of colonial rule.

The economy would be mixed, comprising public, private, co-operative and small-scale family subsistence sectors. In the economy, too, the state would promote skills development among underskilled non-whites and the private sector would be obliged to co-operate with the state to remove inequality and discrimination from the economy. The guidelines also called for a programme of land reform to redress the dispossession and forced removal of hundreds of thousands of people under the infamous Land Acts and the Group Areas Act. Workers' trade union rights would be protected and women would have equal rights and status in all spheres. The last clause of the guidelines, dealing with South Africa's international outlook, committed South Africa to non-alignment and the principles of the charters of the Organisation of African Unity and the United Nations.

The guidelines therefore balanced claims to fundamental rights and freedoms of individuals, in keeping with conventional liberalism, with the imperative to intervene actively in the organisation of society to redress the systematic inequality among South Africans and the consequent curtailment of their liberty, thus maintaining an orientation toward the oppressed majority. In this spirit, a strong affirmative action component was inserted into the guidelines in the bill of rights.

The guidelines rejected the conventional liberal democratic constitutional model that saw the constitution's role as limiting state power, the chief exemplar of which is probably the US Constitution. Our critique of the various proposals that were being put forward at the time had alerted us to the many tricky ways in which the Nationalist government and its collaborators might use liberal constitutionalism to limit the power of a future post-apartheid state. The ANC had always argued that rebuilding South Africa after the abolition of apartheid would require investing the state with an appropriate measure of power to transform the legislated racial caste system into a just society based on freedom and equality. This kind of state power is central to the Freedom Charter and became central to the guidelines, ensuring the continuity of the people-oriented constitutionalism that was fundamental to the ANC's struggle.

Also crucial to the ANC's struggle was the emphasis on restoring political power to the people. But while not seeking to undermine the legitimacy of this imperative, the guidelines were circumspect about people's power constitutionalism. In its simplest terms, the imperative of people's power was fundamental in the way that it continued to organise, mobilise and especially legitimate the struggle for freedom in South Africa. However, it was not necessarily appropriate to building a just society based on freedom and equality and promoting national unity. We argued that a people-oriented constitution founded on a progressive bill of rights would transmit this power to the people more effectively and with better long-term prospects.

The Constitutional Committee continued to meet regularly in Lusaka, except for one meeting in 1988, soon after Albie Sachs survived a car bomb attack in Maputo by the South African security forces, in which he lost his right arm and the sight of one eye. Because he was too weak to travel, the entire committee relocated to London to enable Albie to attend. Some time after he was released from hospital after the horrific attack, Albie flew to Dublin to work with me on the draft ANC bill of rights. As always it was raining in Dublin, and I remember having my repeated smoke breaks outside in the rain because the smoke hurt Albie's damaged eyes. Seated at my kitchen table, with Albie struggling to learn to write with his left hand, we resumed work together on drafting our country's bill of rights. We decided that Albie would start first on the substantive rights and I on their mechanisms for enforcement. Then we would read each other's drafts and integrate them into one document. Albie and I worked without any sources – on purpose. We didn't want our thinking to be predetermined in any way. We wanted to put down what it meant to be a human, a South African, who has fundamental rights. We were strongly aware of being part of a process of writing history; this was going to be the text of a document that would become a lodestar for the ANC during the negotiation process. It was also the precursor of the Bill of Rights that now proudly adorns South Africa's democratic Constitution. I will forever remember those interactions and arguments with Albie, which often went on deep into the night.

Nevertheless, although we had drawn up the draft bill of rights, we kept it close to our chests through most of the negotiations period. Only its bare outline was included in the 1993 Interim Constitution because we didn't want it to be anticipated at a subsequent stage. It then became one of many documents drawn on at the time of writing the final Bill of Rights, and we wanted it to be incorporated in a way that would best serve South Africa. There were indeed changes that we included in the final Bill of Rights – for instance, the section on equality was extended to include rights of sexual orientation, something we hadn't considered back in 1988. I am pleased that the ANC as a whole later accepted this principle without a murmur of dissent.

The ANC was unbanned on 2 February 1990. Those were days of great euphoria. Our collective excitement was unrestrained. The ANC immediately busied itself with making arrangements for the repatriation of the full-time ANC cadres, activists, people in the underground and so on. A group of ANC members travelled home as soon as possible after the ban was lifted to take part in the first two preliminary rounds of negotiations, the Cape Town and Pretoria Minutes, and to smooth the process for the returnees. Arrangements were made to provide houses, families were contacted and all cadres intending to return to South Africa were required to fill out a form indicating their intentions. I don't know where my form is, but if I'd waited for a formal decision, I might still be in Dublin.

Though my immediate inclination was to rush home, the decision to pick up sticks after almost thirty years in Ireland was a difficult one. Louise, of course, is not South African and had never been to the country. She would be leaving her own life behind, and it was a substantial and important life. She was a national figure in Ireland and was involved in a range of institutions, committees and programmes. Emigrating would mean leaving her sons behind. Yet we hardly discussed it. Louise told me afterwards that she knew if she was not willing to go, I would go without her.

When the Constitutional Committee of the ANC met in Lusaka at the end of April 1990, we took the exciting decision that we would next meet in South Africa. This was to be in the middle of the year. The British Airways flight from London caught a tailwind and arrived early in the airspace above Cape Town. The pilot said, 'As we are here ahead of schedule, we're going to take you on a tour of Robben Island.' There, far below and nestled just off the coastline of Cape Town, was the infamous prison island on which Nelson Mandela and others had spent the best part of three decades. We circled around a few times. It was a memorable moment. Then we landed on South African soil. It was raining, as it often is in Cape Town in June, and hundreds of people were at the airport to meet us, waving ANC flags. It was very moving. Dullah Omar, soon to be Minister of Justice in the first democratic government, led the welcoming committee.

Topping my list of priorities on my first days in Cape Town was a visit to District Six, once a vibrant mixed-race community in central Cape Town. Under the Group Areas Act, it had been rezoned for whites and cleared of its residents, despite militant resistance when the bulldozers moved in to destroy their homes. I also had to sample snoek, a traditional Cape dish of salted fish that had been popular among Cape slaves in the eighteenth century. And of course I had to visit the naval base in Simon's Town to see for myself the effects of the arms embargo on South Africa. I recall attending a welcome home dinner for returned exiles held in Athlone by the local ANC branch. Sandile Dikeni, barely known as a writer at that time, recited extracts from his writing. It was a very emotional event. Although something of an outsider – I came from Natal, had spent my entire adult life abroad, and wasn't known in Cape Town – I was truly moved by the warmth with which I was received, especially after the United Democratic Front leader Cheryl Carolus introduced me to the ordinary citizens who made up the mass democratic movement in the country.

When the first South African meeting of the Constitutional Committee was over, I sought permission from the ANC to visit my family in Stanger, and set off for an emotional reunion. In nearly thirty years, I had seen my two sisters and one brother once only, on separate occasions. At Durban airport to greet me was my brother Dawood, the aspiring cricketer whose sporting career had been cut short by the sports boycott. Yet there he was, kitted out in the same Springbok blazer that he had worn when he toured Kenya in a team led by Basil D'Oliveira so many years previously, before there was even talk of a boycott. The vivid green symbolised more than anything else the changed South Africa to which I had returned.

Of course, if I was to return permanently I would need a job, so I wrote to Professor Jakes Gerwel, the Vice-Chancellor of the University of the Western Cape (UWC), whom I had met in Dakar and said: 'I want to come home.' At the time UWC had formed a committee, chaired by Renfrew Christie and co-ordinated by Allan Taylor, later to become one of my political advisers and close friend, which actively sought to recruit the skills and expertise of returning exiles. He and Gerwel replied that the law faculty would almost certainly have something for me. I also had a job offer from the University of Durban-Westville in what was then still the province of Natal.

What with two job offers, Louise came for a two-week visit in January 1991 to help choose between Durban and Cape Town, and for her to meet my family in Stanger. It was suffocatingly hot in Stanger, hotter than in Durban – a preparation for the life hereafter, as one of my friends observed. Louise wilted under the heat. When we got to Cape Town, it was no contest. Back in Ireland I approached the Trinity College authorities for leave of absence for a term, as UWC had offered me a visiting professorship. Later on, after I formally resigned from Trinity College, I took up UWC's offer of a chair in human rights.

It was almost a year before Louise was able to sell our house in Dublin and join me in South Africa. So for a long time after my return I lived a fairly unsettled life. For the first three months I was generously made welcome in the Rondebosch home of Allan Taylor and his wife, Viviene. For me, those three months were unforgettable, though I suspect Allan and Viviene remember them most for the almost constant smell throughout the house of my Silk Cut, which I chain-smoked for years. I believe they had to have their house cleaned by a firm of industrial office cleaners by the time I left. When Louise arrived at the end of 1991, we were welcomed into the home of the former Congress of Democrats stalwart and key figure in the United Democratic Front, Amy Thornton, and enjoyed her hospitality until an extensive hunt, mainly by Louise, turned up our current home, a lovely Victorian house in the quiet suburb of Rosebank. Our sons, who were adults by then, eventually joined us, and they both settled in South Africa, one in Cape Town and the other in Johannesburg.

The first ANC national conference to be held inside South Africa since 1959 took place in Durban from 2 to 6 July 1991. I didn't know what to expect as I had been away from the country for so long. But my conversations in the pub after long sessions or in plenaries, especially with the young comrades who had returned from MK camps in the bush, were every bit as challenging as those I had held for so long with young people at Trinity College – except that this time I was engaging with young people who were products of the struggle. I was truly moved to learn that they had read some of my work which had been distributed in the camps, and their enthusiasm to discuss my views renewed in me my lifelong passion for engaging in debate with young people.

At that first national conference I just made it onto the National Executive Committee of the ANC, coming in at number forty-five of the fifty-person body. ANC branches and regions throughout the country nominated delegates and each had to vote for fifty people, so the counting took hours and hours. It really was an example of democracy in action. Even the misspelling of my name on the ballot paper couldn't dampen my joy. I had come in one vote ahead of Saki Macozoma and two places behind Jeremy Cronin, well-known activists who had been at the forefront of the struggle. It was heartening to know that exiles like myself were known, remembered and recognised by ANC members who probably weren't even born by the time I left home. At the next national congress, I was voted in at number nineteen – and this time my name was spelt correctly. Over the years I made steady progress up that list, coming in at second place (after the highly popular Cyril Ramaphosa) in 1997, during my term as Minister of Water Affairs and Forestry. In 2002 I came eighth, but did not make myself available for the 2007 NEC election.

By the time of its first conference in South Africa, the ANC had formulated what was known as the Harare Declaration, which was adopted by the Organisation of African Unity in 1989 and then, unprecedentedly, by the General Assembly of the United Nations. It listed the five minimum requirements that had to be met before negotiations could begin: the release of all political prisoners; the lifting of all bans and restrictions on people and organisations; the removal of all troops from the townships; the ending of the State of Emergency and the repeal of all repressive legislation; and the cessation of all political executions. Only then, it was argued, could a climate suitable for negotiations be deemed to exist. Of course, this was easier said than done. President F.W. de Klerk felt he had granted enough for the moment by unbanning the ANC, SACP, PAC and other bodies in February 1990.

Among the more practical challenges was how to get negotiations started and actually bring the right people around a table. Most of the key negotiators on the ANC side were wanted men and women. Moreover, the country was still under a State of Emergency, which resembled martial law: there were troops in the townships, the police force was unaccountable and acted with impunity, thousands of activists remained imprisoned, and the law was entirely oriented towards maintaining this massive repression. Much stood between talking about negotiations and actually getting negotiations started. In a major concession for which it did not receive much in return, the ANC suspended the armed struggle in August 1990.

The Harare Declaration was the bedrock of the ANC's position regarding negotiations for a non-racial and democratic South Africa precisely because it represented the interests of the victims of apartheid. In the course of 1990 and 1991 there followed a series of bilateral meetings and accords between De Klerk's government and the ANC, which further committed both parties to a process of negotiation and addressed the obstacles to creating a climate for negotiations, including spiralling violence, intimidation, the issue of political prisoners as well as the armed struggle.

The process of talks about talks culminated in September 1991 in the first multilateral agreement of the transition, with the adoption of the National Peace Accord. At each vital step during those two years of bilateral meetings we in the ANC were guided by the basic objectives, principles and minimum requirements stipulated in the Harare Declaration because we knew these best served the interests of the oppressed.

Formal constitutional negotiations began on 20 December 1991 and took place under the name of the Convention for a Democratic South Africa, or Codesa. Delegations from nineteen political organisations took part, including naturally the ANC. Five working groups were established, each made up of thirty-eight delegates and thirty-eight advisers. These working groups had, as their themes, the creation of a climate for free political activity; the determination of basic constitutional principles; the establishment of transitional procedures for the homelands of Bophuthatswana, Ciskei, Transkei and Venda; the setting and overseeing of timetables for the transition; and the creation of procedures for dealing with new problems that would arise during the transition itself. I was part of the negotiating team at Codesa and served on the fifth working group.

I was also still closely involved with the deliberations of the ANC's Constitutional Committee, which had been hard at work since the mid-1980s drafting constitutional guidelines. It continued to meet regularly on South African soil and served as an advisory body to the party's negotiating team, providing it with discussion documents, briefs and other assistance. By then it was a broader committee – Mandela had invited the prominent South African lawyers Nicholas (Fink) Haysom, Arthur Chaskalson and George Bizos to join and contribute their renowned skills as leading anti-apartheid figures in the country – and it continued to work on drafting a fledgling constitution, which effectively informed the ANC's negotiation team.

Drafts of the constitution would be passed on to the National Executive Committee, where they would be thoroughly debated. Mandela would chair these meetings and he was very meticulous about noting who voted for what position. He was also a stickler for punctuality. Anyone arriving after the starting time of half past seven was made to feel it, even though Mandela never said a word. All he did was look at his watch. Jacob Zuma noted the hands that went up, and people were allowed to speak in that order, and strictly only for their allocated time. Debates could get very heated. I recall it was at one of these NEC meetings that the issue came up of the moral accountability of those responsible for the crime of apartheid. We were struggling at the time with our own reports of transgressions on our side in the ANC camps, and whether these could be compared with the daily injustice of apartheid, not to mention the violence with which it had been imposed. It was then that I proposed the idea of a truth commission.

At one of the NEC meetings Albie Sachs came up with a proposal for a government of national unity and reconstruction. I supported his proposal at the meeting, but wanted to take it one step further. I stood up and suggested it embrace a programme of reconstruction *and* development. This was unanimously supported by the NEC and later became the ANC government's Reconstruction and Development Programme, known popularly as the RDP.

The role of the NEC was to steer the negotiation process. Albie Sachs described it well when he said that we had had the time of the campaigner, followed by the time of the soldier, but this, he declared, was the time of the lawyer. The lawyers like myself felt the responsibility for getting it right; our long history of struggle demanded this of us. There were four members of the Constitutional Committee on the NEC, Zola Skweyiya, Dullah Omar, Albie Sachs and I. We had extraordinarily democratic debates within the NEC. All of these meetings were held in Johannesburg and we purposely chose faith-based community halls as our venues, like the Anglican church in Soweto, not only to save money but to reassure these communities that the ANC was not anti-religious.

The debate on the negotiating process was not confined to the NEC and the Constitutional Committee. It was being played out all over the country. It is perhaps ironic that the two universities that occupied the greatest role in South Africa's constitution-writing process were the rather innocuous University of Potchefstroom, De Klerk's alma mater, which employed some advisers for the National Party's negotiation team, and the University of the Western Cape, once a coloureds-only university created by apartheid, which had become a centre of resistance during the struggle. The Community Law Centre at UWC became an engine room of lively debate, drawing on a group of us UWC academics. We worked closely with the Centre for Development Studies and sometimes the Johannesburg-based Centre for Applied Legal Studies to run a series of countrywide workshops on the issues central to the negotiations at Codesa – should there be a constitutional court, should social and economic rights be in the constitution, what type of electoral system would best suit a country in which almost half the population was not literate? The last was one of the topics that preoccupied us intensely.

When the venerable Walter Sisulu, a Rivonia trialist along with Mandela, was released from prison in 1989, he was asked what electoral system he supported. He opted for the first-past-the-post system, on the grounds that what was good enough for the whites should be good enough for everyone. But it soon proved to be a far more complex question and became the subject of lively debate.

I had done extensive research on the electoral system and had written a little booklet in the late 1980s on what might work best for a democratic South Africa, which Walter Sisulu insisted be published. My own direct role in the process of choosing our electoral system was to produce a study of different systems around the world. I thought through all the electoral possibilities, from Britain's first-past-the-post system to the single transferable vote currently used in Ireland and Malta and for the Australian Senate. I had originally thought that the first-past-the-post system should continue, but soon came to realise that this would deprive Parliament of a number of smaller voices whose exclusion might create difficulties. I found myself gravitating towards the proportional list system in which parties are allotted seats in the National Assembly in proportion to the number of votes they win, and parties allocate seats to members according to a democratically drawn-up party list.

The ANC Constitutional Committee called a conference on the subject in Stellenbosch in 1992, which was open to all political parties. Madiba did not attend, but he asked me to tell him what I thought was the advantage of the proportional list system. I told him that if you got only a quarter per cent of the national vote, you would nevertheless get one seat in Parliament, which would give your party a voice. President Lyndon B. Johnson was right, I told Madiba, when he stated that if there is a son of a bitch pissing, it is better to have him inside pissing out, than outside pissing in. Madiba agreed with what he drily remarked was a very rational argument.

I was truly concerned, as was Mandela, that if we opted for a constituency system, the possibility existed that, apart from the odd ward in urban areas, the ANC might win every single constituency in the country. That clearly wouldn't be good for our fledgling democracy and would undermine the legitimacy of our new state. We instead took the principled decision that it was far more important to ensure that our National Assembly be as representative as possible. We did not set an actual threshold, as in other countries, so consequently a party with just one per cent of the votes would still secure seats in the four hundred-member Assembly, an easy challenge for any party.

At the time there was talk of conducting a national census in order to draw up a voters' roll. I was strongly opposed to the proposition. In fact the NEC had asked the ANC's secretary-general to oppose the census due to be conducted by the apartheid regime as the authorities did not intend to do a headcount in the townships. I was a member of the delegation, together with Walter Sisulu, Joe Slovo and Alfred Nzo, that went to see the Minister of Internal Affairs at the time. The poor man was rather taken aback by our strong opposition to the census, but if it had been the basis of a voters' roll for the first democratic election it could have seriously compromised the inclusivity of the first National Assembly.

It was essential that we came up with a system that was relatively simple, and didn't require major administration – such as the creation of electoral registers or the delineation of hundreds of constituencies – and would provide some representation for the minority parties that gained an effective minimum threshold. A constituency system in any case would be much too large in South Africa, and it is very likely that there would have been more disagreement and fighting over constituency delimitation than over policies and principles. Anyway I believe constituency systems exaggerate the link between an MP and a voter. All that happens is the MP becomes a messenger. Edmund Burke once asked: Are you a messenger or a representative; are you at the beck and call of the electorate or are you making policy? I could see no other way for the duration of the first few elections than proportional representation. At the time of writing, South Africa has held four general elections since it became a democracy in 1994, and I think it is fair to say that our system has been a great success in ensuring the representation of diverse interests within as well as between parties.

However, this does not mean that the system should stay as it is forever. My own long-term preference would be for the German system, which consists of sixty per cent of MPs elected by constituencies and forty per cent elected according to proportional representation. In my view, if we want change – and there is a sound basis for seeking change so that constituency members have a more direct connection to their representatives – then we need real debate. An attempt at that came much later when Dr Buthelezi, the Minister of Home Affairs, appointed the Van Zyl Slabbert Commission to investigate exactly this question. However, the Cabinet, as it was entitled to do, decided to continue with the existing system of proportional representation for provincial and national elections, with local government having a mix of first-past-the-post and PR representation. For some odd reason it was reported to Slabbert that it was I who had rejected his revisions. In fact, Cabinet felt his proposals were too complicated, and that there was not sufficient time to change the system – by then, the 2004 elections were pending. The matter ended with Slabbert accepting my good faith, but without changing his mind. But all that came much later.

During the negotiations another big sticking point was how the regions would fit into the national dispensation. For ages we couldn't even agree on what they would be called. The ANC called them regions to emphasise the unity of the South African state. The National Party wanted them known as states, which suggested far too much autonomy for the unified South Africa we envisaged. At the very last moment we decided on the compromise name of provinces, a term that had been used since Union in 1910.

We also had debates on a parliamentary versus a presidential system for the future South Africa. At first I was strongly in favour of a presidential system because it seemed to most closely reflect the traditional African culture of personalising leadership, in which a strong leader embodies the state. I later changed my mind to favour Parliament as the repository of the elected will of the people and eventually accepted that the President should be indirectly elected, for the same reason. This was a principled position taken by the ANC at the time to recognise the central role of Parliament, with the President having a larger range of powers compared with those of the traditional prime minister.

We thought at the time it was essential that the negotiations be as inclusive as possible, not only for the sake of representivity. With nineteen parties, it became much easier to be quorate and to get some discussion going on important issues. Of course, it soon became clear that some parties were more relevant than others. Still, it was electrifying to see Codesa under way and all those people sitting side by side, deciding the future of our country. Mandela was also able to use his charm and charisma to persuade many of the smaller parties to toe the line and vote with the ANC. Ironically, the Conservative Party, a right-wing Afrikaner political organisation, never objected to a single proposal during the negotiations. They were more of an ally of the ANC than they were of the NP government.

Nevertheless, tension at these talks could sometimes mount. In the early days, possibly the only point on which we ever gained an agreement among parties was in voting on whether to allow smoking in the room. In a rare moment of cross-party solidarity the non-smokers asserted their majority. As a chain-smoker at the time, this frustrated me greatly. When tension built up, my need for a smoke would drive me from the room, but I was so engrossed with the debates I couldn't go far. Sometimes I was reduced to holding my cigarette behind my back while I positioned myself at the open door from where I could still participate in the proceedings. I could not tear myself away from these debates.

Throughout these difficult negotiations we were guided by our version of a post-apartheid bill of rights. The bill of rights was crucial here because it would be the most powerful vehicle for the aspirations of the oppressed in a democratic, non-racial South Africa. That is why we so vigorously opposed the notion of group rights proposed by De Klerk and the National Party. Under their proposals, whites who chose to live together as a self-defined group would be constitutionally protected. The effect would have been to continue apartheid's segregationist vision even after the repeal of the most iniquitous of all apartheid laws, the Group Areas Act. This was completely unacceptable, and it was Tambo who first argued that the concerns of those clamouring for group rights were covered in the provisions of a bill of rights. The regime's conversion to a bill of rights was seen by it as a way to protect and enhance white privilege. It certainly would protect all South Africans, even whites. So, the centrality of a bill of rights in a new constitution was paramount because it reflected the needs of the oppressed as well as providing a suitable vehicle for the concerns of the former oppressors, provided they were committed to peace.

But even a bill of rights was not enough to allay white fears. Whites in the civil service, military and police force were worried about their jobs and pensions. We also recognised that a democratically elected government would need the co-operation of the existing civil service to implement its policies, albeit policies that would be the antithesis of those that had been implemented for decades under apartheid. We did not have a new civil service waiting in the wings, and the South African army and police were not simply going to hand over their equipment, bases and uniforms to our forces. In other words, to run the country effectively, the new government would need the co-operation and skills of the beneficiaries of apartheid. What made things even more complicated was the fact that South Africa did not have a single civil service but a multiplication of civil services for each race, or 'population group' in apartheid parlance, as well as for each 'independent homeland', or bantustan, and for each self-governing territory, all duplicated for the different 'races'. These had to be merged into one civil service, while retaining suitable skills. This was a major challenge.

Our transition was and remains rife with deep and often hopeful ironies. One of these was the so-called sunset clauses, which broke this major deadlock. We proposed the restructuring of the civil service, police and army in a way that honoured existing contracts and provided for retirement compensation. Our proposal allayed white fears because it guaranteed that whites in the public service would not be summarily dismissed or have their pensions expropriated. The sunset clauses were proposed by the ANC, after extensive debate within the National Executive Committee, as a solution that took into account white fears while ensuring the retention of a civil service that would deliver effective governance for the majority of South Africans. The sunset clauses allayed white fears about being swept from power and overwhelmed by majority rule. They also went a long way to securing whites' commitment to the process and their loyalty to a peaceful post-apartheid state.

In retrospect, I think at the time we didn't realise how weak the Afrikaners actually were during the negotiation period. We were warned of disobedience in both the public service and the military, and this was a terrifying prospect, but I am not sure anything would have materialised. I was personally approached by the brother of Constand Viljoen, who had been head of the South African Defence Force. He warned me that Constand was 'threatening all kinds of violence. You must talk to Madiba [Mandela].' Constand Viljoen was a grey-haired, steely-looking Afrikaner general who had purportedly gathered many supporters around him, including a good number of former and serving SADF military men and women, with the idea of establishing an autonomous Afrikaner homeland, a *volkstaat*. An army of tens of thousands of well-armed and highly trained Afrikaners was clearly something we didn't want as we prepared to go to the polls for our first democratic election.

I passed on the message to Joe Nhlanhla, the ANC's head of intelligence. This was the protocol: even I, as an NEC member, felt I couldn't contact Mandela directly. Mandela then spoke to Viljoen, clutching the ANC's plans for proportional representation with which he could demonstrate that by voting *en bloc* the Afrikaners could secure for themselves a whole group of MPs in the new Parliament, who could then work to entrench and expand their representation and protect their cultural and linguistic identity. In the end Viljoen became a Freedom Front MP in the new democratic Parliament.

The issue of the public service, police and army was not the only major sticking point, or even the most significant. A greater obstacle remained De Klerk's insistence that his National Party be granted a special role at the highest level in a post-apartheid government. Mechanisms touted for such participation included power-sharing or minority vetoes or both. Much of De Klerk's effort in 1992 was directed at appeasing and weakening his right-wing opponents, staunch defenders of apartheid who had broken with the NP during the 1980s. As conservative resistance hardened, he called for a referendum in March 1992 among white voters to test his mandate for change. The outcome was a resounding 'yes'. Election analysts reported that support among Afrikaners was even slightly higher than among English speakers.

Buoyed by the result, De Klerk presented Codesa with proposals for a two-phase transition, the first phase managed by transitional councils appointed by Codesa, and the second phase – the constitution-writing process – managed by an elected transitional government headed by a multi-person presidency and a bicameral legislature. The ANC's counterproposals called for a single-stage transition and a committee elected by proportional representation to draft the constitution, with a two-thirds majority needed to pass constitutional provisions. Negotiations were suspended as both sides sought to refine their proposals and to unify their constituencies.

Meanwhile, in the Inkatha stronghold of Natal, and also in the townships of the Witwatersrand, Inkatha militia, clandestinely backed and armed by right-wing elements within the government's security forces, were conducting a campaign of brutal attacks on ANC supporters. It was a time of escalating violence, which posed a serious threat to the successful outcome of negotiations. The inter-party conflict being conducted outside the negotiation process culminated in a brutal massacre which threatened to derail negotiations altogether. On the night of 17 June 1992, supporters of the IFP and (the Truth Commission later found) members of the government's security forces attacked residents of the township of Boipatong. They murdered thirty-eight people in what became known as the Boipatong Massacre. I was in Derry, in Ireland, on that night in June and heard about the carnage while attending a meeting with hostages returning from Lebanon. The meeting organisers asked me if I wanted to return home immediately. In the end I made the difficult decision to see through my obligations to my Irish hosts and the visiting delegation.

After the Boipatong Massacre, the ANC threatened to pull out of the negotiations entirely unless the government made greater efforts to end the violence and curtail covert police support for the IFP. Mandela took his complaint to the Organisation of African Unity and the United Nations, where, on 15 July 1992, he accused the government of 'a cold-blooded strategy of state terrorism'. The impact of Boipatong on the negotiations marked an extremely important shift from formal negotiations to person-to-person, behind-the-scenes informal discussions. Cyril Ramaphosa, the ANC's chief negotiator, called it the 'War of Memoranda'. In particular, the famous 'channel' between Ramaphosa and his counterpart, De Klerk's right-hand man, Roelf Meyer, became a vital avenue for discussion and negotiation.

Finally, in September 1992 De Klerk and Mandela arrived at a Record of Understanding affirming police responsibility for protecting residents in workers' hostels, where support for the ANC was high. In protest against the Record of Understanding, Mangosuthu Buthelezi established the Concerned South Africans Group (Cosag), comprising white conservatives and black homeland leaders whose power bases were being eroded at Codesa, to press for a federal constitution to preserve the rights of ethnic minorities, especially the Zulus and whites.

Negotiations resumed on 5 March 1993, but the fragile process was again threatened a month later when Chris Hani, the popular general secretary of the South African Communist Party, was murdered by a member of the extremist right-wing Afrikaner Weerstandsbeweging. I heard about the murder on my way home from a river-rafting trip with a number of foreign ambassadors. The excursion had seemed like a convivial way to answer the endless questions that these countries were putting to the ANC at that time and, in deference to the French ambassador's need for a cup of coffee, we stopped at a tiny café. There we saw the headlines about a disaster. For a moment I hoped it was a reference to some cricketing event under way at the time. Then the appalling reality dawned. The journey back to Cape Town took place in a subdued and apprehensive atmosphere. ANC leaders joined the government in trying to stem outbreaks of retaliatory violence, and several white extremists were arrested within weeks after the murder.

With a new sense of urgency, political negotiators tried to speed up the process and set the date for nationwide elections no later than 27 April 1994. As Mandela said to me at the time, 'Nothing concentrates the mind like the fixing of a date.'

The most important question of course was who would then draft the constitution. This was crucial because it went to the heart of a fundamental conflict between the negotiating strategies of the ANC and the De Klerk government. The government wanted a multi-party conference to draft a new constitution. But without elections, such a multi-party forum could not be considered representative of all South Africans. We wanted a democratically elected constituent assembly to draft the constitution because only then could the resulting document enjoy legitimacy. In other words, the question of who would draft the constitution went to the heart of whether our new democracy would emerge suddenly complete with a single new constitution or would develop in two or more stages involving transitional authorities and an interim constitution leading to the adoption of a final constitution. At some point there would have to be elections and these would have to be non-racial, free and fair – but how would we achieve that after centuries of colonial and white supremacist rule?

Throughout this process, proposals and counterproposals were taken back to the NEC sitting in Johannesburg, and there they would be debated intensely. The NEC debated for a day and a half before opting for an interim constitution to be drafted by a multi-party conference. This became the Multi-Party Negotiating Forum, in which I played an active part. It was this proposal that eventually won the day. We conceded that the regime would not give way to an interim government, as De Klerk would not waver from his attachment to the legitimacy of his government.

The reasoning behind our insistence on a multi-stage approach was not simply because we knew we would win far more votes in a general election and would therefore have a stronger hand in drafting the final constitution. Nor was our insistence based on concern that at a multi-party convention we would be just one among many parties negotiating with the ruling party.

Our commitment to the principle of a democratically elected constituent assembly to draft the constitution was based on the foundational principle of the Freedom Charter adopted nearly four decades previously, namely that only a democratically elected government can legitimately claim to represent the will of the people. If our new constitution was to enjoy legitimacy, if it was to belong to the people and hold their interests in the highest regard, it had to be drafted by the people's democratically elected representatives. A constitution drafted by a multi-party convention would be an elite pact and could not legitimately claim to represent the interests of the dispossessed majority. Yet, to hold national, non-racial, free and fair elections for a constituent assembly would require a new constitution.

At the end of 1993, Mandela went to see De Klerk about a few outstanding issues that still needed to be resolved. It took some intense negotiation and compromise, though far more on the National Party side. Eventually De Klerk agreed on every single one. So I myself think it is a historic triumph to have achieved power in a democratic South Africa through tough and principled negotiation when the National Party tried every trick in the book to retain as much of their power as they could. There had to be compromises and it was not a dishonourable way to bring peace to South Africa. Nobody but the ANC could have done it; nobody else was supported by the bulk of the people.

The draft constitution was published on 26 July 1993. Many have claimed to have written its preamble. For my part, I put in a claim for the author André Brink. Within its simple but powerful words is contained the clarion call for South Africa's newly minted democracy. 'We the people of South Africa', the preamble says, 'Recognise the injustices of our past; Honour those who suffered for justice and freedom in our land; Respect those who have worked to build and develop our country; and Believe that South Africa belongs to all who live in it, united in our diversity.' The final Chapter 16 contained words just as moving as those in the preamble. It described the Interim Constitution as 'a historical bridge between the past of a deeply divided society characterised by strife, conflict, untold suffering and injustice, and a future founded on the recognition of human rights, democracy and peaceful coexistence and development opportunities for all South Africans, irrespective of colour, race, class, belief or sex.' Then it goes on to say, 'With this

Constitution and these commitments we, the people of South Africa, open a new chapter in the history of our country.' Beautiful, resonant words.

The Constitution contained a federal-style system of regional legislatures, equal voting rights regardless of race, and a bicameral national legislature. Many of us had chipped in during the drafting process, but I am especially proud that I proposed the creation of a Constitutional Court as well as the electoral system based on proportional representation, which was incorporated. Negotiators were undeterred by the storm of protests that followed, and went on to establish a Transitional Executive Council (TEC), a multi-party body that would share executive responsibilities with President De Klerk during election preparations. The Concerned South Africans Group, consisting of Buthelezi's IFP and the white right, demanded equal status with the government and the ANC. Sensing new momentum, however, the government cracked down on this kind of right-wing opposition and tried to reason with white extremists, without slowing the pace of election preparations. Only days before the election the IFP reversed its decision and decided to participate in the end, which required a costly and inconvenient revising and reprinting of the ballot papers, but this was accommodated in pursuit of full inclusivity.

The Government of National Unity was to be a power-sharing government, and the legislature would double as a Constituent Assembly for the purposes of drafting a final constitution, which was adopted in 1996. But a unique South African compromise was proposed. The Constituent Assembly would be bound by over thirty constitutional principles, which would be judicially enforced. Now we had a route to national, non-racial, democratic elections. We also had a draft bill of rights on hand, surely the first liberation movement to have such a document prepared and waiting before negotiations began in earnest. The Government of National Unity was elected into power in April 1994. At last we were moving towards our goal.

During the negotiation period, which ran in earnest from shortly after the unbannings in 1990 through to 1993, when the Interim Constitution was approved, and then on to 1996 when the final Constitution was adopted, our main challenges were several and were not always complementary. Probably foremost among them was the imperative to meet the needs of the oppressed. In political terms, the oppressed were our constituency. But the struggle against apartheid could not be reduced to mere political posturing in negotiations. Apartheid was and remains a crime against humanity and our struggle to defend South Africans black and white, but particularly black, we undertook in the name of humanity. That was an awesome responsibility. In negotiating for justice and peace in South Africa, we had to live up to that responsibility.

This balancing of the needs of the oppressed with the fears of the oppressors permeated the negotiating process from beginning to end. Sometimes maintaining this balance required negotiators to tread softly and handle issues delicately. But the stakes were high and we could not afford to fudge the issues. Balancing the needs of the oppressed with the needs of the oppressors required frank negotiations. We had to remember Edward Said's injunction: Our duty was to capture the imagination not just of our people but also of our oppressors.

There are few examples in the world where a very powerful regime has handed over power without self-destruction (or compromise). Anybody who says that the apartheid house was a pack of cards that would have fallen down at the slightest touch is suffering from political amnesia. The National Party knew they were going to lose power and could see apartheid crumbling around them, but they were still going to fight. We were told again and again: 'Unless you concede on this, you can't rely on the civil service. Unless you concede on that …' In fact, though we conceded on issues like the sunset clauses (it was the ANC who proposed them in the first place to break the deadlock), in the end it was the regime that capitulated.

If there is a single lesson that our remarkable transition can demonstrate for the benefit of humanity, it is that the transition from an unjust to a just society succeeds or fails on the strength of its participants' commitment to peace. Where there is a commitment to peace, there is *always* a way. But beware of the corollary: where such commitment is lacking, the process is imperilled. The transition to democracy in South Africa is often characterised as a negotiated settlement. Maybe a more apt description would be a successful negotiation of a peace treaty between warring parties. White South Africa had waged war against non-white South Africa – and it wasn't even confined to the territory of South Africa: successive apartheid governments had invaded neighbouring countries and sent assassins as far afield as Maputo, Paris and London. Negotiations to end apartheid peacefully pivoted on the imperative to end the war in South Africa.

In retrospect, there are a few further aspects of negotiations that make all the difference between a successful transition to democracy and a collapse into disaster. First, it is vital that negotiators work toward a specific goal. Our vision at the outset of the negotiations was to establish a non-racial, multi-party democracy in South Africa. But a vision is not enough. You must identify and work towards substantial and measurable goals. We worked toward holding national, non-racial, democratic elections for a constituent assembly that would draft the final constitution. When we went into negotiations we were prepared – not entirely – but we knew what we wanted and what we didn't want.

Second, it is axiomatic of negotiations that they involve give-and-take and compromise; that is the substance of bargaining. However, to find a middle road, to negotiate through seemingly irreconcilable differences, you have to know your objectives. You have to be acutely sensitive to the reasoning behind your particular position on an issue so that you may modify it as need be without compromising your vision or end goal. The sunset clauses are a good example of this. We learnt that trust is the outcome of, not a precondition for, negotiations. Within the ANC, too, we thrashed out all our differences during the negotiations until we reached unanimity on our side. I do not recall a single member of the NEC, from Chris Hani to Harry Gwala, opposing any proposal or decision reached through our wider discussion. That is how we approached all the intractable problems along the road to the adoption of our final constitution in 1996.

Finally, we underestimated the importance of a strong bilateral trust between the two major parties. This was probably the most important lesson we drew from the first round of negotiations, which really amounted to discussions, at Codesa. Bilateralism had been downplayed at Codesa in the interest of inclusivity, particularly because inclusivity went some way toward overcoming the inequality of negotiations between the ruling party and the forces of liberation. Yet even as Codesa was collapsing, a place for a bilateral initiative emerged, with direct talks between the ANC's Cyril Ramaphosa and the National Party's Roelf Meyer, backed of course by their respective parties. It was this initiative that eventually delivered the Record of Understanding late in 1992, which got negotiations back on track and led to a new multi-party effort. That bilateral initiative became invaluable at the Multi-Party Negotiating Forum because it maintained the momentum of the negotiations, while the forum still ensured that everyone had an opportunity to present their views and make their contribution.

As an addendum, it is worth noting that the public participation process that accompanied the drafting of the final Constitution exerted massive influence over the Constituent Assembly. This was perhaps not surprising as I believe it was the most extensive exercise in public participation ever undertaken anywhere on this planet. This was a fitting heir to the Congress of the People's instructions back in the 1950s and fully lived up to the need for a mass mandate. Thus the final Constitution contains provisions and mechanisms designed to 'check and balance' the legislative and executive branches of government not because of some theoretical distrust of either, or some reactionary concern about the potential excess of our governors, but in order to ensure that the principle of social transformation is sustained and that the rights and duties that are accordingly enshrined in such distinctive detail in our Constitution are respected by all.

This, for me, was the defining moment of our democracy, when we launched South Africa's new Constitution with a bill of rights following multi-party negotiations and broad-based public participation. As a life-long campaigner for human rights, this moment was one of the highlights of my life.

6

Three Great South Africans

I have been fortunate in my life to have encountered many extraordinary men and women, some South African, some African, some British, some Irish, others from different parts of the world. Of this collection of passionate, principled, talented individuals, three stand out: Albert Luthuli, Oliver Tambo and Nelson Mandela. These three are men of such quality and character that I feel compelled to devote a small part of this memoir to mark their deep impact on my life. They were in large part responsible for making me into the political animal that I have turned out to be. Why their lives intersected with mine will always be a mystery, but I got to know each of them at different stages in their lives and at different stages of mine, and they, each in their own way, guided me and made me the man I am today.

I met the larger-than-life Albert Luthuli when I was only a child and spent many, many hours with him during my adolescent years. He was the midwife of my political awakening and was a towering presence who greatly assisted my comprehension of what was happening in the world and in South Africa. I came into contact with Oliver Tambo shortly after he went into exile in London in the early 1960s. And while my own period of exile was spent largely in Ireland, our paths crossed periodically. In spite of these infrequent, often short interactions, he had a major impact on my thinking. I first met Nelson Mandela in 1990 in London and then a few months later when he visited Ireland. I then went on to serve in the Cabinet of Mandela's first democratic government. We worked closely together for five years.

135

Here, I want to pay tribute in turn to these three great South African leaders. Each in his way has made an indelible imprint not just on my own life but on South Africa and indeed on the history of humankind. Two of them, Mandela and Luthuli, have won due international recognition by being awarded the Nobel Peace Prize. Tambo never earned that distinction, but none who knew him doubted his extraordinary qualities.

Tambo, Luthuli and Mandela were all men of enormous depth, conviction and dedication. They led by example, acknowledged their frailties where necessary, and never backed down from the beliefs and principles they held most dear – not even if it meant great personal sacrifice, as it often did. At heart, each was a deep humanist, totally convinced of the equality of all men and women, appreciative of the inherent worth of every individual, and committed to improving the lives of the poorest and most vulnerable. At a personal level, they were deeply empathetic, kind, compassionate, wonderful men. It was a very great privilege indeed for me to have known each of them.

Albert Luthuli was a teacher by training, although he resigned from the teaching profession when he was elected by his people as Chief of the Umvoti Mission Reserve in 1936. Through his experience of the problems of his community he became politicised. In the 1940s he became actively involved in the ANC. He was an eloquent speaker, with a commanding presence and a formidable intellect. His qualities of leadership were recognised when he was elected in 1951 to the presidency of the Natal ANC and, soon after, to the presidency of the ANC itself.

This new political role precipitated a crisis when the government demanded that he choose between his chieftainship and his political activities. Refusing to resign from either, he was deposed as chief by the government, although throughout his life his friends and followers continued to address him by that traditional title, indicating that Luthuli was not to be defined by the apartheid regime. Luthuli's statement in response to the government's denial of his traditional authority was a resounding assertion of his moral authority:

'Who will deny that thirty years of my life have been spent knocking in vain, patiently, moderately and modestly at a closed and barred door?

'As for myself, with a full sense of responsibility and a clear conviction, I decided to remain in the struggle for extending democratic rights and responsibilities to all sections of the South African community. I have embraced the non-violent passive resistance technique in fighting for freedom because I am convinced it is the only non-revolutionary, legitimate and humane way that could be used by people denied, as we are, effective constitutional means to further aspirations …

'It is inevitable that in working for Freedom some individuals and some families must take the lead and suffer.'

In 1952, as the Defiance Campaign gathered pace in South Africa, Luthuli was banned by the government. Stripped of his chieftainship, he was now restricted to Groutville, where he was born, and the surrounding area of Lower Tugela. As Stanger was fortuitously the only big town in Lower Tugela, Luthuli became a frequent visitor to my neck of the woods. He seldom visited Stanger without stopping by a bookkeeper named E.V. Mohamed. 'E.V.', as he was called, was a very gentle, pleasant man. He didn't actually have any strong political affiliations, but he clearly had his own personal strengths and convictions, and Chief Luthuli valued his friendship enormously. As Luthuli didn't have an office in Stanger, E.V. let him use his garage for this purpose. It was a brave act at the time because Luthuli was a banned person and to consort with him was bound to lead to Special Branch interest and, usually, harassment of some kind.

My father's fruit shop was where many like-minded people met. He knew E.V. very well and one day E.V. asked him if I would like to meet the Chief. I must have been about thirteen or fourteen years old. I felt like I'd been asked to meet the King – I was then still in my royalist phase. For me, it was a most stirring experience. I was in total awe of the famous visitor from Groutville. He was the first African I met who wasn't a cleaner, a gardener or a night-soil remover. Over time, I too became a regular visitor to E.V.'s house and Luthuli became my mentor.

Luthuli was a large man, and when he laughed, his whole face was suffused with smiles. I asked him many questions, some of them hugely naïve. He answered gently and patiently. He spoke in this extraordinary, beautiful voice with a lilting timbre and a rhythm that was intoxicating. He may have been a very large man, but he never made you feel small.

I became then a creature of the ANC, even though it was some years before I was able to join the organisation. Like many of my generation. I was moulded, influenced and deeply affected by the party and its policies. In fact, all my fundamental assumptions came through the ANC, starting with the profound wisdom and deep humanity of Albert Luthuli. He gave me and others a vision of South Africa that overcame the prejudice of one's cultural, ethnic, social and particularly religious background. He made me feel that we were all products of a shared society, despite its welter of prejudices. Luthuli, the Chief, made me into a South African.

I remember his telling me he had visited Johannesburg in an attempt to engage with white South Africans. Luthuli wanted to speak to whites, even though his banning order meant he wasn't allowed to. During the meeting, a young white Pretoria University student had kicked him under the table. It seemed that when he did get the opportunity to communicate with white South Africans, many just didn't want to hear him.

A few years after meeting him, I asked Luthuli to visit my home. He gracefully accepted and was soon welcomed into the tidy sitting room of our small house in Colenbrander Street in Stanger. Luthuli was the first African who had come as a visitor to our home. He brought some mangoes and I gave him a plate with a fork and knife. He ignored the cutlery and took a big bite out of a mango. The juice ran down his chin and onto his shirt. He didn't care in the least. He was thoroughly humble. He had no pretensions or pomposity. He just enjoyed the fruit. This amazing man introduced me to a political sensibility that I would hold close to my heart forever.

During the 1950s, the apartheid government considered it a criminal act to address Luthuli as Chief. In Alan Paton's novel *Ah, But Your Land Is Beautiful*, the police interrogate a leader of the National Union of South African Students (Nusas) after the organisation had congratulated Luthuli on his election to the presidency of the ANC. The police insist that it is 'subversive for a students' organisation to continue to give a man a title which has been taken away from him by a Minister who ultimately derives his power from Parliament. It is in fact contempt of Parliament, which is a serious offence indeed. The penalties are heavy, and could be crippling for you and your organisation.'

Ironically, around this time, F.W. de Klerk, who was later to become President of apartheid South Africa, invited Luthuli to speak at Potchefstroom University, on behalf of his student organisation, the Afrikaanse Studentebond. Although he regarded the ANC as dangerous because of its co-operation with communists and its proposals for a universal franchise in South Africa, De Klerk was interested in Luthuli because 'we respected his position as a Zulu chief'. It appears that De Klerk was quite unaware that the government he supported had deposed Luthuli as chief, or that addressing him as 'Chief' might be a criminal offence. Despite the objections of his university, the Afrikaanse Studentebond held the meeting off campus. 'It was a strange experience,' De Klerk relates in his autobiography, 'for young Afrikaners at the time to converse with black South Africans on an equal basis.' These students might have respected the Chief, but, De Klerk reports, 'his message that all South Africans should have the right to one-man one-vote in an undivided South Africa was at the time utterly alien to us'. In view of their insistence that Afrikaners had the right to rule themselves, while Zulus and other Africans should be relegated to 'homelands', this exchange with the students left Luthuli, so De Klerk imagined, 'despondent about the possibility that Afrikaners would ever accept his message'.

Luthuli, however, possessed a remarkable generosity of spirit, although he was never tolerant of injustice. He was a Christian, with very deeply held beliefs, but his Christianity was modelled on the Jesus who threw the moneylenders out of the temple. Throughout his active political life, Luthuli was a committed and disciplined member of the ANC. He articulated the movement's non-racial policies with the same deep conviction he vested in his religion.

'Our interest in freedom is not confined to ourselves only,' Luthuli said in his ANC presidential address of 1953. 'We are interested in the liberation of all oppressed people in the whole of Africa and in the world as a whole.' Clearly, Luthuli's vision of freedom in South Africa was advanced in solidarity with the struggle for freedom throughout Africa, because he and the movement were internationalists.

In his testimony during the Treason Trial, Luthuli invited the government to participate in negotiations, observing that 'one really can't anticipate and say what will happen at negotiation', but proposing that the ANC 'would be very, very happy if the government would take up the attitude of saying, come let us discuss'. When the court insisted that there was 'very little hope of negotiation', Luthuli responded: 'There were no signs, my lords, in that direction … [but] hope is always there.' Far ahead of his time, even under the most hopeless of conditions, Luthuli held out hope for a peaceful resolution through negotiations.

In a speech in Johannesburg in 1958, Luthuli challenged any assumption that South Africa, with its complexity of race, colour, creed and culture, could not develop into a democracy. 'I personally believe', he declared, 'that here in South Africa, with all our diversities of colour and race, we will show the world a new pattern of democracy. I think there is a challenge to us in South Africa to set a new example for the world. We can build a homogeneous South Africa on the basis not of colour but of human values.'

In that same speech, Luthuli called for an international boycott of South African products. This call for international pressure on the apartheid regime was heard in London, where I began studying a year later, and inspired the Boycott Movement, which was to develop into the British Anti-Apartheid Movement. Despite the attempts by the government to silence him, Luthuli announced the ANC's human and humanising values of non-racialism, freedom and democracy in such resounding tones that his words reached all over the world.

When Louise and I decided to marry in 1961, the news created a sensation in Stanger as the apartheid prohibition on mixed-race marriage meant I could not return home – unless I left Louise behind. Before we did anything I wrote to my family. I believe it was my eldest brother, Ebrahim, and my second sibling, Mohammed, who approached the Chief to write to me. I received a beautiful message from Luthuli, who said he was looking forward to my return so that we, together, could set up a strong political centre in Stanger, where I would provide legal services to the indigent. I imagine it was a painful response to a dilemma posed by the intervention of my family.

Luthuli was nominated in February 1961 by the Social Democrats in the Swedish Parliament for the 1960 Nobel Peace Prize. At the time, he was still entangled in the five-year Treason Trial, which finally resulted in his acquittal on 29 March 1961. Under renewed banning orders that restricted his freedom of speech and his movement to the Lower Tugela magisterial area, Luthuli was confined to his home in Groutville when he learnt on 12 October 1961 that he was being awarded the Peace Prize. In a public statement, he thanked the Nobel Prize Committee, but said that the award was being given not only to himself, 'but also to my country and its people – especially those who have fought and suffered in the struggle to achieve the emancipation of all South Africans from the bonds of fear and injustice'.

The apartheid regime reacted with outrage to the award. B.J. Vorster, then Minister of Justice, grudgingly allowed him to travel to Norway, 'notwithstanding the fact that the government fully realises that the award was not made on merit'. The Cape Town newspaper *Die Burger*, a National Party mouthpiece, said the award of the Nobel Peace Prize to Albert Luthuli was a 'remarkably immature, poorly considered and fundamentally un-Western decision'. With characteristic humility and humour Luthuli observed that this was the first time he agreed with the government as he also thought himself unworthy of such a great honour.

Although the government was prepared to let him go to Norway, it would not grant permission for him to attend the celebrations that were held in nearby Stanger. Buses were prevented from transporting people to the occasion. Nevertheless, a celebratory event was held. Fatima Meer spoke and Alan Paton read his 'Praise Song for Luthuli'. The praise singer Percy Yengwa received the biggest response for his tribute to the 'great bull that our enemies had tried to enclose in a kraal, the great bull that had broken the strong fence to wander far – as far as Oslo!' Yengwa concluded by praising Luthuli as 'Nkosi yase Groutville! Nkosi yase Afrika! Nkosi yase world!' (Chief of Groutville! Chief of Africa! Chief of the world!)

Luthuli received the Nobel Peace Prize on 10 December 1961, a significant day, for in 1950 it had been declared by the United Nations as International Human Rights Day. He made a brief acceptance speech. The next day, he delivered his lecture 'Africa and Freedom'. Wearing his traditional Zulu headdress, he was very much the Chief. But he surprised the audience by singing the national anthem, 'Nkosi Sikelel' iAfrika', demonstrating that he was also the leader and president of the ANC.

Luthuli made a tremendous impression by bringing Africa to Europe. As a Norwegian newspaper reported on Luthuli's lecture, 'We have suddenly begun to feel Africa's nearness and greatness. In the millions of huts of corrugated iron, mud and straw lives a force which can make the world richer ... Luthuli, the Zulu chieftain and school teacher, is an exceptional man. But in his words, his voice, his smile, his strength, his spontaneity, a whole continent speaks.' But although his words and voice could be heard in Norway, they still could not be legally heard in South Africa. 'Albert Luthuli must now return to his people in chains, to his guards in exile,' the Norwegian report concluded. 'We have never seen a freer man!'

The last time I saw Luthuli was at Heathrow Airport in London on a cold, dark December night in 1961. He was on his way to Oslo to receive the Nobel Peace Prize. A small group of South African exiles, students and anti-apartheid campaigners had assembled in the hope of greeting him and his wife, Nokukhanya, but we could only wave our placards and ANC flags from the other side of a wire fence. The South African regime had given him a passport on condition that he did not engage in any political activities. Accordingly, he was forced to pass by without speaking to us, only casting a wistful look in our direction, while we were left feeling elated that after so many years we had at least had a view of our 'Chief'.

Returning home, Luthuli was again confined to Groutville. With the Nobel Peace Prize money, he bought two farms in Swaziland which he hoped would provide a safe haven for ANC refugees escaping from the increasingly violent repression of the movement in South Africa. Any profits from the farms, he intended, would go towards supporting the ANC in exile. As Luthuli was restricted to Groutville, the responsibility for overseeing the farms fell to his wife. Nokukhanya travelled every spring to Swaziland to spend six months sowing and reaping in the fields. Enduring tremendous hardship, she demonstrated why she was held in such high regard as a force in her own right, being affectionately known as the Mother of Light.

In 1963 the American journalist, interviewer and oral historian Studs Terkel met the Chief. In his interview, Terkel was impressed with Luthuli's extraordinary generosity of spirit. Although blacks had suffered greatly under apartheid, Luthuli said, 'The white is hit harder by apartheid than we are. It narrows his life. In not regarding us as humans he becomes less than human. I do pity him.' Luthuli's vision for the future, a non-racial democracy, was the only hope for the human spirit for all South Africans, black and white.

Apartheid, as Luthuli saw so clearly, was a tragic failure of imagination. As he observed in his autobiography, *Let My People Go*, 'We Africans are depersonalised by the whites, our humanity and dignity is reduced in their imagination to a minimum.' Recovering human dignity required imagination and courage, 'uniting all resisters to white supremacy, regardless of race'. Non-violent resistance, as Luthuli often observed, was his preferred strategy. He came from a neighbourhood in Natal where the Indian activist M.K. Gandhi had lived and where the Mahatma's idea of *satyagraha* had taken root. Luthuli advanced this non-racial, multi-religious tradition of non-violent resistance in his political work.

To advance a 'relatively peaceful transition' Luthuli advocated economic sanctions against the apartheid regime. Yet he was not a pacifist. He once observed that anyone who thought he was a pacifist should try to steal his chickens. I believe that he came to appreciate, under the pressure of events, that some measure of force was inevitable, but he felt that any use of force should be wielded through a military formation separate from the political movement of the ANC.

I know that the plans for an armed struggle, under the auspices of a new military formation, were submitted to Luthuli for his approval. Just days after Luthuli received the Nobel Peace Prize, the newly founded military wing of the ANC, Umkhonto weSizwe, engaged in its first act of sabotage of a state installation. In pursuit of peace, the armed struggle had begun.

A few months before his death in 1967, Luthuli welcomed to his home the Africanist researcher and bookseller Donal Brody, who reported that Luthuli was still actively imagining a political future for South Africa. As Brody recalls, Luthuli said, 'I will not live to see everything that I and my friends have fought so hard for, but I think you will.' In prophetic terms, according to Brody, Luthuli observed: 'There will be enormous, peaceful change in South Africa before the end of this century. People of all races will eventually live together in harmony because no one, white, black or brown, wants to destroy this beautiful land of ours. Women must play an increasingly important role in all areas of the life of the future. They were and remain the most loyal supporters in all our struggles. The big powers will eventually turn away from all of Africa, so we must dedicate ourselves to solving our own problems.' Certainly, these reported observations by Luthuli anticipated a unified, democratic, non-racial and non-sexist society, a new South Africa working out its own destiny in the continent of Africa and the larger world. They are consistent with his vision of South Africa's past and future.

Looking to the future in his autobiography, Luthuli affirmed the principle of non-racialism, which was clearly identified in concrete terms in the Freedom Charter and eventually enshrined in the Constitution of a democratic South Africa. 'The task is not finished,' he wrote. 'South Africa is not yet home for all her sons and daughters. Such a home we wish to ensure.' As he imagined such a home for all, he faced and embraced this challenge: 'There remains before us the building of a new land, a home for men [and women] who are black, white, brown, from the ruins of the old narrow groups, a synthesis of the rich cultural strains we have inherited.' This new land, this new South Africa, he foresaw, 'will not necessarily be all black; but it will be African'. In such an inclusive, expansive vision of what it means to be African in South Africa, Luthuli imagined this new land as a home for all.

Although he envisioned this new land for all of us, and gave so many of us the imaginative capacity to share that vision, Luthuli did not live to see its realisation in a democratic South Africa. Struck by a train in 1967, he died while those who upheld his vision were still embattled, underground, in prison or in exile.

In Ireland we kept the Chief's beliefs alive by inaugurating the annual Albert Luthuli Memorial Lecture in Dublin, where so many ordinary people had devoted themselves to the isolation of the apartheid regime through the boycott of goods and trade, which Luthuli had been the first to articulate.

In our gratitude and love, Luthuli lives. The central offices of the ANC in Johannesburg were named Luthuli House, at my request. The government has decided that the watermark on our South African passports must bear his image, so wherever we travel, anywhere in the world, we carry Luthuli with us. Further afield in Africa, the University of Jos in Nigeria has established the Albert Luthuli Professor-at-Large, a position held by the great scholar Ali Mazrui.

For those of us who now live in a unified, non-racial, non-sexist and democratic South Africa, we keep his memory alive because we live in the home that was designed and built by Luthuli.

In 1955 Chief Luthuli informed me that the ANC had recently elected a Johannesburg lawyer named Oliver Reginald Tambo as its secretary-general. He broke into laughter when he told me that Nelson Mandela's law partner was quiet and modest but a man of steel who would galvanise the ANC. I was to hear little more of Tambo until the early morning arrests of the 156 Treason trialists in 1956.

All of us involved in the ANC followed the vicissitudes of our heroes and heroines in the charade that passed as a trial and we celebrated their acquittal in 1961. However, what struck me afterwards was the way Tambo's life resembled the fortunes of the main character in a book that Luthuli had lent to me, John Bunyan's *Pilgrim's Progress*. Luthuli's words to me were: 'Read this book as it reflects a life of struggle. We will face similar struggles to those of the hero, Christian, before we win our freedom.' At the time, for me as a budding rationalist, the book was a revelation, and even now provides fresh insights.

Both Luthuli and Tambo were profoundly religious, though neither allowed his beliefs to obtrude on personal relations. Both travelled along Christian's allegorical road – the slough of despond, the hill of difficulty, the valley of humiliation – and neither reached the 'celestial city' of freedom. Both were strong men, and though they must at times have despaired, we who knew them, mostly from a distance, were never aware of this.

Tambo lived his life by the injunctions given to Christian: not to surrender to the forces of evil and not to be deflected from the path of righteousness. Life was not given to him 'merely for ease and pleasure but for the realisation of ideals of high endeavour and noble service', in the words of one edition of the book. Indeed, Tambo sacrificed his life for our freedom, and his life really did reflect these ideals.

I identify two phases of Tambo's life that relate to my own. The first was when he was in exile and based in Britain. He mobilised people to break the walls of ignorance about apartheid South Africa and he advocated sanctions. This culminated in his star performance at the first international conference on sanctions in 1964. This event also promoted the campaign on behalf of political prisoners, which saved the lives of the Rivonia trialists, and then, most important of all, arranged for military and other forms of assistance to the ANC.

I was a student when Tambo arrived in London and was already deeply involved in the Boycott Movement. Tambo showed us that it was possible to arouse public consciousness about the evils of apartheid by reaching out to ordinary people, by working with civil society in all its manifestations, including political parties, to put pressure on governments. He was at the centre of our activities. We were all involved with him, either through the Anti-Apartheid Movement or through the ANC, or both. The loneliness of exile was largely dissipated for those engaged in solidarity work by the comradeship that grew between us all. Of course, Tambo was busy with a multitude of concerns, so as young people working at grassroots level we did not meet him often, but we followed his doings eagerly. His stature grew with each appearance at international forums and we revelled in his triumphs.

For all of us he became our lodestar, who guided us through the maze of exile politics and the complex relations with governments and domestic organisations. He introduced many of us to the burgeoning anti-apartheid and solidarity movements in Europe and elsewhere in the world. He showed us by example the necessity to remove any political or sectarian approach from our solidarity work. His humility drew us to him and strengthened our own understanding of our work for a non-racial South Africa. He was a truly modest man: for years, he insisted that he was only the acting president of the ANC, and nothing was to detract from Nelson Mandela's pre-eminent role.

A lesser man might have abandoned what must have seemed a hopeless task after the incarceration of so many of the experienced leaders in the 1960s and the suppression of resistance. Bunyan's 'hill of difficulty' proved long and steep, but Tambo's steadfastness helped us to believe that it was not insurmountable.

After I moved to Ireland and Tambo moved to Lusaka to be in closer contact with the struggle, our paths did not cross again directly for a while. Contact was never lost, though, as we celebrated the ANC's diplomatic and political victories and worked with him in the seminal conferences organised by the UN and solidarity organisations.

We all understood the intense pressures brought to bear on Tambo by the conflicting demands of the Cold War externally and by the war in southern Africa internally, which had echoes within the structures of the liberation movement. The unity and integrity of the ANC were his paramount consideration. Uniquely, compared with the fortunes of other liberation movements, he managed to keep us together.

I can attest to his moral courage and pertinacity. In 1979 he came to Ireland to speak at the first conference on the European Economic Community (the EEC) and apartheid South Africa. His words have stayed with me: 'The struggle in South Africa is one between the forces of national liberation and democracy on the one hand and the forces of colonial domination, racism and fascism on the other. Between these forces there can be neither compromise nor peaceful coexistence.'

Though the Irish government's opposition to apartheid was clear, it was reluctant to impose economic sanctions and would not support any resolution at the UN that intimated support for the struggle led by the ANC. The IRA campaign in Northern Ireland was at its height at that time. How could the Irish government support the armed struggle of the ANC when, it was argued in some quarters, the IRA was conducting a similar armed struggle against a similar colonial master? Such an extrapolation from South Africa to Northern Ireland I considered to be invalid, but the Irish government was afraid that the argument would result in a loss of support among its voters. Tambo understood the reasons for this approach, though he might not have agreed with it.

Prior to the Dublin conference of 1979 he met with the Minister of Foreign Affairs, Michael O'Kennedy, who was to open the conference with him. These meetings usually last for an hour, but this one went on for two. Such was Tambo's persuasiveness that the Foreign Minister undertook to provide direct assistance to the ANC, much to the chagrin of his officials, whose body language spoke volumes. Ultimately, the Irish Anti-Apartheid Movement was not able to hold the government to this undertaking, which was made on the spur of the moment in response to Tambo's force of argument and quiet passion.

At the conference, Tambo's speech galvanised the delegates to action. A structure was soon established to co-ordinate the activities of the anti-apartheid movements in the EEC. There was a striking phrase that Tambo used in Dublin when he described the EEC as the 'life-blood of apartheid' because of the prominent role it played in military, financial, strategic and economic relations with South Africa. This was history in the making: as a result of the conference, the focus of anti-apartheid activities would no longer be limited to national work but took on a collective European perspective through lobbying the EEC institutions in Brussels. Tambo provided the impetus for such an innovative development.

Another insight into Tambo's remarkable brand of leadership was provided by the events leading to the signing of the Nkomati Accord between Mozambique and South Africa in March 1984. My personal involvement arose from a telephone call from Tambo, requesting my presence in Lusaka for an urgent extended meeting of the ANC to discuss the legal and political implications of this agreement for the movement. This was a difficult request for me to meet. My students at Trinity College were to write an international law paper the following week and there was no guarantee that I could be back in Dublin in time for their examinations. University protocol decreed that the examiner had to be present at the examination.

This was the first time I had been invited to a meeting of the ANC's National Executive Committee (NEC) and I wanted to take part. I explained my dilemma to Tambo. His response was understanding and provided me with an instant solution to my dilemma. Stay in Dublin and do your duty, he advised me, but promise that in the next day or two, you will write an analysis of the Accord from an international law perspective.

This I did in time for the NEC meeting, drawing attention to two features of the agreement that rolled back all the gains that had been made as regards the status of the ANC at the level of international law. Firstly, it implied that combatants of the ANC were terrorists. Secondly, the agreement compelled both parties not to provide any form of assistance to these 'elements'. Apartheid South Africa had rejected the series of UN General Assembly resolutions that accepted the right of states to provide assistance to liberation movements combating racism, colonialism and foreign occupation; and now it was demanding that allies of the ANC also reject the demands made on them by these resolutions.

The Nkomati Accord stated that all ANC members should be

My father, Ahmed Asmal, and I

Clockwise from top left: My mother, Rasool Asmal; My father; With my mother;
a toddler in the backyard of our Stanger home

TOP: Louise and I at our wedding, 30 December 1961   ABOVE: With Louise and our young sons, Rafiq and Adam

TOP: The Asmal family in Dublin   ABOVE: With my granddaughter, Zoë

TOP: The staff of Stanger Secondary School, with me seated on the far right
ABOVE: Embarking for England on the Edinburgh Castle, December 1958

the anti-apartheid movement

173 barton road east, dundrum, dublin 14

phone 983703

CHAIRMAN:
Professor Patrick Lynch

ACTING HON-SECRETARIES:
Brendan Scott & Niall Greene

VICE-CHAIRMAN:
Kader Asmal

HON. TREASURER:
Dermot O'Connor

ANNUAL REPORT 1969-1970

January 10th, 1970 — the day Ireland marched against the Ireland v all-white Springbok rugby international.

Photo: Irish Times

protest march in London on behalf of Fidel Castro, with Louise and me in the centre

TOP LEFT: With the eminent Algerian jurist Mohammed Bedjaoui
TOP RIGHT: On holiday in France
ABOVE: At a conference with Enuga S. Reddy and Diana Collins

hearing the news of Mandela's release, at our Dublin home

TOP: Meeting Mandela on his first visit to Dublin after his release, June 1990
ABOVE: Nelson Mandela meets members of the Irish Anti-Apartheid Movement in Dublin

The years of democracy

P: My first public meeting in South Africa after my return, at Stanger, in 1990

OVE: With Louise and my grandson, Oisin, on our way to the opening of the new Parliament, 1994

The first Mandela Cabinet. Seated in front (from left to right): Sipho Mzimela, Jay Naidoo, Trevor Manuel, Joe Modise, Mangosuthu Buthelezi, Thabo Mbeki, Nelson Mandela, F.W. de Klerk, Dawie de Villiers, Joe Slovo, Kader Asmal, Roelf Meyer.

The Mandela Cabinet after the withdrawal of the National Party. Seated in front (from left to right): Joe Modise, Mac Maharaj, Nkosazana Dlamini-Zuma, Kader Asmal, Thabo Mbeki, Nelson Mandela, Mangosuthu Buthelezi, Sibusiso Bengu, Derek Hanekom, Trevor Manuel.

Clockwise from top left:
With Thabo Mbeki and Al Gore;
Renaming the Verwoerd Dam, with Evita
Bezuidenhout; The millionth recipient of tapped
water; The Minister of Water Affairs opening a
rural water scheme.

ry Robinson, Nelson Mandela and I on the Irish President's visit to South Africa

TOP: Meeting Mrs Nokukhanya Luthuli, widow of my mentor Chief Albert Luthuli
ABOVE: At our Dublin home with Albie Sachs while we were drafting the bill of rights

TOP: A newspaper photo of Albert Luthuli arriving at Heathrow Airport en route to Stockholm to receive the Nobel Peace Prize, December 1961. I am holding a welcoming placard on the left.
ABOVE: Yusuf Dadoo and his wife at our wedding ceremony in London, 1961

TOP: Unveiling a bust of Oliver Tambo in London, with Mike Terry of the Anti-Apartheid Movement
ABOVE: Oliver Tambo and I at a conference in Dublin, 1979

P: In conversation with Walter Sisulu
OVE: With Nelson Mandela

TOP: Joe Slovo, Louise and I   ABOVE: An animated moment with Thabo Mbeki

ria Ramos, Trevor Manuel and I finding warmth in the chill outdoors

The Minister of Education with grandson, Oisin, and young learners in Khayelitsha, Cape Town

TOP: Greeting Yasser Arafat at Mandela's inauguration in 1994
ABOVE: Fidel Castro and I getting to know each other with the help of a translator

: Thabo Mbeki, Julius Nyerere and I putting our heads together
OVE: The Queen admires the handiwork of local residents in Khayelitsha, Cape Town

Rhodes University confers an honorary doctorate on me in 1997

TOP: Receiving the Légion d'honneur in Cape Town from the French Ambassador, 2005
ABOVE: The Swedish king, Carl Gustaf, conferring the Stockholm Water Prize in 2000

On the occasion of the award of the Stockholm Water Prize

Archbishop Tutu and I, with Louise in the background

removed from Mozambique. In turn, Mozambique would be eligible for various economic and other benefits from South Africa, which would also halt its support for the rebel group Renamo. The Accord caused a great deal of anger at what we considered to be a betrayal of the legitimacy of our struggle. Another very serious bone of contention was that our president had not been fully informed by the head of state of Mozambique.

Yet the NEC statement on the matter was a sober and firm reiteration of the role of the ANC. Tambo, who had been slighted by Mozambique, refused to condemn that country. If he felt pushed into the valley of humiliation, he never showed it. At the time South Africa was actively assisting the forces fighting the Frelimo government in the civil war then raging in Mozambique and he understood the murderous pressures being exercised by P.W. Botha against its neighbour. He also recognised the enormous sacrifices that Mozambique had made in support of the ANC.

In the event, it was South Africa that violated the agreement by cynically continuing to support Renamo rebels. No serious injury was done to the ANC. Rather than driving Mozambique into a corner, Tambo's calm and collected approach had been the right one. He ensured that an unequal and forced treaty would not result in a breach of our relations with a valued partner. There is a place for hotheads, but this was not the time. Tambo's sense of history and his innate decency provided the correct response.

Following the 1976 Soweto uprising, there was a surge of resistance in South Africa. This was followed in the 1980s by the formation of the United Democratic Front (UDF), in which Tambo played such an important role. Delegation after delegation from inside South Africa came to Lusaka to seek his opinion and advice, even when it was still very dangerous for them to do so. In effect nothing ever happened 'at home' without his approval. I recall one such occasion when I was in Lusaka attending an ANC Constitutional Committee meeting. I was invited to attend a meeting of a large delegation of traditional leaders who were waiting to seek Tambo's advice on some matter. At the meeting, he listened to them patiently, took on board a number of their suggestions about how to organise in rural areas, and quietly put some challenges before them. Their respect was given to him not simply because he was an older person or because he was president of the ANC, but because of their admiration for the man he was. Openness to others and their ideas was never an excuse for him to revise or weaken his principles.

The second phase of my relationship with Tambo has to do with the events in South Africa in the middle of the 1980s, when the situation in the subcontinent once again came to occupy the centre of the world stage. The State of Emergency, the emergence of the UDF, and the dramatic success of Umkhonto weSizwe attacks reflected a changing country and required a collective response from the movement. So, it was decided that a second consultative conference would be held in Kabwe, near Lusaka, in 1985. The first consultative conference, held in Morogoro, Tanzania, in 1969, had adopted the 'Strategy and Tactics' document, which provided the foundation for the ANC's activities in the 1970s. Because it was in exile, the movement could not call a national conference, which would have constitutional authority, but it was felt that the time was ripe for a second consultative conference. Though I hadn't attended Morogoro, I was present at Kabwe.

News of the conference was met with disinformation from a panicky apartheid South Africa. The Afrikaans newspapers and the 'liberal' white press were full of stories about a putsch against Tambo and the rest of the leadership because of alleged dissatisfaction among the rank and file, especially in the ANC camps. In fact, more than three hundred ANC delegates from every part of the world where the movement had a presence assembled in Kabwe in June 1985. Tambo introduced the political report of the National Executive Committee, which was wide-ranging and comprehensive. While there was overwhelming support for it, some vexed issues needed to be discussed, such as the increasing impact of the armed struggle and whether membership should be 'open' to all the so-called races defined by apartheid laws.

The ANC constitution did not refer to race at all. However, in the Congress movement, there were different structures for the various groups (such as the South African Indian Congress) and an understanding that the ANC would above all be representative of the most exploited section of our country's population, the African majority. In his political report, Tambo carefully referred to the membership issue and asked whether 'we still felt justified to keep the restriction on membership'. Even more carefully, so as not to pre-empt the right of the conference to decide, he felt we could reach agreement on a decision that 'will take our movement and struggle further forward'.

The following day we all broke into commissions. I spoke against opening up the membership, partly because some elements who argued that the ANC was already dominated by whites and Indians might use this to incite further hostility. Chiefly it was because I felt that the ANC should continue to be representative of the vast majority of the most oppressed and nothing should be allowed to dilute this representative capacity.

I was in a small minority of dissenters. In the middle of the night, I was quietly educated about the nature of the ANC. A group of young combatants from the camps who came to talk to me firmly told me it was wrong that while whites and Indians could lay down their lives for our freedom in the service of the ANC or MK, they were not good enough to become full members. On my way to the plenary, where I intended to speak before the vote was taken, Tambo happened to pass by me. He stopped and took me by the arm and, without any hint of trying to persuade me, drew my attention to the need to recognise that the ANC represented all oppressed blacks and also those progressive whites who had accepted the policies and programmes of the movement.

At the plenary I subsequently withdrew my objection, and the motion to admit all South Africans to membership, including the right to become members of the NEC, was passed overwhelmingly. Tambo had great respect for lawyers, especially those in the movement. He therefore proposed that Albie Sachs and I oversee the election of the NEC – not an easy task in the absence of secretarial services. It was Tambo's unobtrusive leadership that enabled all of us to affirm the non-racial character of the ANC, and the organisation emerged from the Kabwe Conference more united than ever.

Even more significant was the adoption of a Code of Conduct, promulgated after the conference. This code established a system of justice for the ANC that was unique among liberation movements in southern Africa, even though we were engaged in a situation of war. Insisting on proper legal procedures, including the appropriate burden of proof, meant that arbitrary arrests would be reduced and improperly prepared cases thrown out at hearings. I am not aware of any partisan movement in Europe or liberation movement anywhere that emphasised, as the ANC did, the need for restraint and respect for proper procedures during the conduct of hostilities while its very existence was at stake. This was Tambo's legacy.

One aspect of Tambo's work as president that has received little acknowledgement is the outstanding role he played in ensuring that internal controls were put in place concerning the treatment of members of the ANC, especially in the camps in Angola where our combatants were stationed. This was a sensitive matter as the security department of the ANC had to ensure the welfare and safety of our members and especially of the core leadership, but its behaviour had given rise to criticism. The Pretoria regime had made no bones about its all-out war against the ANC. Apart from the assassination of our leaders, such as the outstanding Joe Gqabi in Harare in 1981, attacks on the frontline states like Angola were part of the destabilising process against the ANC. Even more dangerous was the infiltration of agents into the ranks of the ANC with a mission to sow confusion and to attack the leaders. In this murky world, abuses by our security elements did take place.

Soon after the Kabwe Conference, new allegations of abuse arose, especially at the Quatro camp in Angola. Against the advice of his security staff, as the situation was fraught with danger, Tambo visited the camp to investigate matters. The combatants had requested Tambo's presence as they felt that no other leader would be able to deal with their grievances. Tambo the lawyer, with his overpowering sense of justice and his infinite capacity to listen to everyone, even to occasional hostile outbursts, was able to reunite the forces in the camp. The result was that the leadership of the ANC's security department was replaced and a restructured directorate of intelligence and security was created to assume responsibility. As a commission of inquiry later established, there was never a pattern of systematic abuse of rights or a policy of violations in ANC camps.

Although Tambo always insisted that he was part of a collective and that he acted on the advice of the National Executive Committee, there can be little doubt that the initiatives the ANC took were inspired by him. There was always a delicate balance to be maintained between the need for security and transparency and the morality of the movement. In one case, the decision of an ANC judicial tribunal to recommend capital punishment was rejected by the NEC and by Tambo, in line with our historical opposition to this obscene form of punishment. Capital punishment was of course eventually abolished by the Constitutional Court of a free South Africa. Our liberation movement's hostility to capital punishment was reflected in an early draft of the country's Bill of Rights, produced in 1991, which abolished the death penalty. No international covenant on human rights had renounced the obscenity of capital punishment in such a forthright manner. Tambo approved of such an approach: this was real leadership.

By the 1980s, not many of our comrades who remained in South Africa had actually met their acting president. When some had the opportunity to do so, it was electrifying. Those of us who witnessed their response were deeply impressed. This happened once in Harare in September 1987 during a breakaway session of an international conference dealing with the appalling treatment of children in South Africa, thousands of whom had been detained, tortured or imprisoned during the 1980s.

The organisers had expected a handful of people to attend because of the State of Emergency in South Africa. Yet more than three hundred people came, many of them children. During the first day, we heard their harrowing testimonies. At the opening session, Tambo made one of his most moving speeches. He began by reading Ingrid Jonker's touching poem 'The Child Is Not Dead'. In his concluding statement he talked about cherishing children. Those views of his are now, in my opinion, reflected in the unique provisions on the rights of the child in the present South African Constitution. 'We cannot be true liberators unless the liberation we will achieve guarantees all children the rights to life, health, happiness and free development respecting the individuality, the inclinations and capabilities of each child,' he said, drawing attention to the urgent task of a free South Africa to attend to the welfare of the millions of children whose lives had been stunted and 'turned into a terrible misery by the violence of the apartheid system'.

Later that afternoon, a call was made for all South Africans to gather together, away from the conference. Tambo had been out of the country for more than twenty-five years by then. Very few would have seen him, as his photograph was banned, as were his speeches. He spoke without notes, welcoming first by name the new members of the National Executive Committee who had been elected at the Kabwe Conference of

1985, and drawing attention to the non-racial composition of that body. There was silence when he spoke about violence by the regime and then about 'necklacing', the practice emerging in the strife-torn townships of killing state informers by using burning tyres. 'This must stop,' Tambo said. There was a hush: exiles did not know what would happen next. Then there came a dramatic, full-throated roar of approval. Tambo's was a cry that drew on the humanism of our struggle and the need to relate means to ends.

In the public eye, Nelson Mandela is most closely associated with reconciling white and black in post-apartheid South Africa, but long before that Tambo had made the case for reconciliation. I recall this vividly. I had prepared an opening speech for the children's conference in 1987 in Harare. My address was a legal indictment of apartheid's criminal leaders, based on the Nuremberg Principles underpinning the trials of Nazi leaders after 1945. I had intimated to some ANC leaders at the conference that I would call for the prosecution of apartheid's leaders, after our freedom, for crimes against humanity and war crimes.

Tambo took me aside before the opening session and, with quiet persuasiveness, informed me that Nuremberg was 'victor's law'. There was already talk about negotiations with the apartheid regime, and he made it clear that it would be provocative in the extreme to announce that we would negotiate with the regime and, following successful discussions, we would try them for crimes against humanity.

The Nuremberg Principles were very important to me. They also came to form the basis of the International Criminal Court's jurisdiction. But the facts on the ground in South Africa led all of us to a different conclusion, guided by Tambo. We were engaged in talks about talks and were planning to negotiate on the basis of a predetermined agenda. We could not demand prosecution and the infliction of punishment as a condition for negotiations. If the ANC had done this, there would have been no talks or settlement. For me, ten years' work went down the drain after Tambo's intervention and I hurriedly changed my speech. Subsequent events showed the correctness of Tambo's approach.

By the time the subject of negotiations was first broached – and also in large part as a result of it – the boycott movement had spread to countries around the globe, and the pressure on governments to impose sanctions against the apartheid regime was meeting with increasing success. These pressures were also beginning to have an impact inside South Africa. By the middle of the 1980s, the ANC was talking with white individuals and organisations who desired some form of progress away from apartheid. Also, under the leadership of the ANC and the UDF, initiatives were being taken to incorporate trade unions and education, religious, cultural and sports groups within the growing movement of resistance.

What, we asked, should we do when some of these bodies wanted to establish links with overseas affiliates or make overseas visits? What would become of our isolationist policies? Tambo resolved this dilemma when he spoke at the Canon Collins Memorial Lecture in London in May 1987. There he laid down a policy that had enormous implications for our solidarity work. His timing was brilliant. He first traced the effects of the State of Emergency and the way our people were responding. He looked at the serried ranks of anti-apartheid activists before him and then, quietly and firmly, told us: '[The] moment is upon us when we shall deal with the structures our people have created and are creating through the struggle and sacrifice as representatives of the masses. Not only should these not be boycotted but more, they should be supported, encouraged and treated as the democratic counterparts within South Africa of similar institutions and organisations internationally. This means that the ANC, the broad democratic movement in all its forms within South Africa and the international solidarity movement must act together.'

It was a dramatic change from the way in which we had operated previously. Tambo's message reflected the growing opposition to apartheid in South Africa. We had to respond, as he had taken us into his confidence. While the isolation of apartheid must continue and there was to be no let-up, we had to treat these 'people's movements' in a different way. This was a direct challenge to those of us in the Anti-Apartheid Movement. Strict ideology and dogmatic policy had to take into account developments at home.

In all my association with Tambo, his constant refrain was the need for equality. He insisted that we should reach out to all South Africans, in contrast with the apartheid regime, which violated every canon of equality and thrived on separating our people from each other. In hindsight, his reaching out to all the communities in South Africa made Tambo one of the principal architects of reconciliation. It meant that he took great care to maintain and strengthen the ANC tradition of non-racialism, and knew that our struggle relied for its success on inclusiveness.

He also applied the principle of inclusiveness to gender issues and was instrumental in placing women's demands before a largely male-dominated ANC. History will honour him as the first leader of a liberation movement who argued passionately for gender equality. On more than one public occasion I heard him express his support for the Women's Charter, adopted by the Federation of South African Women in Johannesburg in 1954, which in many ways was a more revolutionary document in its approach to women's issues than the Freedom Charter of 1955.

One of Tambo's abiding qualities was the trust he placed in those who worked with him. This in turn evoked a deep respect, even love, for this highly principled leader, who was able to draw on the talents and capacity of so many of the South African men and women in exile in different parts of the world. Tambo possessed more than the ordinary virtues of leadership. I realised in my contact with him that his distinguishing quality was his accessibility, not simply in the sense that he was available to meet South Africans whether he was in Accra, Lusaka, London or New York. It was not his style to be protected by a phalanx of private secretaries or a guard of minders. If you had something to discuss with him, he was there for you.

By accessibility I mean something more. He had an openness to ideas and a capacity to respond to changing circumstances. Tambo gave us many gifts: selfless leadership, an extraordinary capacity to listen to others and consider new ideas, humility, compassion, and a belief in the capacity of people to be their own saviours. In the hell-holes of apartheid's prisons, in the countless villages and barren townships of South Africa, in the loneliness of exile and in the isolated camps of our combatants, his was the voice that spoke for us and provided the hope – no, the certainty – of the freedom which he would, sadly, not live to see.

The poet Seamus Heaney's famous line that once in a lifetime, justice can rise up, and hope and history rhyme, was written in response to Mandela's release in 1990. There is no doubt that Tambo's extraordinary determination to uphold the values of inclusiveness, non-racialism, non-sexism and justice, and his capacity to imbue others with the same values, made an incalculable contribution to that sentiment. Tambo was a true hero of our struggle, who helped us all to reach the 'celestial city' of Bunyan's parable: a free and democratic South Africa.

Few individuals have had as great an impact on their nation and on the world as Nelson Rohlihlahla Mandela. South Africa's political transformation was at least in part the result of Mandela's personal capacity to purge any poison of hatred or revenge from his soul, to rise above bitterness, to demonstrate a generosity of spirit, and to reach out to others, all the while remaining true, even under the harshest conditions of injustice, imprisonment and oppression, to his political principles. Those principles, Mandela himself would argue, were not his alone. They were the shared achievement of a political movement, the ANC.

I met Nelson Mandela at a gathering for ANC members during his first visit to London after his release from prison. It was quite clear to everyone that he was going to be the next President of South Africa, but Madiba himself acted like any other visitor. On being introduced to me his first words were, 'How is Louise?' To this day I remain moved not only by his knowledge of the details of the personal lives of so many of us in the ANC, but also by the importance he placed on our families. Despite being deprived of family relationships for so many years, he had clearly not lost sight of the importance of them in even the most political of lives. I was totally taken aback, especially when he went on to say, 'Oh Kader, I have been reading your work in prison on the Island.'

A few months later I met Mandela again when, in mid-1990, he at last received the freedom of the city of Dublin, an award that was made while he was still in jail in 1988. Francis Devine, author, now retired academic and former president of the Irish Labour History Society, wrote a poetic letter to Louise and me on that occasion: 'That Mandela was actually here, a Dublin Freeman, is tribute to your energy, cause of the grey salting your moustache, the tears salting your black, sparkling eyes … You wrapped the world in your dream and it is proud to have believed you, warm in the scarlet glow of other people's struggles, cheering him.

'Tomorrow morning you will be again left with true friends to clear away the chairs, the tattered bunting, making ready the platform for the next campaign, not acknowledging the riches your comradeship has given Ireland. You will pluck for us wayside flowers that will lighten our lives with the fragrance of freedom.'

Such kind words. It was mostly luck that enabled us to host Madiba in Dublin. He had accepted an invitation to attend an ANC fundraising concert in Oaklands, California, but he assured me that he would honour the promise he had made to visit Dublin, so he cut short his US visit and stopped over on his way home. We met him at the airport at two in the morning. Also there to greet him in force was the Irish press, including a young journalist from one of the daily papers, who thrust a microphone in Madiba's face and demanded to know what he thought of the IRA. Mandela's response was typical of him. 'You must talk to them,' was his reply. Well, not only the tabloids turned this into headline news; even the BBC led with the story. I had organised the trip and it was left to me to do some damage control.

I visited Mandela's hotel early the next morning, to find him still in bed. 'Madiba,' I said, 'we have a problem.' He invited me to sit down. There was no seat in the hotel room so I had no option but to perch at the foot of his bed. I was surprised again at how tall he was: there was little room for me. 'Kader, why are you so uncomfortable?' he said, shifting to make room for me. I explained why I was really uncomfortable. 'Madiba, we have a problem. It's like a ton of bricks falling on our heads.' I explained that the British and US governments didn't talk to the IRA. We were in something of a quandary. While we did not want him to repudiate his words, the British Anti-Apartheid Movement was seriously perturbed.

In the end we came up with a simple solution. He was due to speak at a dinner that night with the Taoiseach (the Irish Prime Minister), so we inserted a sentence into his speech. 'It is not my job to prescribe to anyone else how to behave in their own countries,' said Mandela. 'But all my life I have believed that it is important to talk to people, to negotiate. You don't negotiate with friends. You negotiate with your enemies.' A few years later, of course, the Good Friday agreement was signed in Northern Ireland. That day my secretary put through a call to me. She was taken aback. 'It's from the President.' It was indeed Madiba, and he was chuckling. 'Hey, Kader,' he said, 'is there a ton of bricks falling on your head?' He was as delighted as I was that negotiations had taken place in Northern Ireland and that they had ended in an agreement.

I think it was on that very trip to Dublin that Mandela again went a little far in breaking the unwritten rules. RTE, the Irish television channel, had asked a bright young TV journalist, Olivia O'Leary, to interview him. Of course, Madiba was his usual charming presence, until she posed her last question, asking what he planned to discuss with Margaret Thatcher at his meeting with her the following day. Mandela's response was tart: 'Young lady, I don't believe I should tell you what I shall discuss with the Prime Minister.' It was mostly the reference to this highly acclaimed reporter as a 'young lady' that got people bristling. I suppose we can forgive him that *faux pas*. The years of the feminist revolution had completely passed him by on Robben Island, and he could be excused for not knowing that 'young lady' was no longer a politically correct way to address a woman, even if she was really very young.

Madiba had his own way of doing things. I had done what I could to prepare him for the television interview in Dublin, even taking the liberty of unbuttoning his jacket, which had bunched up rather scruffily, but as the cameras started to roll I noticed he had buttoned himself all up again.

But these episodes were soon forgotten as the world followed South Africa's progress in the negotiations. Few people know that the ANC's National Executive Committee did consider disputing the outcome of the elections in 1994, questioning the Inkatha victory in KwaZulu-Natal and the ANC's loss of the Western Cape. At a tense meeting of the National Executive Committee immediately after the poll, Madiba allowed members to speak, but stuck to his conviction that further violence had to be avoided. The new Parliament had to be as representative as possible, even if meant a loss for the ANC in some parts of the country. Madiba seemed to have a way of cutting through the excess right to the heart of the matter, and I admired his decisiveness. Stanley Greenberg, the American pollster who assisted the ANC in preparing for the 1994 elections, wrote this of Mandela's crucial decision not to contest the result:

'As each person spoke, Mandela circled the table, thinking. Barely noticed by the others, he took up the coffee pot and my eyes followed him as he went around offering to pour coffee for each person, an offer I accepted. Such a simple gesture but, I thought, a measure of his thoughtfulness and courtesy that made him even larger in scale. Mandela had said nothing during the discussion. Then he brought the room to a full stop. "Tell the comrades to cancel the press conference. We will not do anything to make the election illegitimate. The ANC will not say the election is not 'free and fair'. Prepare our people in Natal and the Western Cape to lose." ... As if waving a wand, he made everybody seem small for not thinking bigger, including me, who should have known better than to get caught up in the war room hothouse. He embraced and thanked each of us as he departed, without any further discussion of the issue.'

That, too, was the Mandela I knew: prowling, decisive, compassionate and always with the big picture in view. He also had an instinctive sense of the mechanics of politics and of effective negotiation strategies. Mandela was a renowned boxer in his youth and, in his political sparring, thrusting and counter-thrusting, feinting and then going for the hammer blow, he reminded me of what the young Mandela must have been like in the ring: a wily and dangerous adversary. Like all good negotiators, he only got angry intentionally.

Not long after his release from prison in 1990, it became necessary to suspend the armed struggle. There were people, powerful people, within the ANC who didn't want to do that. They were anxious to keep the military formations in place and the caches of arms and munitions concealed, just in case De Klerk and the National Party reverted once more to oppression and war. In August 1990 Mandela set up a committee that would go round the country explaining to the provincial and military structures why the armed struggle had been called off. He appointed the three ANC leaders who were most critical of the decision to suspend the armed struggle, Joe Slovo, Chris Hani and Joe Modise, to sit on the committee and undertake the work. Their co-option was crafty politics.

I worked intensely and in close proximity with Mandela for five years during his first and only term as South Africa's democratic President. He was not a perfect person or above making mistakes. For me one of his greatest *faux pas*, as President, was his advocacy of the scheme to lower the voting age in South Africa to fourteen years.

I wrote a letter to him urging him to drop the notion. 'Lowering the voting age in South Africa to fourteen is, currently, not practical politics because it will not command sufficient consensus for its introduction,' I said. To his credit, he listened to us and the idea was dropped, but not before he had subjected himself and the party to a wave of criticism and ridicule. Mandela always had a soft spot for the youth and was fully supportive of the idea of a Youth Commission to look after the particular interests of young people. The commission was intended to be part of our constitutional dispensation's Chapter 9 institutions, which were established to deepen and protect our democracy. He was deeply disappointed when our later report on these bodies showed that the Youth Commission was not doing its work.

Certainly I will never forget the extraordinary magnanimity of spirit he displayed when he was called as a defence witness during a legal case involving Louis Luyt, who was eventually sacked as president of the South African Rugby Football Union. Mandela was summoned to appear in court in connection with the setting up of a commission to investigate racism, graft and nepotism in rugby. There can hardly have been two characters more unalike than Luyt and Madiba. Yet out of respect for the judiciary, Mandela agreed to appear in court, the first time a South African President had done so, so determined was he to bolster the legitimacy of the country's courts. There seemed to be no limit to this man's largeness of heart, and no lengths to which he would not go to ensure his country went forward proudly and peacefully towards equality and dignity.

South Africa had been very keen on capital punishment during the struggle years. Many ANC cadres and other liberation movement members had been executed by the hangman at Pretoria Central Prison in the 1970s and 1980s. In his moving collection of poems *Inside*, Jeremy Cronin wrote of how the prisoners at Pretoria Central could hear the trapdoors of the gallows slamming open one after the other, like wooden seats at a cinema. I have been an abolitionist my whole life and was delighted when the Constitutional Court ruled in 1995 that capital punishment was contrary to the new Constitution.

In spite of this, the idea of reintroducing capital punishment cropped up from time to time in the Mandela Cabinet, especially from the National Party members, who continued to view the noose with nostalgic fondness. What once had been totally ineffectual in deterring freedom fighters, they now thought for some reason would work with criminals. I recall on one occasion that a National Party minister again made the case for capital punishment. Mandela intervened. I think he spoke for about four minutes, but in that time he demolished the case for capital punishment in a devastating way. 'The death sentence is a barbaric act,' he said. 'It is a reflection of the animal instinct still in human beings.' When he did speak in Cabinet, Mandela did so with great humanism, feeling and understanding, and on this subject I had never heard him talk with such passion. His was a brilliant, determined, unemotional rebuke. If the debate does ever emerge again, there couldn't be anybody with a more compelling testimony than Mandela to speak against it.

Later, Mandela asked me whether we shouldn't consider passing a law on capital punishment, rather than leaving it to the Constitutional Court. I said that for one thing I was not the Minister of Justice, and this was a political decision. And secondly, I told him, if you leave it open to Parliament to vote on the issue, a majority would probably vote in favour. At a later stage I went to him again when there was some pressure to hold a debate on capital punishment. I told him that if such a debate were allowed, I would resign. I had fought against capital punishment my whole life and was totally committed to opposing it. 'Oh no, no, Kader. There is no question about this. We are not having a debate about capital punishment,' Madiba assured me. And that was the end of it, at least for the rest of my time in public office.

While his loyalty to the ANC was always paramount, this didn't stop Mandela from questioning ANC decisions or leadership. In doing so, he effectively protected the ANC when proposals or practices threatened to derail it from the course the Freedom Charter had set out for us. I remember his reservations about the election of the firebrand KwaZulu-Natal ANC leader Harry Gwala to the position of ANC Chief Whip in the KwaZulu-Natal legislature. Even though they had spent years together on Robben Island and retained a comradely bond, Mandela was uncomfortable with Gwala's uncompromising and militant stance in the conflict between the ANC and the Inkatha Freedom Party in the KwaZulu-Natal Midlands, in which hundreds had died in the run-up to the first elections. The importance of maintaining peace and preventing further violence took priority for Madiba. Later, his concern was borne out when Gwala, who liked to be known as a Stalinist, was suspended by the Communist Party for six months and eventually passed over for provincial leader by the local ANC.

Mandela was a magnificent fundraiser and made the most of his international reputation to meet and greet his presidential and royal counterparts from all corners of the globe. While this did much to assure South Africa of a place in the world, it also kept the ANC's coffers full. During his five years as President he hosted sixty heads of state, compared to the four or five who visited his successor in close to ten years. For his part, though, he didn't always stick to protocol. On a trip to England in 1996, at a meeting with the Queen, I saw her give way to Madiba. He had a way of turning protocol on its head. As a senior Cabinet minister accompanying him, I travelled with Louise in the second carriage behind his, and our official driver told us repeatedly that in all his years he had never enjoyed such a relaxed state visit. As we drove behind him and the Queen down The Mall we passed a group of cheering South Africans. Their spirit was so overwhelming I found it difficult to hold my right hand firmly down at my side. I longed to thrust an exuberant clenched fist into the air. When we encountered a group of schoolchildren who had come from all over Britain to catch a glimpse of Mandela, I just knew his instinct would have been to get out and greet them. But of course protocol and security provisions forbade this, although he did stop his carriage to wave to them.

On the same visit to England, Mandela broke with the long-held practice that visiting heads of state never travelled south of the Thames. He rode as far as the rough, working-class suburb of Brixton, I think because he understood that ordinary citizens wanted an opportunity to see him. When he addressed the crowds that gathered at the local town hall, he included some warm praise for Prince Charles, who at that time was in the process of divorcing Princess Diana, a subject that raised much controversy in England. His words, if I recall, were along the lines of how lucky the Queen was to have such a wonderful son. You can imagine how the British establishment must have been taken aback at the praise heaped on one who had so recently embarrassed them.

On the way back the crowds were so huge that there was no way Madiba would have been able to reach central London. Prince Charles then sent his own Rolls-Royce to fetch Mandela, driving him through a back route, while a police escort struggled to clear a path for the official car in which Louise and I were travelling.

At our next port of call, St James's Palace, the foreign ambassadors represented in the UK were lined up to be presented to Mandela. Normal practice is for a visiting head of state to shake each hand and move on. But that wasn't Madiba's style. He engaged with each one in turn, displaying his most remarkable memory as he asked after the health of their president or commented on their country's state of affairs. I watched with much amusement as the British government flunkeys looked increasingly uncomfortable, glancing at their watches, as Madiba took his time greeting each ambassador in turn.

Later, he attended a banquet where the freedom of the City of London was to be conferred on him. As he took his seat, the hundreds of dignitaries present rose as one and banged their knives on the table – not for one or two minutes, but for what seemed like a very long time. The memory of that tribute still moves me today, and even Madiba, whose stately presence was rarely disturbed and who always maintained his dignity, appeared visibly moved at the time.

Mandela has an extraordinary humility, which is the more remarkable in view of his own royal presence and his reputation and achievements. There was no quicker way to get Mandela's eyes to glaze over than to start telling him how wonderful he was. The celebration of his own qualities made him deeply uncomfortable. Perhaps that is why he loved being with children. For them, he was just a kind, lovely man with a big smile who was seemingly as old as the hills. He laughed at their questions and insights. They gathered round him like a swarm of bees and he basked in their simple affection. He was never happier than when he was in the company of children, most especially his own grandchildren. When he was at home in Qunu in the Transkei, the house was always full of people and particularly children.

On one occasion, I went to see him at his Qunu home, which was deep in the countryside, surrounded by rolling hills and villages of small, thatched huts. I was surprised to discover that his house was an exact replica of the one allocated to him in the grounds of Victor Verster Prison, where he had spent his last years of imprisonment, and where he had started to engage in the politics of reconciliation and negotiation.

He always said his home in Qunu was a replica of that prison house because it was where he had had his first taste of near-normal living, of freedom, in almost three decades.

At times Mandela made fun of his own humility, which was even more disarming. Once he came to me, when I was the Minister of Education, shortly after he had retired as President, and asked for an appointment with me at my office. I told him I would come to his home to discuss the matter. He was very formal, but he had a twinkle in his eye and the hint of a smile on his lips. 'You are a minister,' he said to me. 'I am just an ordinary, plain person.' His sense of humour never failed to impress me. He knew me as one who would stand my ground and, when he asked for my opinion, would always give him a straight answer. I was never one for saying what he wanted to hear. I recall attending a meeting of two or three Cabinet ministers where Madiba had a proposal for which he was seeking support. Then, just as he was about to put it to us, he stopped suddenly, looked up and said with a wicked grin, 'No, I can't do that. Kader is here.'

Mandela is first and foremost a loyal member of the ANC. Still, as former presidents Fidel Castro and Bill Clinton have recognised, the political assumes a distinctively personal quality in Mandela. He has proved, as former UN Secretary-General Kofi Annan once observed, that one individual, with such courage and tenacity, dignity and magnanimity, can actually make a difference in political struggles. Providing a focal point for a sense of human solidarity, Mandela changed the way people experienced South Africa and the larger world.

Whether you are a child, a king or an employee, Mandela has a way of making you feel important. He holds your gaze. He squeezes your hand. I feel very fortunate indeed to have spent time with him. He is truly a great man. His life will cast ripples across the pond of humanity for all time.

7

Truth and Reconciliation

When I was about ten or eleven, I used to love going to our local cinema, the Stanger Picture Palace. Of course the cinema was segregated by race in those days and our section was invariably dirty and uncomfortable. There were even holes in the screen. But it was a wonderful treat to sit with my friends and watch the film of the week. It was here I saw the stars of Hollywood, from Judy Garland to Mickey Rooney. A newsreel always preceded the main feature, as was usual at that time. On one occasion, as I settled down in pleasurable anticipation of the escapism and adventure to come, the newsreel ran a report on the recent liberation of a Nazi concentration camp.

I will never forget the sight of those emaciated people in their striped, ragged clothes stumbling into the daylight. Nor will I forget the horror of the piles of human corpses. One image that will live with me forever was the sight of bulldozers being used to push dead people into a pit. I thought at the time that they were all Jews, but of course there were communists, gypsies and gays who were made to suffer the same fate. Faced by the enormity of this crime, I decided then and there, oddly you might think, that I wanted to be a lawyer. I wanted to fight this kind of evil, just as Zorro coralled the baddies in the town jail.

At first, I didn't make the connection with South Africa. The link between the dehumanising prejudices of South Africa's racism and the fact that the genocide of the Jews happened because they were considered inferior, only came later. Those few minutes of grainy film changed my life. When the Nuremberg Trials began at the end of the Second World

War, there was nobody more enthralled than I was. I was fascinated by the connection between that awful, vivid crime of which I had witnessed only the tiniest glimpse and the meting out of justice.

Nobody with any experience or knowledge of South African history will be unaware of the scale of the crime that took place in our country under the guise of colonialism and then apartheid. How can I even begin to recall the slavery, abuse, oppression, dehumanisation, violence or the scope of the indignity that was perpetrated against our people for year after year, decade after decade, century after century? There can never be full recompense for the totality of apartheid.

Even when ordinary people were not being imprisoned, tortured or killed, everyday life for black people in apartheid South Africa was a sequence of constant embarrassments, deprivations and humiliations. It felt, said Mandela in his autobiography, as if each day you received a thousand pinpricks. Each prick on its own was relatively insignificant – a look, a curse, a sign saying 'Europeans Only' – but together they made a clawing, painful assault on one's humanity and self-worth. How can there ever be justice for the infliction of such an experience on generation after generation?

Nuremberg set a precedent, of course. Here at last the perpetrators of crimes against humanity were brought to account and, in some cases, executed for their complicity in these crimes. The process was by no means perfect, in fact it was deeply flawed, but suddenly regimes and their lieutenants could no longer commit gross acts of violence and inhumanity against their own people and expect to escape punishment. This, naturally enough, motivated the liberation movement – and myself in particular – to start planning our own Nuremberg Trials, to be instituted the moment the walls of apartheid could be pulled down. From about 1973, when apartheid was declared a crime against humanity in terms of UN Resolution 3068, I started work on an indictment of apartheid's criminal leaders in terms of the Nuremberg Principles.

The framework for the ANC's attitude towards justice and human rights goes further back into the organisation's history. As early as 1955, with the adoption of the Freedom Charter, the ANC had described its vision for a future South Africa as a non-racial, unitary and democratic state. I have recounted in an earlier chapter the work of the ANC's Constitutional Committee and our efforts to articulate in constitutional language the Charter's demands, an effort that produced the Constitutional Guidelines of 1988. Against the charge that the Charter was an impractical blueprint for post-apartheid South Africa because it remained silent on crucial constitutional issues, we could now point to the Guidelines as the guarantor of the Charter's vision.

The Guidelines also responded to the regime's newfound love for human rights, or at least a version of human rights that emphasised the rights of minorities. Against Pretoria's advocacy of the human rights of minorities, we insisted on an inclusive bill of rights that would protect the universal rights of all people. Being activists, human rights lawyers and constitutional experts thoroughly versed in the ANC's human rights tradition, we were unanimous in our view that a post-apartheid constitution drawn up in accordance with the Guidelines would be the foundation of a new South Africa and its bill of rights the axis on which our new society would turn.

However, our reasoning contained a weakness. Decades of National Party tyranny had led to an entrenched culture of impunity and disregard for human rights as well as a humiliated, deeply wounded and traumatised population. Though a new, rights-based constitution might fundamentally transform the prevailing culture, would it truly lead to reconciliation? How far would transformation really go? If we could be certain of one thing, it was that our efforts to transform society would be challenged. I began to appreciate that the conditions of possibility for realising the ANC's vision would be as much a part of the final settlement with the regime as the technicalities of a new constitution.

Surprisingly, though, it was not the latest outrage from the apartheid regime – a recent assassination, torture or murder – that ushered into existence the body that became known as the Truth and Reconciliation Commission (TRC). It was the painful acknowledgement of our own frailties within the liberation movement. During 1991 and 1992 it was widely reported in the media that serious violations of human rights had been committed in ANC camps in Angola. The 'revelations', as they were billed, centred on allegations that the ANC was responsible for a range of abusive practices, including detention without trial, beatings, solitary confinement and executions. The story provoked a media frenzy in which the basic contention was that the ANC was guilty of the same crimes as those we accused the Pretoria regime of – and thus implying an equivalence between the National Party and the ANC. One commentator in the *Sunday Star* even went so far as to suggest that 'When the securocrats of both sides get together [in the envisaged Government of National Unity], they could return to their old bloody habits in their eagerness to reduce the political violence gripping the country'.

Of course, the allegations *were* very serious and the ANC did not shy away from investigating them. However, the allegations were also not new. During the preceding decade, the ANC had appointed several commissions of inquiry into allegations of human rights abuses within the organisation. The first of these, the Stuart Commission, presented its report to the National Executive Committee (NEC) in 1984. It concluded that there had indeed been abuses and ill-treatment of soldiers and suspected enemy agents detained by the ANC's security department. Among the commission's most significant recommendations were that the organisation's leadership become more closely involved in the running of the camps (as had been the case during the 1960s and 1970s), and that the head of the ANC's department of intelligence and security be redeployed, Umkhonto weSizwe's organisational structure be reformed, and the logistics of camp life – including the provision of food, transport, health and welfare services – be improved.

The Stuart Commission also recommended that a national conference be convened. At the national conference held the following year in the Zambian town of Kabwe, the issue of political accountability and oversight in the camps was debated at length. Delegates were unanimous in their view that the viciousness of our enemies did not justify ill-treatment on our part and emphasised that our struggle was in defence of human rights.

The conference then adopted a Code of Conduct binding on every member of the ANC. The code was designed to promote human rights within the organisation, protect the rights of all our members, and outline procedures for complaint and recourse when violations of the code were alleged. Significantly, as the code emphasised, the fact that we were at war with a powerful and brutal enemy in no way lowered the standards against which we measured ourselves. The preamble to the code insisted, 'We do not take our standards from the enemy, we do not simply turn the glove inside out, but rather we create our own standards within our traditions of struggle and in the light of our goals for the future.' The introduction to the code emphasised: 'If we fight for justice in our land, we must ensure at all times that justice exists inside our organisation – our members, the people of South Africa and the world must know and feel that for us justice is not merely an ideal but the fundamental principle that governs all our actions. Accordingly, we must at all times act justly in our own ranks, train our people in the procedures of justice and establish the embryo of the new justice system we envisage for a liberated South Africa.'

The Code of Conduct – and the system of justice it represented – was a first among liberation movements and became the measure of accountability within the ANC. When a commission of inquiry was appointed to investigate the death of the MK commander Thami Zulu, it directed itself towards determining whether the Code of Conduct had been violated and whom to hold accountable. Similarly, the Skweyiya Commission, appointed in 1991 to investigate allegations of abuse and torture levelled by several former ANC prisoners, also assessed the gathered evidence against the Code of Conduct in its effort to hold the ANC and its operatives accountable for their actions.

So when allegations were again reported in the course of 1992, we were not surprised. Indeed, we knew terrible things had happened in our camps; we knew that the remedies we conceived and the systems we instituted, while improving the situation, had not had the range of impacts for which we had hoped. Of course, this did not minimise the seriousness of the allegations or diminish the ANC's responsibility to investigate and, where necessary, hold our members to account. In this effort, however, we had at our disposal the experience of three preceding commissions. Most significantly, however, by 1992 the notion of holding ourselves to account was not as foreign or novel as many at the time assumed. Indeed, for several years already the notion of accountability had been formally constituted in the Code of Conduct, revised and superseded in 1992 by the Constitution of the ANC and the disciplinary rules and procedures which it outlined.

Mandela, in his capacity as president of the ANC, appointed a new commission of inquiry in January 1993. This commission was instructed to investigate the allegations, determine whether the Code of Conduct had been breached and recommend disciplinary measures where these were determined necessary. Additionally, the commission was instructed to consider what publicity should be given to its findings and recommendations. The three-person commission would be chaired by Dr Sam Motsuenyane, assisted by Advocate David Zamchiya and Judge Margaret Burnham.

The commission's work was distinguished by two features. First, it was independent. None of the commissioners or their supporting staff were members of the ANC. Though the ANC provided what resources it could, the commission was not beholden to the ANC for its financial and material resources and received assistance from the United Nations High Commissioner for Refugees (UNHCR). As the commission subsequently noted in its report: 'This is a historic event insofar as it is the first time that a liberation movement has engaged an independent commission to review allegations that its members violated human rights guarantees within its ranks.' Secondly, the work of the commission was conducted transparently, involving some fifty witnesses at public hearings in Johannesburg. Several witnesses travelled specially to South Africa to give testimony. The commission also made an *in loco* inspection of two former ANC camps and communicated with officials of the Tanzanian government, the UNHCR and the ANC.

In its report the commission noted the National Executive Committee's interventions, particularly the adoption of the Code of Conduct and creation of the Officer of Justice, but found that these measures had ultimately failed because insufficient attention was given to following up with material resources and other forms of support. Additionally, the ANC's security department adopted an adversarial posture regarding the Code of Conduct, seeing it as a criticism of its operations. The commission was not unsympathetic to the extremely difficult circumstances in which the ANC had waged its struggle against the apartheid regime. However, despite the difficult conditions in the remote camps and relentless persecution by a ruthless enemy who would and did stop at nothing to compromise the forces of liberation, the commission averred that it did not matter who was the perpetrator and who the victim; there were no special circumstances under which torture is permissible.

The commission submitted its findings to Mandela on 20 August 1993. Among its recommendations were that the ANC apologise to all individuals whose rights were violated at any stage by the ANC, establish mechanisms whereby victims might be compensated, and institute disciplinary proceedings against all those named in the report as responsible for violations. The ANC was also urged to improve accountability within the organisation. Furthermore, the commission recommended that, in the interests of accountability and transparency, the ANC make public the report in its entirety.

On 23 August the NEC convened to consider the commission's findings and decide its response. Certainly we knew before 1993 that the rights of some held captive in our camps had been violated. Yet there was something distinctly different about the Motsuenyane Commission. For a start, the earlier commissions had been appointed internally, conducted their work internally and reported to the leadership. They represented sincere efforts to hold ourselves accountable to ourselves within the structure and organisation of our movement. Though the Motsuenyane Commission emerged out of this tradition of accountability, it was very differently constituted and operated in an altogether different manner.

If I had to reduce the difference to a single factor, it would have to be transparency, not simply in terms of the commission's work (the hearings were held in public and closely watched and reported on by the media), but particularly in terms of the commission's recommendation that the report be made publicly available. There is something particularly shaming about acknowledging one's mistakes and shortcomings publicly.

The NEC meeting of 23 August was one of the most difficult, heated and painful meetings of the leadership in nearly a century of struggle. Ostensibly we were gathered to discuss the commission's findings, yet the issue of whether to affirm or reject the recommendation that we publish the report rapidly came to dominate discussions. Naturally, this debate turned on the political implications of such publication. Yet as the meeting continued and the exchanges became more heated, it became apparent to me that the real issue at stake was the sense of disbelief and shame we felt at what appeared to be a betrayal of all we held so dear. Though the debate was generally couched in terms of political implications, each of us was grappling with our personal and collective moral accountability.

It goes without saying that everyone present was deeply committed to the struggle to liberate our country, and all had suffered for their convictions. Every one of us, whether as soldiers, lawyers, trade unionists, ministers of religion or innumerable other roles, had made huge sacrifices because we were committed to the cause of justice and human rights for all South Africans. Our faith in and commitment to human rights were the reason for our organisation's existence and the source of our strength and unity in the face of massive repression, vilification and persecution. Yet here we sat, the National Executive Committee of the ANC, the heirs and custodians of a human rights tradition that predated even the Universal Declaration of Human Rights, confronted by a report commissioned by ourselves that, firstly, confirmed our responsibility for violations of human rights and, secondly, recommended that we publicly acknowledge the facts in all their horrible detail. After all we had endured and sacrificed, this was asking a lot, perhaps too much.

The debate came to pivot on two competing views. On the one hand, it was argued that the violations were anomalies in a movement that was on the whole very disciplined, despite the very difficult conditions in the isolated camps. The abuses were not systematic and did not form part of official policy. When the incidents became known, the leadership had taken steps to address the issue. Reforms were implemented and abuses were reduced, though regrettably not eradicated. In any event, the movement had not shirked its responsibility to account for itself, as the several commissions had amply demonstrated. Our cause was just and, though these violations were deplorable, they did not diminish the legitimacy of our struggle. On the other hand, it was argued that human rights are human rights and violations remain violations no matter who commits them. Mitigating circumstances are relevant to the extent that they help us understand why certain rights were violated and perhaps assist us to prevent recurrences. But it is an axiom of our rights tradition that no circumstances can ever justify or excuse violations of human rights.

These arguments are not necessarily contradictory, but emotions ran high all the same. Some comrades tried to justify the abuses with the argument that we were at war with a vicious enemy; we were infiltrated; we knew there were enemy agents in our ranks. Our cause was just and breaches in our security had to be plugged at any cost in the interests of the greater good. This line of reasoning prompted Pallo Jordan to stand up and say: 'Comrades, I've learnt something very interesting today. There is such a thing as regime torture and there is ANC torture; and regime torture is bad and ANC torture is good. Thank you for enlightening me.' Whereupon he sat down again.

We knew the report's findings would be used to diminish the legitimacy of the struggle against apartheid. Anticipating the reception it would receive in some quarters, some argued that publishing the report would lessen the sacrifices of all who had supported our struggle and desecrate the ultimate sacrifice of fallen comrades. Others countered that since the commission held its hearings in public, the violations were already public knowledge. Failure to publish the report would be interpreted by some as the ANC's refusal to accept responsibility for what amounted to ANC crimes. And so the debate went back and forth.

The elephant in the room was the issue of moral accountability, and as the debate became still more mired, so did the outline of this imperative become clearer to me. At a certain point, someone stated the basic dilemma at which our deliberations had arrived: why should we confess our sins, accept responsibility for our failings and expose ourselves to the harshest public scrutiny while the real evildoers – perpetrators of a crime against humanity under international law, people for whom torture and indefinite detention were matters of policy and daily routine – were permitted to avoid accounting for their crimes and sheltered from the shame of public disclosure?

It was at that point that I stood up. I proposed a national commission of truth for South Africa. I argued that a truth commission was the only solution to this dilemma and the best way forward for a nation as deeply divided as our own. A truth commission would serve the complicated demands of justice for the crimes of apartheid and would offer a basis for national reconciliation. I based my arguments on a lecture I had given some eighteen months earlier at the University of the Western Cape (UWC). Though I had not intended using the occasion of the NEC meeting about the Motsuenyane Commission's report to propose that the ANC call for a South African truth commission, it became clear to me during the course of that painful meeting that the time was right.

Yet the origins of my proposal to the NEC predate my UWC lecture. As mentioned earlier, in 1987 I had put my thoughts on Nuremberg-style trials to Oliver Tambo. At that stage, negotiations seemed increasingly likely and Tambo replied in his quiet but persuasive way that if apartheid was to be defeated at the negotiating table, there could not be Nuremberg-style trials. He pointed out that we couldn't announce our intentions to try apartheid's leaders for their crimes and still expect the regime to meet us at the negotiating table. Negotiations were unlikely to begin, let alone succeed, if the regime knew they faced criminal trials once they had given up power. Clearly, some other means of accountability that still satisfied the demands of justice would have to be found.

In the interim, the Constitutional Guidelines had been adopted and the Harare Declaration signed. F.W. de Klerk replaced P.W. Botha as President of South Africa and unbanned the ANC. The world's attention had turned to South Africa and hopes and fears were kindled anew. Amid relocating from Dublin to Cape Town and continuing my work for the ANC – now more demanding and stimulating than ever before – I continued to grapple with this fundamental problem. To my mind, it was not enough that a non-racial democracy founded on a justiciable bill of rights be installed in South Africa. While that would correct the crime of apartheid in a formal sense, it would not serve justice for the crime against humanity which was at the root of apartheid's inherent criminality. Yet how to hold the regime accountable in a manner that did not jeopardise the transition to democracy?

Of course, the ANC also wanted more than merely a formal corrective to apartheid governance. As I have explained, since the adoption of the Freedom Charter, the notion of a human rights culture had been fundamental to the ANC's vision of a non-racial, post-apartheid democracy. Now that we were home in South Africa and apartheid's demise seemed imminent, the difficulties, limitations and challenges of realising that vision became palpable. I began to appreciate that the two problems, justice for apartheid's crimes and the prospects for a human rights culture taking root, were intimately related in several ways. The most obvious connection was that if justice for apartheid's crimes was not seen to be done, then the prospects of a human rights culture taking root would be so much poorer. A more significant connection, however, was that the imperatives of transparency and accountability, the twin pillars of our envisioned human rights culture, constituted a basis for justice. We would seek justice for apartheid within the framework of the human rights culture that we sought to create.

I used the occasion of my inauguration as Professor of Human Rights Law at UWC on 25 May 1992, the anniversary of the signing of the African Charter on Human and People's Rights, to present my thoughts on these issues. Though founded as one of apartheid's 'bush universities' for non-whites, UWC was respected for its history of anti-apartheid activism and scholarship. I began by questioning whether a static state-based approach to human rights in political life was a satisfactory basis on which to build the future. I posed the question whether a formal commitment to constitutionalism was sufficient to make our fledgling human rights system work and wondered what place there was in it for the history and legacy of pain, humiliation, alienation and dispossession as well as the demands for justice for these crimes. I cautioned that making a formal constitutional settlement the only measure of justice for apartheid would produce a culture of exculpation, and a shallow, tenuous and racially exclusive one at that – certainly nothing like reconciliation between the fractured parts of our nation and definitely not a solid basis for a new, rights-based political system. The proper approach to political life in our new democracy, I suggested, should be founded on a moral sense of personal responsibility for our common history. Only when apartheid's evil legacy had been repudiated in this way would the demands of justice be served and our nascent human rights culture flourish.

Accordingly, it was vital that the past not be ignored. First and foremost, there was the imperative to recognise apartheid as fundamentally illegitimate, for only then could the assumptions and 'old ways' of doing things be challenged and transformed. I pointed out that history remained contested and argued that we needed to know our past if we were to resist any efforts to sanitise it. The regime's tendency at that time to hold up its minority rights proposals as evidence of a longstanding commitment to human rights demonstrated this danger. Reconciliation in our divided society required that we recognise the past for what it was in order to understand apartheid's terrible legacy and draw together as a society and nation to respond positively to the future challenges this legacy posed. What we needed, I suggested, was a time of debate and opening up, what the Chileans call *reconvivencia*, a period of getting used to living with each other again. In order to consolidate the new order, we could not afford to deny the effects of the old order.

I went on to recall the experiences of other countries and cautioned against remedies such as Czechoslovakia's lustration law. This law prohibited a range of former officials of the old order from being employed in schools or holding government positions. Instead, I suggested that we pay careful attention to the debates about indemnity, restitution, justice and reconciliation. I spoke about the experience of many South American countries in the late 1980s and early 1990s when new democratic governments found themselves under considerable pressure to investigate, prosecute and punish the crimes of former regimes. At the same time, however, a new consciousness was forming among citizens in these young democracies. They were beginning to understand that truth was indispensable to reconciliation and that punishment of offenders was insufficient compensation to their victims.

I cited other examples that we might follow and argued that numerous precedents around the world provided us with enough experience and guidance to lessen the daunting expectation that we needed to be creative and innovative to provide redress to apartheid's victims. As it turns out, we have been enormously innovative in how we have chosen to deal with the past, which bears testimony to our determination to confront our terrible history, however painful that reckoning was. In 1992, however, it was sufficient that the bogeyman of 'dealing with the past' could be cut down to size. Yes, it would be traumatic, but it was possible.

Nowhere in my lecture did I speak specifically or directly about truth commissions but the implication was quite clear: something had to be done. Albie Sachs, who was at my inaugural lecture, which by the way I didn't get to finish because I ran out of time, says he can't remember if I actually proposed a truth commission as such in that lecture, but he asserts, 'Kader put this issue on the agenda. He put it on the map for the first time.' He has described my proposal for a truth commission as a 'paradigm shift and the introduction of a whole new theme' and as my 'most distinctive contribution to South Africa's history, producing a unique result that is spoken about all over the world as something special'.

Back in May 1992 we were still a long way from a settlement. Codesa – the Convention for a Democratic South Africa – had deadlocked not two weeks before my address and some of the most intractable problems that would repeatedly stall the negotiations in the months and years ahead, problems that the future TRC would go a considerable way towards resolving, were only just beginning to take shape. At one level, my lecture was concerned with these problems and the underlying issues they signified: justice, accountability, reparation, reconciliation, citizenship and so on. At the same time, I was concerned with what I saw as a solution at a fundamental level: the urgency and necessity of reviving a moral conscience in South Africa. My arguments about dealing with the past and the examples I cited of other countries' experiences were addressed to the space in between. Though the nature of my argument implied something like a truth commission, I did not at that stage go so far as to formally propose one.

I think there are several reasons why my ideas were so well received. To begin with, it coincided with the moment that Alex Boraine, the co-founder of the Institute for a Democratic Alternative for South Africa (Idasa), and others began searching for ways to manage the dilemmas of justice in times of transition. For this group, most of whom had opposed apartheid in one way or another but were neither members of nor associated with any particular political party, I think it was encouraging to hear a member of the ANC National Executive Committee put forward an argument that spoke to many of the issues that preoccupied them.

During the next eighteen months I had time for further reflection. I attended a conference on truth commissions organised by Boraine, who by this stage had canvassed interest and some support for a South African truth commission. Being a member of the NEC, I was aware of the Stuart, Thami Zulu and Skweyiya commissions and, along with the rest of South Africa, the Motsuenyane one. These resonated with many of the issues raised at the conference and in the subsequent debates on the desirability, appropriateness, form and structure that a South African commission might take.

Given the hectic workload of the ANC's Constitutional Committee, I could not give these debates all the attention I would have liked, though I was convinced that South Africa desperately needed a truth commission. Yet as I reflected on the proposals, listened to objections and spoke with friends and colleagues, it became clear to me that our truth commission would have to depart in significant ways from the generic model based on experiences in Latin America.

I was concerned that the emphasis on the proposed truth commission as primarily a moral instrument that would investigate all parties to the conflict downplayed the importance of some hard political facts which justice for apartheid demanded be acknowledged – and which other truth commissions in their particular circumstances had shied away from confronting. It was vital that the proposed commission demonstrate unequivocally that the doctrine of apartheid was a crime against humanity, in accord with the 1973 UN ruling, and was illegal under international law (a historical fact little known to most white South Africans); that the National Party, in power since 1948, was an illegitimate regime; and that it was this regime that was ultimately the source of violence in our country because it had insisted on implementing and defending at all costs a crime against humanity.

Blanket amnesty would be intolerable because it would obscure too much of what was inherently criminal about apartheid and would fatally subvert the just demand that perpetrators of crimes against humanity be held accountable. Whereas a criminal trial would seek accountability within the framework of the law, such as I envisioned prior to Tambo's sage advice, our truth commission would seek it within the framework of truth telling. One way or another, there had to be accountability – and not of the soft kind that depicted apartheid as a kind of structural error similar to poor economic policy, something for which no one in particular was to blame, while agreeing that the resultant suffering was appalling and regrettable. There had to be accountability of the hard kind, the kind that asks, 'Who attended the meeting, who signed the orders, who made the parcel bomb and who posted it?'

This desire for hard accountability stemmed from the model of criminal accountability from which my view of a truth commission was adapted, as well as the ANC's various internal commissions that named names and recounted events and allegations in considerable detail. It was this kind of accountability that was at the heart of the NEC's dilemma about how to respond to the Motsuenyane Commission's findings. Here we were holding ourselves to the hard measure of accountability, all the while knowing that unless some mechanism was devised, the perpetrators of apartheid – the ultimate source of all the violence and turmoil in South Africa and the frontline states – would suffer no more than general and collective condemnation – something they'd lived with for decades already – and that considerably softened by ringing applause from the international community for finally seeing the light.

All these issues were ringing in my head as the NEC, on behalf of the ANC, drafted a statement outlining its response to the Motsuenyane Commission. In the statement we recognised that abuses did occur and expressed 'our profound sense of regret, collective moral responsibility and apology to all who suffered as a consequence'. The statement went on to stress that human rights violations should be condemned regardless of who the perpetrator was. We pointed out that the ANC had taken the first steps to hold itself accountable when we subjected ourselves to objective and impartial scrutiny, the first time a liberation movement had done so. The statement stressed that the human rights violations referred to by the commission's report could in no way be equated with the violations perpetrated by the apartheid state, 'which were gross, systematic and a product of a policy which transgressed not only South African law but virtually the whole range of fundamental rights protected in international law'.

The statement also criticised De Klerk's government for attempting to exonerate itself and parts of the state apparatus by passing the Further Indemnity Act in 1992 and drew attention to the fact that the government had made no attempt to make reparations for its crimes. The statement then insisted that 'any policy on reparations and amnesty must be made as part of negotiations and democratic consultation'. The statement ended by calling for a truth commission: 'We regard the Skweyiya and Motsuenyane Commission Reports as a first step in a process for national disclosure of all violations of human rights from all sides. We accordingly call for the establishment of a Truth Commission, similar to bodies established in a number of countries in recent years to deal with the past. The purpose of such a Commission will be to investigate all violations of human rights – killings, disappearances, torture and ill-treatment – from all quarters. This will not be a Nuremberg tribunal. Its role will be to identify all abuses of human rights and their perpetrators, to propose a code of conduct for all public servants, to ensure appropriate compensation to the victims and to work out the basis for reconciliation. In addition, it will provide the moral basis for justice and for preventing any repetition of abuses in the future.'

The ANC also released both the Motsuenyane and Skweyiya commissions' reports. Thus did the ANC commit itself to a truth commission for South Africa, the only political party to do so during the pre-election period. Dire warnings about witch-hunts, the recklessness of provoking Afrikaners and the dangers of opening wounds only just beginning to heal became commonplace and were widely repeated.

One of the most persuasive of the scaremongers was General Krappies Engelbrecht, head of apartheid's security police. He was an extraordinary-looking man. His face was scarred as if he'd been through many battles. His hairstyle was heavily slicked back like a Brylcreem advert from the 1940s. He reminded me a bit of the cricketer Denis Compton, his wavy hair heavily ridged and parted down the middle. Engelbrecht wasn't someone you would want to meet in the middle of the night in a dark alley, but fortunately our meetings were generally in the daylight hours. I met with him once at the World Trade Centre in Kempton Park in a side room. He told us that if total amnesty wasn't granted, we could not depend on the loyalty of the police or the defence force, or even state employees in the power stations and the railways. This was a very serious matter, and it was only subsequently that we realised how weak these threats were and how little they were based on. But in 1993 they were terrifying.

What made the timing of the announcement of the NEC's backing of a truth commission even more awkward was the advanced stage of the negotiations then taking place at the World Trade Centre. Only a week before the NEC issued its statement, the Technical Committee on Constitutional Issues published the third draft constitution. Would this move scupper the final settlement?

The apartheid regime had never liked the idea of a truth commission. Even in the Record of Understanding of 1992 between the ANC and the government, which got negotiations back on track and led to the commencement of the Multi-Party Negotiating Forum, the issue of amnesty was left open and unresolved. The National Party still hoped that, despite the ANC's statement, De Klerk could secure a general amnesty. In the end, they were mistaken. There were clearly discussions going on at different levels both within the ANC and beyond about whether to concede a general amnesty and, if so, to which categories of perpetrator.

Two other meetings made this very apparent. The first occurred early in 1993 when I was summoned late one evening to the Pretoria residence of Thabo Mbeki. He and Penuell Maduna, a lawyer by training and later the Minister of Justice and Constitutional Development, were busy discussing the amnesty issue. 'Must we give them all amnesty?' Mbeki asked me. I was flabbergasted. This flew in the face of all our agreements, discussions and plans. It also undermined the special committee that Mandela had established, consisting of myself and ANC lawyers Dullah Omar and Bulelani Ngcuka, to consider the question of amnesty. I said, 'No, it's not up to us. It wasn't only the ANC who were affected by apartheid atrocities and we shouldn't be the ones to grant amnesty for everybody. What about Steve Biko's killers? Or Dr Fabian Ribeiro's? They weren't ANC people. How can we just hand out amnesty on their behalf?'

The second meeting took place one day in the heat of the negotiations at the World Trade Centre. I was asked to attend a 'special' negotiations meeting. Intrigued, I agreed, and was soon picked up by one of the state's negotiators, a senior officer in the National Intelligence Agency. We drove round and round Pretoria for what seemed like hours. Suddenly, we pulled into the driveway of a house and there was Kobie Coetsee, the National Party's Minister of Justice. 'Ah, hello, Kader,' he smiled as I entered. Before long, who should walk in but Thabo Mbeki. It was evident that De Klerk didn't want to take up this issue with Mandela and was instead involved in behind-the-scenes discussions with other senior members of the ANC negotiating team. This in itself was an indication of the lack of consensus within the ANC about the issue of amnesty. As De Klerk and his team clearly assumed that they wouldn't get their way through normal negotiations, they were trying to direct things through the back door, through the person of Mbeki. Perhaps they hadn't realised that when it came to amnesty the hard-liner in the ANC was me. Perhaps they thought I would be accommodating, but I was in no mood for that. I felt the agreed route and the agreed policy were being circumvented.

Coetsee and Mbeki started playing around with different categories of amnesty, all based on the assumption that General Engelbrecht was telling the truth and that the whole superstructure of the state would come crashing down if apartheid's villains were required to come clean.

My view was that this was a bluff. I didn't think Engelbrecht had any basis for making these intimations of threats.

In the end, the amnesty idea was not pursued any further and was deferred, as it should have been, to the formal negotiators. The committee which considered amnesty, chaired by me, took the view, after considerable debate and argument, not without ill-temper, that we should not concede and grant a blanket amnesty. In fact, it would have been an act of grave political heresy if an amnesty had been agreed prior to the drafting of the final constitution and at the behest of the apartheid regime. It would have been wrong.

The now famous 'post-amble' to the Interim Constitution of 1993 laid the foundation for what became South Africa's truth commission. It stated in part that 'In order to advance ... reconciliation and reconstruction, amnesty shall be granted in respect of acts, omissions and offences associated with political objectives and committed in the course of the conflicts of the past. To this end, Parliament under this constitution shall adopt a law determining a firm cut-off date, which shall be a date after 8 October 1990 and before 6 December 1993, and providing for the mechanisms, criteria and procedures, including tribunals, if any, through which such an amnesty shall be dealt with at any time after the law has been passed.'

The post-amble left much open to interpretation, and De Klerk and others hoping for a general amnesty found in it succour that their desires would be met. However, the post-amble lacked legal rigour not only because it was the last clause of the Interim Constitution to be adopted at three in the morning by exhausted negotiators, but also because it was deliberately left open to the broadest interpretation.

The Promotion of National Unity and Reconciliation Act was finally passed into law in 1995 after a prolonged period of negotiation within Parliament. By then, the ANC was in power, having won the 1994 elections, and was presiding over the country in a coalition Government of National Unity, which included the National Party and the Inkatha Freedom Party.

Hundreds of drafts of the Act were formulated, discussed and then reworked. It took a whole year for the bill to pass, largely because it was the product of a committee, not of Cabinet, and was heavily reliant on lawyers' interpretations of what the negotiators had intended. It was a compromise between Nuremberg-type trials and a whitewashing amnesia. 'The objective of the Commission', its report explained, was 'to promote national unity and reconciliation in a spirit of understanding which transcends the conflicts and divisions of the past.' Archbishop Desmond Tutu and Alex Boraine were appointed chairperson and deputy chairperson of the commission.

Of course it could not have been expected that the TRC could undo all the evil of the thirty-five years that were the span of its investigations, let alone the centuries of oppression. Yet it did expose the details of large numbers of atrocities previously shrouded from public view, and it afforded victims the catharsis of a public opportunity to tell of their pain. It was said, too, that public confession of the commission of atrocities such as hooding a victim to the point of near-suffocation was a shaming ordeal for perpetrators. The revelations that were aired nightly on television came as a shock to many who had managed to close their eyes to what evidence of injustice and oppression was allowed by the apartheid regime to penetrate the veil of its suppression of information. Thus, inasmuch as the TRC opened wounds but closed books, it was an essential element of the political transition. Its final report provided as authoritative an accounting for the recent past as was possible, so easing the passage of that transition and pointing the way forwards to the transformation that must follow.

In general though, each of the sectoral hearings of the TRC, when business, the media, the legal profession, religious bodies and others were afforded the opportunity to reflect on their roles under apartheid, ended in disappointment. There were high levels of unwillingness to testify and a generally sanctimonious and exculpatory approach by those who did appear. I, for one, could not get my Department of Water Affairs to make a submission to the TRC on how water had been used by the previous regime as an instrument of repression. The forcible resettlement of millions of Africans had taken place not only to impoverished areas far from any opportunity of employment, but also, in order to break their spirits, to areas where little if any water was easily accessible.

Significantly, the military themselves did not appear before the commission. They were too powerful to yield to any moral pressure. And the one prosecution of a general in the South African Defence Force, as it was called then, failed to get a conviction.

Louise attended a few of the hearings that took place in Cape Town and was particularly struck by the contrast between the presentation by the ANC and that by the National Party. The latter was led by De Klerk, who announced that he alone would speak and therefore he alone would take the oath to tell the truth. In contrast, Thabo Mbeki, who led the ANC delegation, announced that all those in the ANC delegation should take the oath, so that they could all speak when they wished.

In his famous poem 'Easter 1916', W.B. Yeats celebrated the heroes of the Easter Rising in his incomparable words 'Too long a sacrifice / Can make a stone of the heart'. Yeats spoke also of the love of these warm hearts that the oppressor sought to turn to stone, the love of their country and of people and, in the end, the love of humanity itself. In our case it could have been that our own hearts might turn to stone, that we inscribed vengeance on our banners of battle and resolved to meet brutality with brutality. When Nelson Mandela used this poem in the Irish Parliament in 1990 – in possibly one of his most magnificent speeches, obviously written by Thabo Mbeki – I could not wait for him to finish as it was all too much for me. I fled to the men's cloakroom.

We understood that oppression dehumanises the oppressor as much as it hurts the oppressed; that to emulate the barbarity of the tyrant would transform us into tyrants. We knew we would sully and degrade our cause if we allowed that it should, at any stage, borrow anything from the practices of the oppressed. We had to refuse that our long sacrifice make a stone of our hearts. Just as important, it was essential that South Africa face up to the atrocities in its past. This was not only true for the agents of apartheid, but it was also applicable to the liberation movement. As Alexander Solzhenitsyn argued: 'By not dealing with past human rights violations, we are not simply protecting the perpetrator's trivial old age; we are thereby ripping the foundations of justice from beneath new generations.'

The TRC represented South Africa's novel way of dealing with its traumatic past. Yet the formula at the heart of the TRC's approach, the exchange of amnesty for truth, is not as simple or straightforward as is often assumed. The TRC consciously eschewed criminal accountability for apartheid's crimes in the recognition that the pursuit of criminal prosecutions, whether or not these were secured, would jeopardise the fragile peace. It wasn't only the peace that was at stake. Criminal prosecutions were not conducive to the desired ends, namely truth and reconciliation, key terms for the entire enterprise, which are considerably more complex than is often recognised. In the book I wrote with Louise and Ronald Roberts, *Reconciliation through Truth*, we made a detailed case against prosecution of apartheid's culprits.

The heart of reconciliation is not the manufacture of a cheap and easy bonhomie. Nor is it an escapist flight from the facts or an arrival at jerry-built consensus through the avoidance of debate and accountability. Rather, it is the facing of unwelcome truths so that inevitable and continuing conflicts and differences stand at least within a single universe of comprehensibility. In a political context, it is a shared and painful ethical voyage from wrong to right. Reconciliation through truth is therefore not about auditing the past so that it can be declared accounted for. It is a journey that rests on acknowledging the facts of the past so that moral accountability can be assigned to them and in this way we may continue into our future on the basis of a new moral consensus.

The TRC played an important role in realising the moral significance of democracy in South Africa. In doing so, it engaged in the work of memory dedicated to the struggle (in Milan Kundera's familiar phrase) of 'memory against forgetting'. This work of memory was important. Although we should be critical of attempts to turn memory into myth-making, especially if such myths are only ways of avoiding historical accountability, the TRC was responsible for important memory work. To create a future, we must therefore remember the past. In doing so, we recognised that a wishful and forgetful approach would simply serve to entrench past inequities, as they would not disappear of their own accord. They must be actively dismantled.

The TRC enabled us to come to a reckoning of our past. This was crucial in ensuring that the processes of corrective action (wrongly described in my view as affirmative action), which flowed from its work of transferring resources to education, welfare and housing, did not lose their historical moorings and condemn South Africa to moral and political drift.

Indeed, the TRC recognised that for genuine and meaningful reconciliation to occur, we had to ensure that moral and political restitution, in the sense of *Wiedergutmachung*, to 'make good again', took place. We could not really enter upon the process of making good the history of South Africa unless we acknowledged precisely what bad there was to undo.

What kind of memory of the past did we need to build a new South Africa? We needed a memory based not on bitter resentment of the past but on the possibilities of reconciliation for the future. In doing so, we had to follow the advice of the Chilean truth commissioner José Zalaquett, who insisted that a 'society cannot reconcile itself on the grounds of a divided memory. Since memory is identity, this would result in a divided identity.'

Memory needs a place, a habitation and a name. While it is a truism that those who forget their past are often doomed to repeat it, the reverse comfort does not necessarily hold. A society may remember its past and nevertheless repeat it – or even surpass it in cruelty. Afrikaner suffering at the hands of British imperialism early in the twentieth century actually fuelled the racial oppression of apartheid, rather than serving as an admonition against it.

Since the devil can quote history to his own purpose, a simple factual record of the apartheid past, devoid of an ethical basis, would be of little value. What matters is not merely the fact that we remember history, but the way in which we remember it. In this context, one where we take full measure of the past, our country can become a safer place for idealism, the sort of place that Seamus Heaney had in mind when he wrote of those rare times and places 'when hope and history rhyme'. And it is only between our divided past and our hopes for the future that we can build such bridges in the present.

There is no question that when the final report of the TRC was received in Parliament in 2003, South Africa had reached a truly historic moment. As Albie Sachs recalls, 'It signified the end of a particularly intense, searching and sometimes painful process in our country's history. But as much as it was the end of a process it also pointed to the dawning of a new chapter for our democracy and the national development and reconstruction needed to fully achieve the ideals we set for ourselves.'

It is important to recall that the TRC was intended to be one initiative among many designed to bring healing to our nation in the wake of the evil years of apartheid. As Albie goes on to say, 'As we entered the closing phases of the work of the TRC, we needed to recall the overall mandate that governed its work. It was to reconcile. It was to heal. It was to repair and establish what happened in the past. The time had come to build a national consensus on how to do so ... Therefore we need to rise above our political differences in pursuit of national inclusivity, redress and restoration that will finally take us across the historic bridge between an unjust and violent past and a future founded on the recognition of human rights and peace and enable us to take forward the challenge of building a united and thriving nation.'

Since the TRC submitted its first report to Parliament in 1998, several excellent (and some not so good) accounts of this cathartic process have appeared, variously examining the commission's strengths and weaknesses, its impact at the time, and its contribution toward strengthening a post-apartheid society founded on the supreme values of human dignity, equality and the advancement of human rights and freedoms. Less attention has been given to the origins and genesis of the TRC itself. When this has been the subject of inquiry, the accounts have tended to focus on the role of South African civil society – vibrant as only years of political agitation can ensure – in supporting and incubating a proposal that, with the notable exception of the ANC, found no official support among political parties and in the main was denounced as dangerously provocative by many political commentators and analysts.

There is another, less often recounted story of the TRC. It involves understanding the TRC process not only in terms of the moral imperative of accounting for apartheid's sins, but as a political imperative of the transition. Certainly, the thorny issue of amnesty for crimes committed during the National Party's decades-long reign of terror was definitely on the agenda at the negotiating table. However, I have in mind a more subtle and politically nuanced interpretation of the TRC and its contribution, even before it had begun its work, towards the larger project of growing a just, peaceful and prosperous post-apartheid society.

As a forum and social process, the TRC, from genesis to conclusion, played a vital role in the ANC's strategy to alter favourably the conditions for nurturing a culture of human rights and realising the Freedom Charter's vision of a free South Africa where all people would live in brotherhood, enjoying equal rights and opportunities. The TRC would be the seal on the peace treaty concluded in November 1993.

In retrospect, there were many aspects of the TRC process that were flawed or that we could have done better. The ANC, and the country's then President, Thabo Mbeki, did the process a disservice by failing to give the delivery of the final report the requisite acknowledgement. Very few ministers attended the official launch of the report in Pretoria. Many in the ANC were still angered by the exposure of ANC violations, by the equivalency this implied with the National Party's crimes – an equivalency which Archbishop Tutu himself encouraged – and were irritated by the sanitising of that aspect of the report dealing with President De Klerk when he threatened legal action. Essop Pahad, Mbeki's right-hand man and Minister without Portfolio in the Cabinet, said that he thought I had been 'too keen' on the TRC.

This lack of wholeheartedness on the liberation movement's side, understandable as it was, was mirrored by the lukewarm acceptance of responsibility by the white community. I am not sure whether white South Africans, as a result of the TRC process, ever got sufficient information about the real human impact of the Group Areas Act, forced removals, the pass laws, Bantu Education, the migrant labour system and the economic war waged against black South Africans. I am not sure they ever really understood or acknowledged the many and diverse ways in which they benefited from apartheid, from excellent schooling and world-class universities to top-notch health care. As a result, it is easy for them to deny complicity, to blame apartheid on someone else.

I must also mention my huge disappointment with the government's handling of the reparations that were promised to victims within the scope of the TRC's work. One of the reasons we never finished making provision for reparations was that the Minister of Justice at the time simply didn't do what was required of him and present to Cabinet the details of the reparations scheme. In addition, it took an inordinate time for financial compensation to be paid. Scandalously, it is only very recently that the government has made attempts to trace those who were due recompense.

The TRC emphasised at the time that financial recompense for the twenty-two thousand individuals who appeared before it was unlikely to be adequate, and that the government should rather concentrate on its programme of reconstruction and development. As I said in a speech at the time, 'We cannot simply limit our response to that of individual reparations. Instead we would do better to continue on our path to achieve sustainable collective redress through socio-economic programmes that invest in people, eradicate poverty, create employment opportunities, and redress the legacy of exclusion.'

Where the TRC proved a disappointment was in the impact that the disclosures of appalling human rights violations had on the broader community of those responsible. We hoped that it would persuade whites of the need for corrective action. We hoped that it would give rise to a shared view of what was necessary to put things right in the future. This has not really been the case.

Then, too, the TRC took evidence from both the victims of apartheid and those who had suffered violations in the ANC camps. Of course the transgressions of the ANC were few and far between as compared to the sins of the upholders of apartheid, but nonetheless the TRC insisted that according to its mandate it had to hear evidence from both sides. Despite the commission taking pains to say that it saw no equivalence between the two, this gave rise to some considerable disappointment within the ranks of the ANC, and a distinct lack of enthusiasm at the launch of the report.

There was also the fact that Archbishop Tutu inevitably gave the proceedings a patina of Christianity, even though after the first session there was a 'moment of silence' rather than a prayer. The idea behind the TRC, that one could obtain amnesty through truth telling, was very close to the Christian idea of redemption through confession. This gave rise to some accusations of 'religiosity', though I thought this to be overstating the case.

Whatever the TRC's shortcomings, few would today deny its impact. Unreconstructed racists apart, no white South Africans can now deny the crimes committed in their name. To be sure, the TRC was not without its limitations and its achievements have not been without great pain. Yet these and a host of further benefits placed our country and society on a secure footing to continue into our brave new post-apartheid future. Had the ANC avoided the imperative of moral accountability and chosen instead simply to close the book on South Africa's brutal past, with what moral authority could we claim to be representing the interests of justice and equality in South Africa? Indeed, it was exactly such a moral dilemma that in 1993 prompted the

ANC to throw its weight behind the proposal for a truth commission process in South Africa.

The TRC gave us the opportunity to come to terms with the past, and provided a foundation for rebuilding the country on the basis of a human rights culture and the values of our Constitution – a new democracy. It is the reconstruction of our society on the basis of a shared vision of the future that best guarantees a peaceful, just, multicultural society in which each is offered an opportunity to flourish and reach fulfilment. The past is, after all, another country.

8

In Cabinet

Following the ANC's overwhelming victory in the first democratic elections of April 1994, Nelson Mandela – as ANC president – soon got down to the business of choosing his Cabinet. This would be Mandela's first, and only, Cabinet as he would retire after his five-year term had run its course. As late April drifted to early May, the rumour mill started to click into high gear.

Quite by chance I read in the press one day that I was to be Minister of Constitutional Development. I was very excited at this prospect, as the legitimacy of the struggle and of the state had been an important aspect of my work as a lawyer in the anti-apartheid movement and as a researcher and teacher at university. Soon afterwards, I read that this ministry was to go to Roelf Meyer, the National Party's capable chief negotiator. The constitutional task was a continuation of his role in the De Klerk government and recognised his part in the negotiations. Still, I was to be an MP in the first Parliament of a democratic South Africa, and I had no doubt this would afford me plenty of opportunities for contributing to the rebuilding of my country.

Shortly before the inauguration of our new President, I was notified that Louise and I must be ready to fly to Pretoria early on 10 May for the ceremony. We were to travel up and back the same day, dressed in our finery, and were not allowed to take any luggage. Naturally, on this occasion at least, we did as we were told. We grabbed my briefcase and Louise's handbag and drove to the airport to catch the first flight to Johannesburg.

It was a glorious day, and there was a huge buzz of excitement when we arrived at the Union Buildings in Pretoria, though we had to complain that the outgoing ministers had taken all the best seats. Eventually the seating was rearranged, and we could wander around greeting comrades in the struggle and leaders of the solidarity movements overseas. Among them were Fidel Castro; Mary Robinson, President of Ireland and a long-time supporter and sponsor of the Irish Anti-Apartheid Movement; and of course the IAAM president, Terence McCaughey. It was an extraordinary array, not only of our supporters, but also of our opponents. The inauguration itself was a breathtaking and emotional event, with the whole paraphernalia of state rolled out to celebrate, and leaders of state mingling cheek by jowl with members of liberation movements from all over the world. Below the Union Buildings huge crowds of ordinary South Africans gathered in the open space to celebrate as jet fighters from the air force thundered overhead and military bands played our new national anthem faultlessly.

When it was all over, I found myself with Trevor Manuel waiting for transport. There was none. The former ministers had left in their official cars, and whatever else was provided was not enough for everyone. By this time I had been told I was to stay the night, and eventually the driver of a bakkie took pity on us and drove us to the hotel. We had no nightclothes, not even a toothbrush between us – and no fresh clothes to put on in the morning to wear to the Union Buildings, where I had been summoned. I did manage to find an acquaintance who kindly bought me a clean white shirt, so Louise stuffed my worn shirt into a plastic laundry bag. Though she tried to carry this about her as inconspicuously as possible, she did stand out somewhat in the company of the immaculately turned-out National Party wives, resplendent in gloves and hats.

When we arrived at the seat of the South African government, the Union Buildings, I could see from its portals Pretoria stretched out before me in the autumn sunshine. I was not sure why I was there. Having seen me, Joe Slovo came over, laughing, and asked: 'What are you doing here?' I felt embarrassed, but Slovo went on to assure me, in an off-hand manner, that Mandela would find 'something or other' for me. From that day on I found it very hard to be collegial towards Slovo. We were both known as strong personalities and it was probably inevitable that at times we would clash.

Inside the Union Buildings we gathered together with our ANC comrades and a group of luminaries from the National Party and Inkatha Freedom Party. As the ANC achieved victory through a negotiated settlement and not through a coup, revolution or military victory, we had accepted the necessity of a Government of National Unity (GNU) under the constitutional compromises of 1993 rather than a government based on our outright electoral victory. The GNU featured ourselves, the National Party and Inkatha in a coalition aimed at building reconciliation and national unity and easing fears of post-election ANC domination. Each of these parties required its seats at the Cabinet table.

One by one the prospective ministers were called in to our new President and were told what posts they were being offered. In the end it was my turn and I was informed that I was to be Minister of Water and Forestry (a title later changed to the more comprehensive Water Affairs and Forestry). I accepted gratefully, and left the room to tell Louise. She excitedly picked up the nearest red telephone, on which it turned out she could dial England, and so she was able to tell her parents the news.

We then all assembled together in the Cabinet room to take the oath of office. The aides helping us find the right seats at first marshalled the men into the front row and the women at the back, as was the old practice. Soon, though, someone realised what was happening, and we sorted ourselves out. The same kind of thing happened later in Parliament, where seats labelled 'Reserved for wives of MPs' had to be renamed 'Reserved for spouses of MPs'.

Being Minister of Water Affairs and Forestry seemed at the time a humble portfolio in the grand scheme of things, and a far cry from the post of Constitutional Development I had hoped for, or Justice, or any of the glamour portfolios. Some questioned how a person with no engineering or scientific background could manage such a portfolio, to which I replied that I would be carrying out the dictates of the ANC Freedom Charter. (In fact, though there is a section in the Charter entitled 'There shall be houses, security and comfort', it makes no mention of water.) Nevertheless, I threw myself into the job with all the energy I had. I didn't in any way feel slighted. I was delighted to have been chosen by Mandela, and elated to work with and for him. I still recall laughing out loud with pleasure when I entered my office on my first day as minister. I was soon to appreciate the importance of clean water to ordinary South African men and women. Later, Trevor Manuel, who was at first made Minister of Trade and Industry and subsequently became Finance Minister, was to say I was the only person Mandela could possibly have chosen to turn Water Affairs into a 'sexy ministry'.

While the ANC's election victory had left the entire movement and its friends all over the world in a state of euphoria and relief, there were some uncomfortable facts underpinning the work of the first Mandela Cabinet. The first was that the Government of National Unity required the presence of a large number of people in our Cabinet whom we would normally have preferred not to be there. First and foremost of these was, of course, F.W. de Klerk, former head of the apartheid state. De Klerk was one of two Deputy Presidents in the GNU – along with Thabo Mbeki from the ANC – on account of the NP having won twenty per cent of the seats. De Klerk was accompanied in the Cabinet by five of his NP colleagues, including Roelf Meyer and Pik Botha, the world's longest-serving Foreign Minister turned Minister of Mineral and Energy Affairs.

After several years as State President, De Klerk found it very hard to play second fiddle to anybody, including Mandela. When he became upset in Cabinet meetings, as he occasionally did, he used to slam shut the lid of his bomb-proof briefcase and then march out of the room. He also didn't like the style of discussion that took place and the free flow of debate or the policies that we adopted. After one Cabinet committee meeting in which De Klerk had been unusually obstreperous, Mandela called the ANC leadership to his office at Tuynhuys. 'I want to remove De Klerk from chairing the Cabinet safety and security committee,' he told us. While all the brown noses in Cabinet muttered, 'Yes, Madiba,' I said quite frankly, 'No, you can't.' Mandela turned to me and requested, 'Write down your reasons. I have a meeting in ten minutes' time. You have to explain it to me by then.' I thought that removing De Klerk from Cabinet-level involvement in safety and security would send out a very bad signal to our political partners and to the country, and informed Mandela of this in a few scribbled sentences. 'You were quite right,' he said to me later, and he left De Klerk where he was.

De Klerk had a soft spot for me because I was a lawyer. One day he said to me, 'You know, I knew nothing about Vlakplaas,' referring to a notorious police death squad base. I told him I valued this frankness, as one lawyer to another, but added that there was an old principle in law: depending on the office you occupy, if you don't know about something that happened under your watch, you ought to have known. As head of state and as a member of the NP Cabinet and its Security Council throughout the 1980s, he ought to have known what was happening. I do think, too, that De Klerk's attitude to the Truth and Reconciliation Commission was appalling. He refused to accept responsibility for what his government had done though, in the end, he did express regret.

What De Klerk did in essence was fight for the preservation of white interests. It is doubtful whether he consulted his parliamentary party when he unbanned the ANC and other groups in 1990. It's also not entirely clear whether his fellow NP Cabinet ministers or even his party knew that he was considering leaving the GNU, as he did on 30 June 1996 in a fit of pique. I still believe this departure from the GNU was one of his greatest mistakes. After leaving the GNU, the NP – which changed its name to the New National Party in a vain attempt to conceal its ghastly history – withered and died on the political vine it had nurtured from the bitter soil of apartheid. And rightly so.

That De Klerk was awarded the Nobel Peace Prize jointly with Nelson Mandela was a travesty and still sticks in my craw. In my opinion, it was undeserved. De Klerk and Mandela are simply not in the same league; they are not comparable. As far as I am concerned, the only decent thing he ever did was unban the liberation movements in 1990 and let Mandela out of prison – but even these moves were forced upon him, as so much of our history now makes clear.

Mandela and De Klerk, President and Deputy President, Nobel Peace Prize co-laureates, did not get on well together. I would characterise the relationship as one of 'extreme discomfort'. Ironically, this was the unspoken rubric of our Government of National Unity: that the two top leaders couldn't stand each other. The intensity of their dislike had been captured in various famous outbursts during the negotiations process and was reported periodically in the press. The climax of this occurred in one epic speech delivered by Mandela immediately after the Boipatong Massacre in 1992. Few who were present had ever seen Mandela as furious as when he stormed out of the World Trade Centre and pulled the ANC out of the negotiations. By 1994, there was a quiet, deep-seated antagonism between Mandela and De Klerk that invariably had repercussions in Cabinet.

In Cabinet itself, the culture clash between the NP and the ANC ministers played itself it out fortnightly. The 'Nats' could hardly have come from a more contrasting decision-making tradition than the ANC. The Nats followed orders and protocol. There was little debate and certainly no NP minister challenged De Klerk in Cabinet on anything. The ANC, on the other hand, was used to engaging in heated debate and argument about issues. This was part of the vibrant jostling that occurs in a true democracy. People stated their views, honestly and openly. Consensus was allowed to establish itself in a place where everybody was comfortable, through a process of argument and counter-argument, debate and riposte. The NP ministers were baffled, even alarmed, by the intense debate that took place in Cabinet. During one of these, an NP minister shouted in frustration, 'But the President has already made a statement about it.' In an NP government, that would have been the end of the matter. Not with the ANC. 'We don't believe in *uno duce, una voce*,' piped up Nkosazana Dlamini-Zuma. 'We're different.'

What the ANC did insist on was that once we had decided collectively on a matter and a position had been adopted in Cabinet, that was that. It was expected that all participants would thenceforth accept the decision and refrain from airing any further criticism or unhappiness. We assumed collective, mutual responsibility, in keeping with the Constitution. Most often this was a blessing; at times it was a curse.

But the NP and the IFP, without sufficient numbers to overturn or veto any decision taken by Mandela's Cabinet, did not feel they were bound by this code. Instead, they went along with our decisions with little grace and then vented their frustration and opposition the moment they left the Cabinet office. This annoyed me, and many of my colleagues, greatly. It undermined the dignity and especially the legitimacy of our position as leaders and of our state. It made the foundation of our new order brittle. The other parties would claim that the GNU was not a real coalition but a constitutional provision to deal with an interim phase. So there was a rather direct culture clash between the two main protagonists in the Mandela Cabinet, the ANC and the NP.

The second uncomfortable fact of the GNU was that Mandela's Cabinet consisted of a cocktail of people who couldn't be expected to get along together. Mangosuthu Buthelezi's IFP had been involved in an intense, internecine war with the ANC, mainly in KwaZulu-Natal but also in the labour hostels of the Reef, for the best part of ten years. This war, as the Goldstone Commission of Inquiry confirmed in the early 1990s, had taken place with the backing of the apartheid government in the form of arms and paramilitary support. Literally hundreds of people had died during this conflict, including many ANC leaders – and IFP ones too – in KwaZulu-Natal and elsewhere.

The IFP had three portfolios in the Mandela administration, including the key one of Home Affairs, occupied by Buthelezi himself. Buthelezi's ministry was responsible for such important areas as future elections in South Africa as well as the management of immigration policy. Buthelezi, who had declined the premiership of the KwaZulu-Natal province, clearly recognised the powerful position he had been invited to assume in the national government. However, his antics kept all of us on our toes.

It was a few months after we had assumed office and taken our seats around Mandela's table that the mercurial Buthelezi took centre stage. One Sunday evening in late September, a spokesman for the Zulu royal house, Prince Sifiso Zulu, was being interviewed in the Durban studio of the SABC. The programme, *Agenda*, was one of South Africa's most popular prime-time political discussion programmes and attracted millions of viewers each week.

On the air, Prince Zulu commented about a struggle for political control of the Zulu monarchy and accused Buthelezi of appointing himself prime minister to the Zulu king Goodwill Zwelithini. Enraged by the discussion and by Prince Zulu's views, Buthelezi marched down to the SABC's Durban offices and burst into the studio where *Agenda* was being filmed. On live, prime-time television, and accompanied by his bodyguards, he then proceeded to berate Prince Zulu in an angry confrontation. Buthelezi claimed later he had no idea the cameras were still rolling.

It was an outrageous moment of political farce and as serious an infraction of freedom of speech as it was unbelievable. Here was a minister in Mandela's government doing what the apartheid ministers of old had done when they were unhappy with the views aired on the national broadcaster: they had marched into the SABC or called its director-general on the telephone and sorted things out.

Buthelezi's invasion of the SABC caused consternation within Cabinet and particularly within the ANC. Mandela, who was recalled from a short, well-deserved holiday to deal with the matter, was under pressure to fire Buthelezi from the Cabinet there and then. We all knew that with the profoundly violent recent history of KwaZulu-Natal so superficially held in abeyance by the IFP's membership of the GNU, something like this might have an unsettling effect on South Africa's most populous province. Violence was still simmering in the hostels and townships of the industrial eastern stretches of the Rand on the periphery of Johannesburg, where tens of thousands of IFP-aligned migrant workers from KwaZulu-Natal stayed far from their homes and families.

Mandela called a meeting in Pretoria at the presidential guest house to discuss the matter. He invited members of the National Executive Committee of the ANC, various trusted advisers as well as the ANC's alliance partner Cosatu. At the meeting, Mandela said the Buthelezi assault was a very serious situation that tested the core principles of our nascent democratic state. 'What should be done?' he asked. The discussion continued for two and a half hours. Could he really expel Buthelezi from Cabinet? What steps must Buthelezi take to re-establish public and political trust? Eventually, it was resolved that Buthelezi should be approached and asked both to express his regret for what happened and to undertake not to do anything like that again. I was asked to fulfil this awkward task.

We all approached the encounter with very mixed feelings, from anger to trepidation. As a democrat, freedom of speech and freedom of the press are both close to my heart. At the same time, there did seem to be a great deal riding on the meeting. It felt as if the future of our country was at stake. Buthelezi could be abrasive. In Cabinet, he was a brooding presence quick to take offence. Like De Klerk, if he was ever criticised – including once or twice by me – he reacted instantly, angrily and usually disproportionately.

At the meeting Buthelezi was told that Mandela had discussed the matter with other members of the Cabinet informally and regarded it as very serious. Freedom of speech was a central tenet of our new Constitution. We weren't the only ones who gave it such emphasis.

In the United States, freedom of speech was at times considered more important than the right to life. 'I think ministers and leaders have to help in developing this new tradition of free speech because we don't have a tradition of it yet,' I told him. He was asked to apologise to Cabinet and to South Africa.

To our amazement and relief, Buthelezi agreed with everything we said. I think the only other time Buthelezi has been so accommodating of me came years later on my resignation from Parliament, when he praised me for my 'fierce opposition to injustice or violation of human rights everywhere', saying of me then, 'he must have an anti-prejudice gene'. But at this meeting in 1990 Buthelezi clearly felt contrite about the incident. He probably also thought that he was better off inside the Mandela administration than out of it. He agreed it had been a stupid thing to do. And so after the next Cabinet meeting at the Union Buildings in Pretoria, Buthelezi appeared alongside Mandela at a media conference and made a public apology.

This was far from Buthelezi's most spectacular moment of glory. That particular highlight took place in September 1998 when we invaded the neighbouring country of Lesotho while Buthelezi was Acting President of South Africa – at the time Mandela, Mbeki and De Klerk were all out of the country. Lesotho is a mountainous kingdom entirely landlocked by South Africa and is utterly dependent on South African capital, skills and trade. It exports little more than labour. It had been experiencing domestic tensions for some months following accusations of poll rigging in the August elections. Prime Minister Pakalitha Mosisili had won seventy-eight out of eighty seats, though a commission of inquiry had been appointed, headed by Justice Pius Langa, to investigate charges of irregularities.

In mid-September, according to a report in the *New York Times*, Mosisili contacted the South African government and told them a coup was imminent and he had lost control of the army. Protesters had gathered in the streets of Lesotho's capital, Maseru. Mosisili invited South Africa to come to his aid and uphold democracy in Lesotho. On Tuesday, 22 September 1998, Buthelezi sent in the troops. As a result he gained the unenviable distinction of being the first leader of democratic South Africa to send our army off to war. By the end of the week, more than sixty people were dead. Downtown Maseru had been turned into rubble by looting and burning. Refugees were streaming out of the country, and there were reports of food shortages.

If it hadn't been so tragic, the invasion could have been written off as an appalling joke. Ill-informed, under-prepared and poorly instructed, the South African National Defence Force (SANDF) completely failed in all its objectives. They got lost on the way to the palace in Maseru and underestimated the level of local resistance. I suspect, with hindsight, that anti-democratic elements within the SANDF took pleasure in sowing confusion and inviting disaster and embarrassment. At the time Pik Botha was all for our occupying the Lesotho Highlands Water Project, a lifeline for Gauteng, a suggestion that appalled me as the line function minister.

Only afterwards did we as Cabinet mull over the disastrous sequence of events and rue the things we had not done. In our defence, I should say that we were genuinely concerned about the overthrow of a democratic government in Lesotho, as were many other nations in the sub-region and beyond. It may have been misguided to intervene, but it was after all in accord with the collective wisdom of the Southern African Development Community (SADC) and the Organisation of African Unity (OAU). All the same, you can't send troops into neighbouring countries without agreeing on the rules of engagement. Under what condition can you fire at foreign nationals? You need to clarify the rules of withdrawal. You need to know who is making the operational decisions and how the political leadership can communicate with this hierarchy. We had done none of these, and the results were evident for the world to see: Maseru was burning and we were responsible. The whole affair was an embarrassing débâcle.

After the landmark elections of 1994, our first Cabinet meeting was held in Cape Town on 23 May in Tuynhuys, the presidential office adjoining Parliament. The challenges we faced not only as a Cabinet but as a government were truly daunting. Close to half a century of apartheid preceded by three hundred years of colonialism had caused immense damage to our country and its people.

The democratic government which assumed power in 1994 inherited fifteen distinct systems of government and administration within the country's borders, consisting of the four provincial administrations within the former Republic of South Africa and eleven former 'independent states' and 'self-governing territories' established by the apartheid state. The Interim Constitution of 1993 required that they be rationalised into a single public service operating at national and provincial level, and as a result twenty-seven national departments and nine provincial administrations were created in terms of the Public Service Act of 1994. The new structures were then staffed with the country's 1.2 million public servants. The rationalisation process, which the Public Service Commission justifiably called 'a metamorphosis of epic proportions', had to take place with minimal disruption to the delivery of services.

As well as tackling the extremely serious problems of unemployment, poverty and inequality, we in the new government were expected to satisfy popular expectations raised by the transition to democratic rule; mediate the wide range of competing political, social and economic pressures which continued to be advanced by different social forces in the country; reconcile the almost universal tension between the internal needs of the bureaucracy on the one hand and the needs of clients and customers on the other; negotiate the difficult path between political democratisation and economic liberalisation; and confront the many challenges posed by the increasing globalisation of the economy.

All this was meant to be achieved by a group of people who had very little experience in the business of governing. The ANC in exile was a complex and wide-ranging organisation with its own issues and challenges. How could this compare to managing a country of close to forty-five million people?

The political compromises built into the 1994 democratic settlement (including the 'sunset clauses' in the Interim Constitution designed to protect the guardians of the old order) would inevitably limit our ability to execute an ambitious programme of socio-economic reform as effectively as we would have liked. On top of this we suffered, as the Presidential Review Commission pointed out in 1997, from a very long list of inadequacies and difficulties. Given this exhaustive list, our shortage of experience and the deep rifts that existed within Cabinet, our achievement of any success at all was virtually miraculous. And yet, it is fair to say that Mandela's first Cabinet, and the government that served under it, achieved a very great deal.

In purely legislative terms, the adoption of the Interim Constitution and then, in 1996, the final Constitution encompassed a total overhaul of the country's political culture and its political, social and judicial system. For the first time, South Africans had a Bill of Rights, broad equality and universal suffrage. We systematically recreated the country's entire legislative framework, abolishing, amending or creating hundreds of laws. In fact, South Africa's first democratic government passed 534 Acts of Parliament in its first five years, in itself a great achievement. Nor were these Acts minor technical adjustments. As Nelson Mandela said in his farewell speech to Parliament: 'These have been no trivial laws or mere adjustments to an existing body of statutes. They have created a framework for the revolutionary transformation of society and of government itself.'

Within Cabinet and Parliament, the whole culture of politics changed. No longer were suits and predominantly male representation the order of the day. Many parliamentarians and Cabinet ministers wore flowing African gowns and brightly coloured shirts. Overnight, South Africa's Parliament became one of the most gender-diverse legislatures in the world. We spoke different languages, we debated with an intensity unknown to previous South African parliaments, and established new rules of engagement in debate. We were obstreperous, sometimes downright rude to those whom we considered apartheid apologists, and set up portfolio committees some of which genuinely held the government to account.

More important than enlivening government protocol and changing the dress code, the Mandela administration also achieved some vital milestones that truly improved the lives of millions of South Africans. Little by little, admittedly in only a small but still important way, we began to address the awful legacy of apartheid. Just to quote examples from ministries of which I had oversight, within a decade some nine million additional people had been given access to clean water and sixty-three per cent of households access to sanitation. An integrated education system had been established, and by 2002 secondary school enrolment had reached eighty-five per cent. In a relatively short period of time, and given the scale of the structural obstacles and deficiencies we faced, these and other outcomes were indeed significant achievements.

One achievement of our nascent democracy of which I am particularly proud was the establishment of the National Conventional Arms Control Committee (NCACC). Its story tracks the journey South Africa followed from the immorality of apartheid to an order grounded in respect for human rights. The origins of the NCACC can be traced back to a public outcry that erupted in September 1994 when it was revealed that the parastatal arms manufacturer Armscor had shipped a consignment of weapons and ammunition to Yemen, a prohibited destination for arms in terms of Cabinet policy. Soon afterwards Mandela set up a commission of inquiry headed by Justice Edwin Cameron to investigate the Yemen deal. The commission reported that the débâcle was not an 'unfortunate accident', as Armscor had claimed, but an inevitable consequence of the systemic disregard, over many years under apartheid rule, as to where South African weapons ended up. The commission concluded by arguing that a fundamental review of arms control policy, legislation and decision-making was essential in the light of South Africa's new Constitution and democratic dispensation. This review took place and led to profound changes in policy and procedures. Among other things, a Cabinet committee, the NCACC, was established to formulate and oversee the execution of new policy on arms transfers. I was the NCACC's first chair and served until 2004, when I ceased to be a minister.

I learnt a number of things after seven years of being responsible for arms control in South Africa. The first lesson was that there must be regulatory mechanisms to provide for a policy of restraint. South Africa does not sell arms to all-comers; it doesn't sell arms to those who are considered to be consistently violating human rights. The second lesson I have learnt is that it is vital that there should be real political oversight of the system, unlike in other countries where civil servants effectively decide on every application, except for some of the very sensitive cases. Applications to the NCACC went through a very complex and extraordinary process. No other country in the world had a system where ministers on the NCACC spent, every month, three or four hours going through policy as well as through each and every individual application. The committee reported to Cabinet every three months and we also published the required details on the United Nations Register.

I am satisfied that our system worked well during my tenure of office. We imposed arms embargoes on Sri Lanka, Sudan, Swaziland, Zimbabwe and other countries, and ensured that civil servants were kept under control and did not go off into ventures of their own.

At the same time, I must admit that some ministers with close ties to the armaments industry were pretty gung-ho about arms sales. It was difficult to control the first Minister of Defence, Joe Modise, who never once referred to the criteria laid down in the legislation. Similarly, our ambassadors sometimes contacted their ministerial member of the Cabinet if they felt that I was going to be very strict. In the NCACC we acted by consensus, which meant that the debates were sometimes long and occasionally sharp and bitter. I must confess now that the consensus approach had its drawbacks, when sales to Algeria and Colombia grew apace, much to my regret. We were wrong, but in this activity one won some arguments and lost some.

I believe that it is in South Africa's national interest to have regulatory mechanisms. The definition of the national interest has, of course, been shaped by a combination of factors. It has been in South Africa's interests, for instance – and however much some may regret having an arms industry – to maintain the industry. This is because the Constitution lays down that there shall be a South African National Defence Force. In addition, we are a regional power, and we must take into account the needs of our region. Then, there is the Constitutional assumption that respect for human rights, as a fundamental feature of our domestic policy, has resonance externally.

It was a combination of factors that informed our decisions, chief among them that there had to be a consistent and massive violation of human rights in order for us not to sell arms to the country concerned. And of course we had to take into account that we cannot really act as moral censors of every country in the world. I am convinced, however, that South Africa's record in ensuring that we carried out a proper investigation as far as this is concerned was upheld, at least under my watch. Without question the regulatory system which we set in place strengthened the international recognition that South Africa enjoyed as a responsible country in matters relating to trade in conventional arms.

From early on, the Mandela Cabinet settled into a routine. Mandela himself was rarely present at the fortnightly meetings. As the five years of his administration drew on, he took less and less of a role in the day-to-day running of South Africa and its affairs. This work was mainly taken up by Mbeki, who would soon inherit the presidency. Sometimes even when Mandela was present, he'd ask Mbeki to chair the meetings.

We had to make up the actual functioning of Cabinet pretty much from scratch. There were systems and procedures in place, and committees and a secretariat, but these were designed for single-party Cabinets and not for the broad multi-party Government of National Unity, a concept that both Slovo and Mbeki claimed to have invented.

We met on alternate Wednesday mornings and carried on until two o'clock. We sat according to informal seniority with the President at the head, flanked by the Deputy Presidents. But there was always a bit of a tug-of-war as to where the rest should be. Mosiuoa Lekota, when he took over from Joe Modise as Minister of Defence, felt he should be nearer the President. Manuel, as Minister of Finance, sat close to Mandela. I sat next to Mbeki. Buthelezi sat next to me.

Perhaps the greatest surprise of the new Mandela Cabinet was the exclusion of one of the most able of all the ANC's leaders and its chief negotiator during the critical period of the early 1990s, Cyril Ramaphosa. For many of us, including me, Cyril was a shoo-in for Deputy President and was clearly Mandela's chosen heir. Instead of the capable Ramaphosa, South Africa got Alfred Nzo as Foreign Minister. Nzo was a veteran of the anti-apartheid struggle and was a dear, kind old man. He was no foreign minister, though. He had no experience of international diplomacy and no taste for the rigours of travel, the nuances of multilateral relations or the importance of guiding the new South Africa through a complex, globalised, modern world.

Mbeki was apparently the one who pushed Mandela to appoint Nzo to the foreign ministry. With Mandela spending so much of the next five years out of South Africa on international trips, a high-profile, go-getting foreign minister wouldn't have suited Mandela either. Mbeki was looking for someone who would be quietly amenable to his positions and ideas. Foreign policy was an area close to his heart. Indeed, Mbeki had been pursuing foreign policy for the ANC in exile for most of the preceding three decades.

On the 'Nat' side of the Cabinet, F.W. de Klerk had a large, well-oiled team of assistants and advisers that was highly efficient. He received thorough, timely briefs and he took voluminous notes. This efficiency, combined with De Klerk's willingness to actually read the Cabinet documents, made him a powerful presence and a dangerous adversary.

Manuel read everything, too, as just about every memorandum and document had financial implications. I read them all because I loved the business of government and because I wanted to be prepared. Like a terrier, I am also inclined to make a little trouble. I couldn't do this without the facts at my fingertips. I was almost always the first one to arrive at Cabinet meetings and I always made sure I had gone through the documents and papers before business began.

Early on I suggested that we agree on a code of conduct, but this did not meet with general acceptance. I was appalled by the attacks on the ANC, and even on Mandela, by Buthelezi and by De Klerk outside our cosy Cabinet meetings. I got angry and complained that it was out of order for leaders of political parties within the GNU to criticise us so publicly and vocally. Had not all our decisions been taken together?

I still wonder whether the GNU did not stifle the development of our country. Certainly, the Reconstruction and Development Programme (RDP), the landmark national initiative aimed at reorienting state and private spending to support faster and more efficient social and economic transformation, was a disaster. As the coalition was constitutionally ordained, you couldn't tell the lesser parties to shut up and get on with it. This was no voluntary or dependent coalition, though there was a degree of voluntariness. It was more like a shotgun marriage between partners who could barely conceal their antipathy for each other. Having said that, I have to add that for the first ten years we never voted on a single issue. Everything was decided on the basis of broad agreement.

The ANC had seventeen Cabinet portfolios in total. Some were occupied by cadres of real calibre, others were merely representatives pandering to powerful constituencies within the 'broad church' that is the ANC. Of this latter group, Stella Sigcau, the princess from Pondoland and Minister for Public Enterprises, was the pick of the bunch. Brought in by the ANC to represent the powerful traditional leadership element of the movement, Sigcau contributed hardly anything of value to the Cabinet in her ten years of service.

Like most of her colleagues, including the ANC contingent, Sigcau seldom bothered to read the Cabinet memos or documents that were the lifeblood of our business of government. This was true, sadly, of Jacob Zuma, when he was eventually appointed to Cabinet, and of a number of other ministers who all occupied key posts. Their collective lethargy was lamentable. In fact it was really only Thabo Mbeki, F.W. de Klerk, Trevor Manuel and I who consistently read all the Cabinet documents, which were intended to brief us on important issues and prepare us to make key decisions on behalf of our new country. This preparedness is probably why I was always ready and able to make interventions in debates on all ministries' portfolios – Madiba once called me in jest the 'minister of all portfolios'. I hate lateness, and I hate to be unprepared.

It is difficult to say where power was truly located in the Mandela Cabinet. For the Nats, Cabinet had never been the locus of political power. This resided elsewhere – in the party machinery, in the party council or perhaps even within the secret Afrikaner brotherhood, the Broederbond. In Mandela's Cabinet, the edges were blurred on crucial issues. And, as that first term drew on, Mbeki gained in authority. The national budget was largely a set of Mbeki's decisions, which is a painful thing for me to say in view of my friendship with Trevor Manuel. In truth, Mbeki decided on the important items in the budget for most of Mandela's term and for both of his own presidential terms (the second of which was cut short by a few months following his ousting at Zuma's hands). As competent and amusingly droll as Manuel was – I recall him asking with a smile on his face whether one of the ministers was drunk, given his total lack of understanding on a particular issue – it seemed to me that it was Mbeki who held the purse strings of the first three democratic dispensations. Mbeki's quiet authoritarianism grew steadily in stature and ambit and, by the time he became President, it overawed the executive branch of government in South Africa and every other tier too.

I found Cabinet meetings exciting, provided people had prepared themselves. I loved the cut and thrust of animated debate. When the tension mounted, as it frequently did, I found myself personally struggling with the non-smoking rule. Some might think I ducked out too frequently for a much-needed smoke, but the truth is I never left the building. I always made sure to stay within earshot of the debate. Within Cabinet there was always an air of expectation, and being a minister in a strategic department put you right in the forefront of policy development and implementation. It was an extraordinary, transforming, revolutionary period of governance, the most legislated period in South African history. There were unintended consequences to some of the legislation, which was hardly surprising considering the sheer volume of law that passed through our hands. The prevailing attitude was that we needed the basic law in place before we could even begin to think deeply about its implementation. We would sort out the glitches when they arose, but we couldn't transform a country by leaving in place a whole raft of outdated, racist laws. They had to go, and as quickly as possible.

Departmental memoranda were the currency of Cabinet, and they ebbed and flowed in great waves of paper and cardboard. The flow of memos was so heavy and voluminous that some ministers gave up trying to be *au fait* with their own policy documents, let alone those from other line ministries.

Cabinet memos were generally prepared by the department concerned. The memo stated in broad terms the policy that was to be adopted. These memos were sometimes rejected either because the minister responsible had no idea what was in them, or because they contained an idea that was bizarre or unrealistic, or both. As agreement needed to be reached on everything before proceeding, it only took two or three ministers in opposition to scupper an idea or plan. In order to prevent this or to dissuade the rash introduction of some policy document, lobbying would take place in the lead-up to the fortnightly Cabinet meetings. I might ring up a colleague on the phone and say, 'I have had a look at the memorandum you're tabling tomorrow. Please don't pursue it.' The memo, generally speaking, would then be withdrawn and perhaps reworked for subsequent introduction.

Draft legislation came via two different routes. The first was the tabling of a memo and the reaching of provisional agreement in Cabinet, after which a bill would be drawn up and then sent out to the public and then to Parliament for consideration or to the appropriate Cabinet committee from which it would go to Parliament. The second route involved the department preparing a white paper or discussion paper, out of which a bill would emerge, which would then be placed before Cabinet.

Much of Cabinet's work took place in the Cabinet committees which were clustered around different topics and which processed the draft legislation and policies prior to their being tabled in Cabinet proper. The idea was that these committees would facilitate collaborative decision-making and then make recommendations to the Cabinet. There were six Cabinet committees during the first two terms of South Africa's democracy, namely the committee for the economic sector; investment and employment; justice, crime prevention and security; the social sector; governance and administration; and international relations, peace and security. These committees were chaired by the President or the Deputy President (or the Acting President). I served on four of the six Cabinet committees.

The intention, from the way the Constitution was drawn up and from the way Parliament's method of business was envisaged, was that a genuine process of consultation with the public should take place on all legislation. My own experience of the consultation process was that it was only the interest groups or the people and organisations with money and access to lawyers who took part. Ordinary people seldom participated in the framing of legislation, which I suppose is not a unique trait of the South African legislative system. The consultation process is somewhat chimerical and dilatory.

Indeed, after a court challenge from HIV/Aids activists, the Constitutional Court upheld that consultation must be real, open and transparent. Parliamentary committees, as the HIV/Aids activist Zackie Achmat argued, are not the sovereign representatives of the people, as much as they might like to assume they are. It is Parliament itself that has this role.

The first Mandela Cabinet was very business-like. Every meeting had to find time to adopt the endless legislative proposals that had already gone through the Cabinet committees. If there were areas of actual or potential disagreement, the Cabinet would discuss each issue afresh. This largely depended on the extent to which proposals impinged on policies. One of our first decisions was to provide equal social security benefits to old-age pensioners of all races. We were all very proud of this first decision and there were some wet eyes about, including mine, as the announcement was made. It was an emotional moment.

Though Mandela didn't chair the majority of Cabinet meetings, it was always a great delight to have him there. He rarely intervened, but once he had a particular interest, he would become actively involved. I recall that one topic in which he took a special interest was a controversy in 1996 about whether people were being released on bail too easily. In some cases, people accused of some very serious crimes were being released on bail of little more than R100. Recidivism and further acts of violence by these cheap-bail criminals incensed the community.

Mandela attended a Cabinet committee meeting on the issue, which was chaired by me. There was a long discussion and I was happy to let it run along. As far as I was concerned, the Constitution states you have a right to bail and the right to be presumed innocent until proven guilty. The fact that this was being misinterpreted and that people were being denied bail, or that it was being set too high or too low, was the fault of the magistrates. We could find no area of agreement. Set bail too low and the criminals get out immediately, disappear and resume their criminal activities. Set it too high and innocent people would spend months, sometimes years, awaiting trial. At the end Mandela turned to me. 'It's all your fault we haven't come to a conclusion on this,' he said. But he accepted my response: the matter was too important to be rushed.

In my view, the Chief Justice should give policy direction on these sorts of issues, as they do in many other countries, and the magistrates should implement policy. I couldn't really understand their diffidence in leading on the matter. It certainly was a reminder that issues of policing, security and the criminal justice system constituted a major challenge to the first Mandela Cabinet, as well as to those that followed. As to the stalemate being my fault, I am not sure it was up to the line minister responsible for water provision and forestry to be decisive on this issue.

Serving under Mandela in his one and only period as President of South Africa was a time of great pride for me. It was of course a huge challenge, not only to deal with the dynamics of our fortnightly meetings but to press on with the issues surrounding my own portfolio. The Government of National Unity was hobbled by centuries of colonialism overlaid by almost fifty years of apartheid. It was dependent on a civil service that was undergoing total restructuring and reorientation. And it operated with the plaintive calls of the people for a better life in our ears. Somehow we managed. Out of the confusion of our beginnings we started to build something of value. Piece by piece, we built our new state. And with each brick we put in place, the lives of our people improved.

Thabo Mbeki was sworn in as President of South Africa, and the heir to lead Mandela's 'rainbow nation', on 14 June 1999. In reality he had been in charge for at least two to three years. As a professor, lawyer and an admirer of word-craft, poetry and intellectualism, it might be assumed I readily took a liking to Mbeki. He was engaging, thoughtful and extremely well-read. He peppered his speeches with quotations from fine authors and thinkers. He was totally committed to the ANC and had spent most of his adult life in exile. He was short in stature, enjoyed a smoke and relished a fine whiskey. On the surface, we had a great deal in common.

But though Mbeki and I go back a long way, I cannot say that our relationship was ever warm or affectionate. It was certainly unpredictable. I recall he came to my hotel room one evening in 1991. We were at the Wild Coast Sun hotel and casino in that beautiful part of South Africa known as the Transkei. The ANC's Constitutional Committee had been hard at work all day discussing the bill of rights and the ANC's constitutional proposals. At the end of the day, exhausted, I returned to my room. Before long, I heard a knock. When I opened the door, Mbeki was standing there. He had in his hands the large legal tome on constitutional law that I had borrowed from the Trinity College library. He was concerned it would be stolen if I left it in the meeting room. I thanked him, invited him in and we started talking. In truth, *he* started talking. He didn't stop for over six hours. It was captivating.

I was so enthralled by the spell of his words that, for fear of breaking it, I didn't want to get up even to switch the lights on. Slowly the room was enveloped in near darkness. I don't recall the details of our conversation, but we covered most elements in the politics of the negotiations. What struck me then, as it did when he foolishly allowed himself to be recalled from being President in 2008 by the victors of the ANC conference at Polokwane, was his total loyalty to the ANC. Whatever else one says about the man, you will never take his loyalty away from him. He was an ANC cadre to the core.

For all the camaraderie, the shared commitment to the ANC and the interests and joys we held in common, he could never quite make the leap from colleague to friend. It was as if his feelings were locked in a box and had sat in darkness for a very long time. Many of us made sacrifices in the struggle and Mbeki certainly made his. He barely saw his father when he was growing up, being orphaned by the vital organisational work and constant travel that Govan Mbeki undertook at that time for the movement. Perhaps it was not surprising he seemed incapable of showing warmth or empathy. Not all of us have Mandela's strength of spirit.

Mbeki never once asked me, for instance, about my cancer. Nor did he criticise me to my face. Once, as I recall, he spoke of an 'error of judgement' that I had committed, but even this he failed to elucidate or confront me about. When he told me there was to be no ministry for me in the 2004–9 Cabinet, there was no regretful apology, no 'good luck' or 'thank you'. He did say he needed younger blood in the Cabinet, though at least one of his appointments was older than me.

Mbeki seldom played to the gallery in public and was not very good at gyrating with hip movements on platforms like some of his colleagues. Mandela, of course, was the master at that. His jiggles pushed crowds to rapture. But Mbeki was no Mandela, and he was frequently at pains to downplay the lineage and the expectations. Mbeki was uncomfortable when outdated slogans were shouted by other speakers at mass meetings and almost never punched the air with his fist in the traditional movement salute. He was more at home in a suit, shirt and tie, sitting around a table discussing issues person-to-person – as he was in that dark hotel room on the Wild Coast in 1991. Mbeki had a special talent for identifying issues that other politicians preferred to evade, especially if their personal interests were at stake.

In Cabinet, Mbeki was hawkish in his attention to detail, and I mean that as no criticism. He scrutinised every little detail of the issues at hand in committee meetings. He wanted everything to be perfect. He listened closely during meetings, allowing everyone to make their points. At times he would allow the discussion to continue without much direction. He didn't want to circumscribe the Cabinet by intervening too early or give a sense of direction before it emerged by itself. Then, perhaps when the debate had moved too far off track or was going in circles, he intervened. 'Thabo is not the kind of person who will say that because we have done our work we should rush something through,' I recall one NEC member saying.

As the months went by in Mbeki's first term as President, a climate bordering on anxiety began to settle on the Cabinet. It was suddenly difficult to raise issues because you were unsure what kind of response there would be. You started to think very carefully about which battles to fight and which to let slide. As a minister, you very rarely made any assessment or criticism of Mbeki, if you could help it. You never knew what the response would be. We practised the injunction *maak toe jou mond* (shut your month). But I don't think this climate of silence and obedience within the executive branch of our new democracy was established consciously. All the same, it was not very healthy.

If there was one topic that overwhelmed Mbeki's reign in high office and tarnished it forever, it was HIV/Aids. It is common knowledge now that for many years South Africa's strategy for combating Aids was shaped by an antipathy on the part of Mbeki and his Health Ministers towards antiretroviral therapy. The early years of Mbeki's presidency were framed by Mbeki's questioning of the science of Aids and his support for Aids denialists and dissenters who believed that HIV was a harmless passenger virus and that Aids symptoms were caused by malnutrition and antiretroviral therapy. While Mbeki's scepticism about the link between HIV and Aids is well documented, perhaps an insight into the events in Cabinet during the Mbeki years might be illuminating.

On 22 January 1997, Mbeki – still Deputy President – called a special Cabinet meeting. At the meeting, a presentation was made by two scientists who were introduced as a team from the University of Pretoria: Olga and 'Ziggie' Visser. They told us about a new wonder drug that they claimed could cure Aids. The drug, which was called Virodene, had been making the headlines for some time. A few months before, South Africa's pre-eminent Sunday newspaper, the *Sunday Times*, ran a banner story on the discovery of Virodene by South African scientists, which it said 'arguably matches, or even surpasses, the first heart transplant performed by Professor Chris Barnard in 1967'.

Now here were the Vissers in front of us. They made a number of extravagant claims for Virodene P058, as they called it: that when given to humans 'it appeared to reverse full-blown Aids to HIV-positive', that it fought HIV 'in areas where other drugs cannot reach it, such as in the lymph glands and the brain', and had 'minimal side effects'. Olga Visser contended that her solution 'destroyed' the virus. At the end of the meeting the Vissers received a standing ovation from most of the Cabinet. Perhaps, collectively, we had suspended our disbelief.

Some of us, however, suspected that this Virodene was hocus pocus. As an academic and departmental dean I had sat on countless committee meetings where we considered the ethics and methodologies of proposed research projects. We always gathered enormous amounts of information and subjected the proposal to peer review and authorisation, especially when it involved human subjects. There was no such procedure under way with Virodene. I asked directly whether the University of Pretoria had approved the plan to test, and the answer was evasive. Later, of course, the university rejected the application out of hand. Here were two quacks selling snake oil, plain and simple. But what were they doing in Cabinet?

I looked around the room during that meeting and there was a strange look on people's faces. None were stranger than the faces of Mbeki and the Minister of Health, Nkosazana Dlamini-Zuma. They had the look of acolytes. They believed! They were at once hugely proud and totally impervious to any hint of scepticism. Here was a South African solution to one of the world's most pressing problems.

Virodene's champion was Mbeki himself. He couldn't wait to prove Africa's potential in the field of science and microbiology. When two HIV/Aids sufferers in their final stage of the illness were brought in to give their testimony to Cabinet, evidently as fit as fiddles, Mbeki and the Cabinet rejoiced. As Mbeki commented in a media conference afterwards, 'the Aids victims described what had happened to them as a result of the treatment. They were in the Cabinet room, walking about, perfectly all right. It was a worthy thing to see because the general assumption is that if you get to a particular point with Aids it really is a matter of time before you die.' Jakes Gerwel, the Cabinet secretary, later wrote: 'It was like a church confessional. The patients said they were dying, they got this treatment, and then they were saved! The thing I will always remember is the pride in South African scientists.'

Other than my question about university approval, I sat quietly in Cabinet and looked on in disbelief. Normally loquacious and therefore notable by their unwillingness to take part in the discussion that day were Trevor Manuel and Alec Erwin, silenced in part because of their scepticism. It made perfect sense that the solution to Africa's problems would come from Africa. There was a logic, even an inevitability, about it. It was preordained. Or was it?

We never, ever, in my ten years in Cabinet, agreed there and then to write a cheque for millions of rands for any project. But we did then, that day, and we wrote it out for snake oil. I was shocked. Not even Manuel could resist, as Mbeki promised to find the funds other than from Treasury. Later, at the usual post-Cabinet press conference, Mbeki said the government would 'look favourably' on the researchers' request for R3.7 million to continue their studies. In fact, the deal was already done and for considerably more than R3.7 million. My recollection is that it could even have been four times as much. It was unheard of to make such an award, for anything, at a Cabinet meeting.

In retrospect, we should not have allowed Mbeki, as Deputy President of the country, to have got so personally involved. Mbeki's personal sponsorship of Virodene was a mistake. But once Cabinet had reached agreement, the protocol was that it was not permissible for ANC ministers to subsequently criticise or undermine decisions. In this way we were bound.

The whole Virodene saga ended badly. After evaluating the protocol, the Medicines Control Council refused the Vissers permission to continue testing the drug. Aside from its lack of proven efficacy, Virodene was shown to contain a toxic industrial solvent that was liable to cause liver damage. For some, our worst fears were confirmed; for others, their bright hopes were dashed.

Sadly, Mbeki's engagement with HIV/Aids did not end with the Virodene dalliance. It endured throughout his time in executive leadership, turning like a worm in the rancid soil. By the time he became President in 1999, Mbeki had embraced the dissident Aids literature, which argued that the entire canon of established science on this subject was faulty. Further, Mbeki was in touch with the global dissident scientific community, including Peter Duesberg, a professor of molecular and cell biology from the University of California, whom he appointed to a presidential advisory panel on Aids set up in 2000.

When he was first appointed to the presidency, Mbeki insisted that his Cabinet ministers wear the red ribbon Aids badge as a symbol of our sympathy with and support for those suffering from Aids. On one occasion, rather like a headmaster, he asked us all, going round the table at Cabinet, where our Aids badges were and why they weren't on our lapels. Two years later, his own badge had disappeared along with those of many of the ministers. The belief had clearly waned. I kept wearing mine and did so right until I left Cabinet. My own view on Aids has always been framed by a constitutional law perspective. Our Constitution entitles every South African to dignity and equality. Anything that impinges on these rights, from homophobia to quackery, needs to be contested.

My opinion on the issue was sustained outside Cabinet as well. In early 2002 I arrived early as usual for a meeting of the ANC's National Executive Committee, as I always liked to get a head start on the paperwork. I saw a huge pile of documents on the table. On closer inspection, the documents were titled 'Castro Hlongwane, Caravans, Cats, Geese, Foot & Mouth and Statistics: HIV/Aids and the Struggle for the Humanisation of the African'. Even at first glance it was easy to see that this was an attack on the use of antiretroviral drugs, but it was also evident that the documents were not official NEC papers. In cavalier fashion I picked them up and hid them by throwing them all behind a table.

Before long, Peter Mokaba came into the room. Mokaba was a popular leader of the ANC Youth League and had been appointed a deputy minister under the Mbeki administration. He asked: 'Where are the documents?' When he spotted them, he cried, 'No, no, no, this is an official ANC document. I am entitled to distribute it to the NEC.' And so he did. The rumours doing the rounds at that time were that Mokaba had authored the scandalous 'Castro Hlongwane' attack on antiretrovirals. It was subsequently revealed that it could only have been written by Mbeki.

For some time after the tabling of the 'Castro Hlongwane' document, Mbeki and his Health Minister, Manto Tshabalala-Msimang, continued to fight a rearguard action to resist the introduction of antiretrovirals, to prevent mother-to-child transmission. Even after a Constitutional Court ruling forced her to provide the drugs, her reluctance continued to influence the sector.

But by 2003 Cabinet had had enough. Rebellion was in the air. Tshabalala-Msimang tabled the government's comprehensive policy on HIV/Aids, malaria and tuberculosis, and a famously heated and thorough debate took place in Cabinet. Of special concern was the roll-out of antiretrovirals. The end result was inconclusive. Mbeki, Tshabalala-Msimang and their supporters continued to argue against the distribution of Aids drugs, while the rest of us argued in favour. By the end, we were so exhausted that no summary was offered of our conclusions. Between the lines, just enough had been said for the pro-antiretroviral group to take advantage. Joel Netshitenzhe, head of the Government Communication and Information System, was taking the minutes of the meeting. His creativity in this role, together with the connivance of Trevor Manuel, allowed an agreement to be framed, the money to be allocated by Treasury, and the roll-out to begin. This was never going to be with the full support of either the President or the Minister of Health. Slowly but surely the distribution began nevertheless. At last the tide had turned and we could at last start offering assistance to our suffering people.

Another issue that will forever be associated with the Mbeki government was its handling of the problem of Zimbabwe or rather its ageing president, Robert Mugabe. My own relations with Mugabe were not cordial. I had first met him in 1974 in Lisbon at a conference of liberation movements. He was seated with Joshua Nkomo, with whose Zapu party the ANC at that time had close ties. I went up to Nkomo and invited him to Dublin to address a solidarity meeting. He agreed readily. As I was preparing to take my leave, Mugabe tapped me on the shoulder and asked, 'What about me?' I was taken by surprise as no leader of a liberation movement had actually sought an invitation before. I told him that I would put the question of his invitation to the executive committee of the Irish Anti-Apartheid Movement and then contact him. We never did, as the committee felt that our ties were with Zapu and that we could not invite him. But that was not the end of the matter. After Zimbabwe gained its independence in 1980, Mugabe was invited to Ireland on a state visit. It seems that it is customary for state visitors to be taken to Trinity College, which is redolent of hundreds of years of history. The head of the university asked me to attend because of the Anti-Apartheid Movement's involvement with the Zimbabwean freedom struggle. On the arrival of Mugabe, the Irish side queued up and were presented to him. When it was my turn, Mugabe did a double-take and refused to shake my proffered hand. Needless to say, I had not been invited to the celebrations earlier in the day.

As a Cabinet minister, I was to find Mugabe even more of an intractable problem. From 2000 and the launch of the 'land reform' programme, Zimbabwe sank deeper and deeper into crisis. Such was the assault on human rights, the deprivation of ordinary Zimbabweans and the stranglehold of Mugabe and his Zanu-PF henchmen that calls arose repeatedly for South Africa to intervene. Unlike Archbishop Tutu, I never believed this was possible. South Africa's only hope of influencing events in Zimbabwe was by diplomatic pressures, and Robert Mugabe had shown himself to be largely immune to these. This was not Mbeki's fault. Mugabe was obstreperous and stubborn in the extreme. He wouldn't listen to us, he wouldn't listen to the Southern African Development Community and he certainly wouldn't listen to the countries of the West. It was an untenable situation made all the more embarrassing and awkward for its proximity to our doorstep and for our historical ties.

All the same, I for one cannot remember a full discussion ever having taken place on the topic of Zimbabwe in Cabinet. I do recall, though, on one occasion in 2006 at a meeting of the ANC's National Executive Committee that I risked Mbeki's wrath. In a rare moment of breaking ranks with the ANC, I expressed strong criticism of Mugabe, admitting that I should have done so earlier. There was no reaction.

With Mbeki at the helm, the truly sensitive or difficult topics of state were kept off the agenda even at the level of South Africa's executive branch of government. While power hovered in and around the Mandela Cabinet, by the time Mbeki had assumed the presidency this kind of power resided elsewhere. Cabinet carried on with the day-to-day business of governance and the managing of our individual portfolios, but the difficult, controversial decisions, strategising and policy formulation took place within the rapidly expanding Office of the President.

Mbeki chaired a Cabinet sub-committee that dealt with the arms deal, which I didn't serve on, and great care was taken to ensure its discussions were not allowed to reach the public domain. Documents and Cabinet memos were collected at the end of the meetings and removed. I recall that Treasury, in the person of Trevor Manuel, was unhappy at one point about the cost of the deal. A long discussion took place within the National Executive Committee about it. There was an awareness, too, that while the primary contractors in the arms deal had acted appropriately, it was in the realm of the sub-contractors that difficulties had arisen. Here there were allegations of financial vested interests and profiteering, undue influence and corruption. I didn't take a special interest in the arms deal and the full Cabinet also didn't spend much time deliberating on the issues that came out of it.

It was also Mbeki's decision to elevate deputy ministers to the Cabinet, from which they had been previously excluded, though they would have no voting rights in meetings. The introduction of fifteen or so deputies totally changed the tone and function of Cabinet. From a fairly intimate and collegial arrangement, suddenly there were more than forty people in the room jostling for position and trying to engage on the issues. The geography was all wrong. We couldn't sit around a table any more, we had to sit in rows. It became even more difficult to criticise or debate. This was Mbeki's way of controlling things, of diffusing ideas through the weight of the people present. If you were minister of one of the less prestigious portfolios, you wouldn't get a chance to speak very often.

The supernumerary size of Cabinet once it was inflated to include the deputies made any intimate debate virtually impossible. Power was gathered with greater and greater concentration at the centre, around the Office of the President, with its growing cohort of researchers, advisers and consultants. And, as it did, the President grew more and more isolated and less in touch with the wishes and needs of his party and his people. His recall, at the ANC's national conference in Polokwane in December 2007, was the inevitable conclusion to the path he had chosen.

During the years of the first Mbeki Cabinet, we ministers focused on our own obstacles and constraints, overwhelming as they often were. Under Mbeki, I was Minister of Education, although I was only ever called to Tuynhuys twice in all that time. There was more than enough to keep me occupied in that most challenging of portfolios without trying to take on Mbeki when my counsel was not sought. I already had a reputation as the minister of all portfolios. I could not fight every battle and still reform the education sector. It was something of a blow when I was not reappointed. I found it frustrating not to be given the opportunity to see through the initiatives I had started in my tenure as Minister of Education, though it wasn't entirely unexpected. The statistics clearly showed an increase in matric pass rates during that period from 1999 to 2004, but I became resigned to the decision, although there were many tears in my department when my staff were told of the decision.

I remained an MP after leaving the Cabinet until 2008 when a combination of factors made me decide it was time to resign. A few months later I would have had to vote on the decision to disband the Scorpions, the special agency to investigate serious crimes and corruption, and I felt I could more easily voice my opposition from outside Parliament. I had served Parliament for fourteen years, since the first democratic election, and had continued to serve on the ANC's National Executive Council until its 2007 election, which I decided not to contest.

One of my last tasks I undertook as an MP was to chair an ad hoc committee to inquire into the Office of the Public Protector in 2006. On the strength of my work I was invited the following year to chair a multi-party Committee on the Review of State Institutions Supporting Constitutional Democracy. These are the Chapter 9 Institutions, so called after the chapter within the Bill of Rights in which they were proposed. Many countries in the world have similar bodies to our Independent Electoral Commission, Human Rights and Gender Commissions, the Auditor-General and Public Protector, legislated in the ordinary law of the land. We have gone further and accorded them a high status by placing them in the Constitution, charging them with the purpose of observing and protecting the human rights of all citizens, and requiring them to perform their functions without fear or favour. I have always felt that there has to be a sense of ownership of a constitution if it is to be relevant to ordinary people's lives. The story I often tell in this respect is that of an elderly man who slept in the doorways of shops in Dublin. After one evening when the police were a bit rough with him, he complained that they were in breach of his 'constitutional rights'.

At the time of the review committee's establishment, the National Assembly felt the need to investigate whether these bodies were performing their mandated responsibilities adequately. When we presented our report to Cabinet in July 2007 we made the point that the decision by the Assembly to undertake this exercise reflected well on the democratic order. However, the main proposal we made in the report – for the formation of a cohesive, strong and comprehensive umbrella human rights body with power to direct and influence political decisions with human rights implications – has so far come to nothing. That Parliament has still not debated our report is nothing short of scandalous.

In February 2008, when I retired from Parliament, I gave a farewell speech in which I paid tribute not only to all those individuals I had worked with, but also to the South African Constitution, whose creation I had helped shape. 'Our Constitution is not a dead document,' I said in my speech. 'It applies to all of us today, it urges us to care for all in our country, and to work towards a better life for all. It is our collective pledge. In other words it embodies values which this House must respect, and which permeate the laws we pass and indeed every aspect of our lives. It is a living instrument that enlarges our freedoms and restricts our power to act arbitrarily.'

I left Parliament to return to my first home, academia, having been appointed Professor Extraordinary in the Faculty of Law at the University of the Western Cape and Honorary Professor in the Faculty of Law at the University of Cape Town. By then I had gathered nine honorary degrees from universities in South Africa and Ireland and had been made an Honorary Fellow at my old alma mater, the London School of Economics, as well as the Colleges of Medicine of South Africa and the Royal College of Surgeons in Ireland.

A cartoon by Zapiro published soon after I left Parliament amused and pleased me immensely. In the foreground two citizens are talking. One says: 'He's vacated his seat but somehow it doesn't feel like he's left the building.' And sure enough, there I am, featured larger than life, atop of the parliamentary complex, caricatured as Jiminy Cricket. My top hat reads 'Parliamentary Conscience'. In my other hand I am holding a report called 'Ethics and the Pinocchio Syndrome'.

My good friend Richard Harvey from the Haldane Society of Socialist Lawyers, which I served as vice-president for many years, paid tribute to the cartoon, which he said 'captured brilliantly several facets of your character, including the "Counsellor in Moments of Temptation and Guide along the Straight and Narrow Path" as the Blue Fairy defines Jiminy Cricket's job description when appointing him to be Pinocchio's official conscience'.

In the email from the Haldane Society congratulating me on my retirement, he wrote: 'You have served, among your many other official capacities, as a kind of unofficial conscience of the National Assembly. And, assuming we define "Moments of Temptation" to refer not to whether to add one cube or two to an amber glass, but to the temptations to take short cuts in government and to think that ministers always know best without the need for democratic participation – and if we define "Straight and Narrow Path" to mean defending the path of human dignity and human rights against all who would seek to water down, divert, or redefine "rights" more expediently to suit their own stunted vision of humanity, then Zapiro has got it in one.'

It left me wondering if I was seen by my fellow South Africans, or at least some of them, as a vestige of the conscience that used to permeate the halls of Parliament when we took up our positions as the first democratically elected government. During that first term of office, under Madiba, I had chaired the parliamentary sub-committee on ethics. I spoke specifically to my own party when I reminded Parliament in my farewell speech that we have nothing to fear from pursuing oversight and accountability, and that it remained the responsibility of those I left behind to ensure that the rule of law prevailed and the Constitution was always protected and that the primary task remained to respond to the needs of the most vulnerable members of society.

9

Water and Trees

When Nelson Mandela appointed me as his Minister of Water Affairs and Forestry in May 1994, I could hardly imagine what it would entail. Many have said of me that at the time the only thing I knew about water was how much you needed to add to whiskey, and I suppose when I took up the post there was some truth in that. But I very quickly became keenly aware of the role of water in the quality of most South Africans' lives. I also realised I could put my legal qualifications to use in changing the law to address this problem directly.

In the great drought of 1993, schoolgirls from the Msinga district of KwaZulu-Natal walked many kilometres up into the mountains each day to collect dew. Every dewdrop was precious, all the more so for the fact that on the way opportunistic men often lurked behind rocks and brush to catch and rape the young girls as they searched for water. This daily struggle of life and death, of sustenance and survival, continued in South Africa even after the drought broke, fortuitously soon after I became minister. Nevertheless, the human toll involved in water collection remained unimaginable, even in the tiny district of Msinga.

Water, in Africa, is a story about women. It is women who traditionally collect water for the household, and the consequences of a lack of clean water and sanitation, such as infant mortality, are most keenly felt by them. Making clean water available within a short distance of people's homes is therefore about more than easing inconvenience. It is an act of liberation. If young girls don't have to spend hours and hours every day walking to distant rivers and streams, they are free to pursue other things, such as school. They are free too from the vulnerability of lonely searches and from predation, and not only at the hands of rapists. In one area alone, we found more than a dozen women had been killed by crocodiles while drawing water from muddy rivers. After one such appalling tragedy in KwaZulu-Natal, when a young woman collecting water from a river was killed by a crocodile, the response of one of my officials was to propose that we appoint a consultant. I announced there and then that we would not provide a consultant; we would immediately establish a project to ensure water was made available safely in that area. Fortunately an old 'homeland' project that had long fallen into disuse could be revived for this purpose.

For me, in other words, the question of water provision was not simply about the invocation and use of a right of access to water, the fulfilment of a constitutional provision. It was about the emancipation of women from laborious, time-consuming chores. It was about enabling people to have access to what is literally the source of life.

Even after the drought, the sheer scale of water deprivation in South Africa and the hardship this scarcity inevitably entailed were almost overwhelming. Of South Africa's estimated population in 1994 of just over forty million people, a third did not have access to clean water. More than half did not have access to adequate sanitation. Lack of toilets meant even more rapid pollution of the rivers and streams, more virulent illnesses and widespread human indignity. In the former 'homeland' areas alone, as many as thirty per cent of schools had no direct access to water and, therefore, no toilets or adequate sanitation. How could any government build a school where there was no water or toilets? This was just one more charge on the indictment sheet against apartheid for crimes against humanity. These mind-blowing statistics were made all the more vivid by my own childhood experiences. I could remember all too well the horrors of an outdoor toilet and the lack of privacy and cleanliness.

Almost immediately after the announcement of my appointment, I got a call from the man who was to be my head civil servant, the Director-General, Tinus Erasmus. He advised me that I needed to change the name of my ministry. The President had made me Minister of Water and Forestry. This, Erasmus told me, was 'dangerous'. Most of South Africa's water, and particularly the supplies for the cities of Johannesburg and Pretoria, came from the province of KwaZulu-Natal, which was politically controlled by the opposition Inkatha Freedom

Party. Making me Minister of Water would incur the ire of the powerful federalists in the province, of whom there were many, as I would be seen to be interfering in the provincial governance of KwaZulu-Natal. Better to change the name of the ministry to Water Affairs rather than just Water, he suggested. This made my ambit more national and would include infrastructure and policy. I was not entirely persuaded at the time, but as the 1993 Interim Constitution was silent on the matter, I went along with it. I asked the President's Office to make the change before the proclamation was drawn up and was duly appointed Minister of Water Affairs and Forestry in Mandela's government.

It very soon became apparent to me what the wider ambit of 'water affairs' meant. It was not just about the wet stuff; it was indeed the very essence of the government's Reconstruction and Development Programme. Water and politics are inextricably linked. The right to life and security in a healthy and durable environment has to be one of the basic principles of human rights and development; guaranteeing the well-being and dignity of the individual is a constitutional imperative. Moreover, the needs of future generations rely on responsible management, rational exploitation, and conservation and protection of our resources.

Much, much later, my colleague and friend Trevor Manuel paid me a wonderful tribute in his speech on the occasion of my retirement from Parliament: 'Madiba's faith in Comrade Kader was so completely unbridled. He knew that he could depend on Kader to take on a portfolio whose predecessor few remembered, even then. Kader attacked the portfolio with gusto, hauled out the RDP, calculated the number of miles of water piping – never kilometres, but miles – and the number of taps that the country needed ... Water had just become the sexiest portfolio.'

But at the time, when I first considered the scope of the task I had been set and the personnel I had been allocated to accomplish it, I was horrified by what I found. Apart from Tinus Erasmus's early overture, the reception I encountered in the department was less than friendly. On my first day in the office I think only the cleaning staff greeted me. The senior officials in the Department of Water Affairs were nearly all engineers. This was understandable – after all, the department was run by and on behalf of farmers and urban whites and the provision of water was seen as a technical issue rather than a social one.

Many previous ministers were farmers and fairly nondescript. It was alleged that one minister got the department to build a dam on his farm, but I could not confirm it as everyone clammed up. There was one man who stood out among my predecessors. This was Deneys Reitz, author of *On Commando*, a great, classic account of guerrilla warfare during the Anglo-Boer War, who turned into the epitome of an eccentric Englishman, complete with spats and winged collars. One of his claims to fame is that he was reported to have dived from the top of the achingly beautiful Augrabies Falls on the Orange River.

My engineers were not interested in politics – other than perhaps a fairly unthinking support of apartheid. I would hazard a guess that some of them were members of the secret Afrikaner association known as the Broederbond (the Brotherhood). Some still wore the safari suits associated with the Afrikaners of old and nearly everyone seemed to wear grey shoes. Managing a team of dozens of engineering *broeders* felt a very long way from the halls of Trinity College Dublin and the energy of the anti-apartheid struggle. I don't think my Director-General, Tinus Erasmus, was a member of the Broederbond, in part because of his early civility to me and his warning about the name of the ministry. He was also a keen fan of that madcap BBC Radio group of comedians, the Goons, the epitome of eccentric English comedy. I did not believe that anyone who loved the Goons could keep a straight face through a meeting of *broeders*.

Engineering in the past had been an all-male enclave and the entire top management I inherited comprised white males. Virtually everyone had, at some stage in his career, been a resident engineer at the construction site of one of the many major dams that make up the country's water infrastructure. The management approach was typical of an engineering business and the style, as in the rest of the civil service, was very hierarchical.

A month after I took office, I called my senior staff together and expounded at length on the government's expectations in a country where sixteen million people had no access to clean water. 'This is not going to be a department of engineers only,' I said, 'and there must be total commitment to the government's reconstruction task. If you will work with me, well and good; if not, you should take early retirement or I shall fire you.' This caused quite a stir. I soon realised my job was not going to be so easy. When I presented the first draft of the revised national water policy at a meeting of all the senior officers, it was met with absolute silence. As the only darkie at the meeting, I found the atmosphere distinctly uncongenial. I was placed at the head of a long table. Finally, the silence was broken by a deputy director-general seated at the other end. Without a word of introduction, speaking sharply and aggressively, he said, 'Minister, this is your draft white paper, not the department's.' I had to make it clear then and there who was boss. I knew that the minister was responsible for policy. 'Well,' I said, 'since you don't like the draft of the policy paper and since I will have to work closely with the line functionaries, I am announcing that you will no longer be in charge of the department's finance, staff and the Lesotho Highlands Water Project.' After some silence there came a plaintive query from the other end of the table: 'What is left for me to do?'

It was evident that the department's spending and consumption priorities needed to be revised and that the entire outlook of the department and its staff needed to be shifted dramatically. The old technically oriented and very hierarchical management might have been acceptable in the past, but this was to change dramatically, particularly as the department grew from a staff of seven thousand when I first took over, to twenty-six thousand and, ultimately, to thirty-three thousand through the incorporation of the water- and forestry-related staff of the former 'homelands'.

It was also apparent that this change was not going to occur naturally or by a gradual evolution. Change would need to be imposed. In July 1994, two months after taking office, I established a transformation committee aimed at completely overhauling the department. I also put together a strategic management team and brought in several talented people and organisations to help, such as Trevor Fowler from the Gauteng legislature; Professor Mandla Mchunu, who would head the department's institutional transformation process; Tony Heard, former editor of the *Cape Times*; and a highly professional team from RGA Consulting and Ernst & Young. Among others seconded to the team were Len Abrams, who brought tremendous grassroots experience to the development of water services policy, and Tally Palmer, who brought scientific excellence to the development of water resources policy. I ordered a complete policy and staffing review to address the fundamental problem, that the department was completely out of touch with the millions of South Africans who need clean water and sanitation. It was a problem that might have been noted in principle by the department, but it was not being dealt with in practice. The central focus of the department must be people, I told my senior officials.

Of course there was resistance. Early on, the transformation committee struggled to pin down officials and get hold of documents. The committee members were regarded with suspicion and antipathy, even by members of my senior interim executive team. I had to issue a departmental directive instructing total compliance. The directive stated, 'My advisers will be accepted by the interim management and will not be considered as intruders in the department. From now on they will have full and direct access to every level of the department with my full authority. We are either going to work together on the platform on which the new Government of National Unity was elected or, like the proverbial rats on a sinking ship, we shall go down fighting one another ... Who wants that?'

Gradually, like an oil tanker changing direction in mid-ocean, the department began to turn around. It was to take two years before we were headed in the right direction. By 1998 just half of the senior management in my department were engineers. The balance comprised economists, environmental scientists, geologists, even MBA graduates, former diplomats and urban policy specialists, and obviously the department was no longer an all-white or all-male affair.

My style as minister was soon to shake department officials out of any misplaced complacency. I liked to tell them that I wanted my officials to be always on tap, never on top – and I wasn't joking. I was without fail at my desk in the morning before most of my staff arrived, and was last to leave in the evening. Inevitably I took home with me a stack of submissions that I would usually study at the kitchen table. I insisted on regular, direct contact with my staff. Although I sometimes complained that my office reminded me of a railway station, when once or twice my assistants tried shutting my door I would soon start to feel uneasy about how quiet it all seemed. I insisted on an 'open-door policy', quite literally.

The procedure before I took office had been very clear. Any inquiry or issue was forwarded to the next official up the line, who would then take it to the next in charge, and so on until an answer could be found, and then it would be sent back slowly down the line. I very rapidly brushed all that aside. My staff soon came to realise that if they couldn't give me an answer rapidly, I would get on the phone and find it myself. In what I believe in time came to be known as the 'morning circus', I would have my special adviser call in all those who wanted to speak with me that day, at one time. It took a while for them to get used to my method of holding simultaneous conversations with six or seven people. I would ponder the answer to one as I listened to the question of another, while issuing instructions to a third. I suspect I caused them some confusion, but my memory never let me down. I realise they probably found this disconcerting. I remember an adviser once seamlessly switching midway through his briefing on water conservation to pass some comments about cricket – he knew I have a great passion for cricket – but I was on to him. I knew he was testing me to see if I was listening. I was – and made sure he knew it.

My officials soon learnt that I did not accept any work that was less than perfect. Many memos that fell short of my standards were literally thrown back across the room at their authors for a redrafting, and I never forgot any instruction or order that I issued. I oversaw every detail of the workings of the department. Although there were those who could not accept the changes and left the department fairly soon, I believe I won over almost all of those who stayed, many of whom had probably supported apartheid. I spent time with them, listening to them, debating with them, and explaining what I wanted from them. In the end, I didn't simply out-argue them. I believe I convinced them of the need for our department's commitment to social justice and, I hope, transformed their thinking, winning them over to the higher purpose that could be served through the work of the department.

My advisers have told me they never quite knew who was actually the adviser, because I didn't always take their advice. Though I may have come into the department knowing very little about water management, I made a point of getting to terms with the technical aspects as soon as possible. Maybe it was all those years at Trinity College, but I tended to point out inconsistencies in the arguments of my advisers, perhaps correct some of their facts (even in their areas of expertise), and I couldn't help improving their spelling and grammar for good measure.

My speech writers complained that there was no point to their efforts – I preferred to speak off the cuff. One of them later confessed that he would always include a few split infinitives – something he knew I took great exception to – in the hope of diverting my attention.

There were some fights in my department between the old guard and the diverse range of specialists I had drawn in, but there were also some surprising alliances that the 'bureaucrats' formed when they successfully reined in new staff who wanted to take their innovative schemes too far. A deep (and, on the face of it, unlikely) bond developed between Tinus Erasmus, the Director-General, and Guy Preston, who ran most of the department's water conservation projects, based I suspect to some extent on their shared passion for the Goon Show. Guy came to play an essential role in my department. Slightly eccentric, he could be rather intense. I recall him regaling me at a luncheon with details of a position paper he was working on at the time on water management. It was inappropriate timing, and when he paused to let me respond, I looked pointedly at him for a moment and then asked, 'Do you dye your moustache?' He was suitably amused at the gentle rebuke.

I left no one in any doubt about my management style. Advocate François Junod, who worked on water legislation and had served eight ministers of water affairs, all under apartheid, was pretty unequivocal about me in a 2004 report by the government's Water Research Commission in Pretoria. True, I was described as 'stubborn' and 'ruthless', but I think he was actually endorsing my ministerial performance, calling me 'a brilliant minister with a holistic view, sound approach to water law and with a brilliant mind and legal background that can be very stubborn at times. He is a powerful visionary with a strong political will.'

One of my advisers, Len Abrams, likes to recall the day the Water Research Commission came to present to me. It was immediately clear that they expected little by way of response or direction from me, used as they were to an unthinking and largely uncaring minister who would happily rubber-stamp their proposals. They soon realised that this was not going to be business as usual. I had finished reading their written report long before they finished presenting it, and to speed things along I interrupted them with questions, challenging specific aspects and assumptions. As Len recounts the story, they went away with their tails between their legs.

According to one of my former officials, Eberhard Braune, 'As transformation structures came into being, we started to get a glimpse of the pressure that the new minister was exerting on his managers. Information was needed all the time. Also, he insisted on immediate changes. He would, for example, walk out of a meeting if there was no woman present. It was clear from the very first steps of transformation that the department would have to be more representative and more participative.'

Without being openly hostile, the officials were often sluggish and reluctant. One of the first instructions I issued as minister was to order the department to install water at the home of former ANC president Albert Luthuli's widow. 'Minister,' I was told, 'such a proposal will need far more time than you envisage.' I suppose they imagined this was some kind of stunt or, worse yet, a personal favour. I dug in my heels and insisted: 'Not only will these instructions be carried out speedily but I want you to tell me the date and time when I will be able to go in person to turn on her water supply.' I remember with great pleasure the day I visited the small house in Groutville where Nokukhanya Luthuli lived, to perform this simple action. It was at the same time profoundly symbolic to the officials in my department and to the people they were employed to serve.

I also instructed the department to begin mapping the underground water in KwaZulu-Natal immediately. Six weeks later, after repeated enquiries, I discovered that the work hadn't begun. I was told the department didn't have the R400,000 it needed to undertake the work. I read my officials the riot act. I reorganised the duties of a deputy director-general, chastised him for insolence and issued a memo to all staff declaring, 'There seems to be the mistaken notion that all that is necessary is for the department to adjust to the new minister. This is a grave mistake. Things will never be the same again.'

I then went on to say that these civil servants' jobs were not as secure as they had assumed. 'We are now in an interim phase,' I told them. 'All senior management officials are acting in their present posts in an interim capacity. The Constitution provides for job security, but not retention in a particular job.' A newspaper article appeared at the time in the *Mail & Guardian* under the headline 'Tough-talking Asmal tackles the old guard'. The sub-heading read: 'A frustrated new minister of water affairs warns his civil servants that he expects attitudes to change, or else ...'

One of my first functions as minister was to open an international conference on dams at the International Convention Centre in Durban. The first night was devoted to a social evening, ending with a video of the building of the Verwoerd Dam, the largest structure of its kind in the country and, I was told, the largest dam in the southern hemisphere. The video screened that night was very old-fashioned and reminded me of the Movietone newsreels of my childhood. The voice of the narrator was in that appalling *faux* documentary style. It was public relations at its most obvious and most embarrassing.

I soon noticed there wasn't a single black person in the film. This was particularly ironic given that it was black South Africans whose lives and livelihoods had been most directly affected by the building of the Verwoerd Dam. Of the plight and needs of the people who had lived there before the dam's construction, there was not a single mention. It was a cringe-making, apartheid-like rendition of the story of the dam. Never again would I allow my department to organise a function without my approving the script beforehand. The World Commission on Dams later conducted a study of the consequences of building this dam and only then, when I was already chairman of the Commission, did I learn what had become of the cattle, which were the wealth and livelihood of this displaced community.

One of the first things I did on becoming minister was to rename the dam: after all, Hendrik Verwoerd had been the chief architect of apartheid. I formed a high-powered committee to investigate the options, one of which was to call it the Luthuli Dam. A tribute to Albert Luthuli appealed to me of course, but Luthuli had no historical or political relationship with this part of South Africa, so in the end we named it the Gariep Dam. Gariep is a San word meaning the 'wilderness' and I wanted the long-ignored role of the San people in our history to be acknowledged. At the request of the senior officials I did decide to leave in place a plaque stating that the dam had been opened by Betsie Verwoerd, the wife of the Prime Minister at the time, and I have often wondered if it was the right thing to do. But in those early days of fragile reconciliation between the old and the new we had no desire – indeed no need – to destroy the symbols of the past. From our position of strength, with the clear support of the majority, we did not need to disregard or disrespect those memories that remained important to our former opponents. Louise still has the painstakingly hand-embroidered cushion given to us on that trip by schoolchildren from the local community. That cushion was an expression of the enthusiasm and optimism of these young people and confirmed for me that petty acts of revenge had no place in the new society we were constructing.

When I became minister, not only did I inherit a technocratic department, but I encountered an obsession with a supply-side approach to water management that focused almost exclusively on the needs of the white minority. In 1994 the idea of saving water rather than building new dams was seen as a mere curiosity. The notion of using what water resources you have more efficiently was hardly considered. It was up to me to introduce the idea of directing the budgets into water conservation efforts, which are pro-poor. It took a lot of convincing that money spent on saving water could, in the right circumstances, make available as much water as a dam costing twice the amount. I put public theory into private practice, using grey water in my garden at home in Cape Town, to the amusement of some of my department officials, who firmly believed my plants would die. But they were proved wrong.

It was evident as I began to evaluate my domain that the environment, which included water and forestry, presented very major challenges. It was increasingly being recognised that desertification, unchecked deforestation, soil depletion, the warming of the earth as a result of the 'greenhouse effect', the disappearance of species, the depletion of the ozone layer, pollution and toxic wastes were causing a variety of meteorological and atmospheric changes that were threatening water security and the water needed for the ecological functioning of natural systems. The situation called for urgent measures and concerted action by the entire international community.

In South Africa, unbridled capitalist development had caused untold damage to people and natural resources. The mining sector, for instance, had been South Africa's biggest industrial sector for more than a hundred years. Being a thirsty industry, it placed considerable strains on the water supply and contributed to the degradation of the environment. Furthermore, bulk domestic and industrial suppliers were rapidly outstripping irrigation for agriculture as the major source of demand. Added to that, population growth and rapid urban migration had led inevitably to growing demands for water and sanitation.

Globally, there was a growing trend to build water resource management into environmental policy. In South Africa, though officials and professionals in the water sector were presumably aware of these developments, the issues remained on the policy backburner. By 1994, the provision of water to cities, businesses and farms and the management of the country's forestry resources were in crisis.

The mishandling of the devastating drought in the late 1980s and early 1990s was a dramatic illustration of how poorly equipped the department was to cope with the human dimension of water. I received continuous, plaintive complaints from the new provinces begging for assistance in the face of the drought. One letter from a provincial minister in the drought-stricken north said, 'We have received very little assistance – if any – from the regional management … I do not see us managing to resolve the problem given the pace with which your department is moving.'

While the urban–industrial sector, which had been the focus of the previous government, could cope with the drought as it had excellent bulk water infrastructure, the rural areas were hit severely and were in grave difficulties. The crisis was at its worst in the former 'homelands', where the apartheid government had been particularly cynical when it came to fulfilling its obligations. Looking at the way the sector had been set up, I realised that the legislation we had in place was designed for a water-rich country, though South Africa is dry. The little water we had was appropriated by those who had political power on behalf of the farmers (one of the National Party's key constituencies), white residents and businesses. South Africa's water policy was more interested in catering for the needs of cattle than its citizens.

Millions and millions of people had simply been left, thirsty and dirty, to survive as best they could among the dusty fields and the parched riverbeds. This was apartheid mismanagement at its most grotesque, totally oblivious of the human toll it was exacting on the country's most precious resource, its people. The drought emergency relief programme was not even part of the department's activities but was co-ordinated by other organisations. Government had totally abrogated responsibility. This so incensed me that there were times in management committee meetings that I was driven to the point of bringing out my specially designed sealed ashtray and taking a few calming puffs at a cigarette, despite the 'no smoking' signs that I had insisted be put up in the department.

My new staff members persuaded me that my department could initiate projects that had never before been carried out by the water ministry. What was once an insignificant ministry, to which the disgraced former apartheid Minister of Defence, Magnus Malan, had been relegated, in time became a model of social engineering. I started off with the Community Water Supply Programme, which was initiated as a Presidential Lead Project in August 1994 with an allocation of R282 million. This set a foundation that has been built upon by my successors. Today the backlog of those needing a basic water supply is close to being erased – some have called this the greatest accomplishment in water management of any government in the world.

Back then, I often found myself questioning the approach to basic water supply, in terms of which stand-pipes were installed within two hundred metres of households. The costs were high, and I suspected that some of my officials were not questioning or challenging the engineering solutions put forward by the then largely untransformed engineering companies and engineering faculties in the universities. Another challenge was the cost of water supplied to the poor, usually in urban settings. In many of these badly constructed houses, the metal pipes were laid in concrete, and would corrode on the householder's side of the water meter. The leakages would become enormous, and the householders would be expected to pay for water that they had not used. I refused to accept this, especially when more innovative approaches were being proposed by my far-sighted new officials, with far lower costs, better health implications, improved conservation opportunities and a higher assurance of supply.

One of the initiatives I am most proud of was the National Water Conservation Campaign, which was based at least in part on the simple premise that significant environmental – and social – gains were to be made by clearing alien vegetation. In time, this led to the internationally recognised Working for Water programme as its flagship. But that was only one of fifty-two different national initiatives within this campaign, for which I won fifteen awards during my tenure as minister, including the Gold Medal for Conservation by the World Wide Fund for Nature SA. I was also asked to serve as vice-president of the Independent World Commission on the Oceans from 1995 until 1998.

For me, one of the highpoints of the conservation campaign was the '2020 Vision for Water Conservation', a programme we took to schools to educate young people about tracking water usage, firstly in their schools and also in their homes. Our department officials worked with them, conducting audits of water usage at the schools, working out alternative water conservation strategies, and then measuring the amount of water, and money, saved.

With Nelson Mandela as patron-in-chief, the National Water Conservation Campaign aimed to secure the sustainable, efficient and equitable supply and use of water in South Africa, premised always on the notion that there had to be social justice in access to water in our country. One of the first schemes within the department's campaign was set up early in 1996 as a pilot programme in the coastal town of Hermanus in the Western Cape. Called the Greater Hermanus Water Conservation Campaign, it was a twelve-point programme to ensure the long-term water security of the Greater Hermanus region as a cost-effective alternative to diverting water from the Theewaterskloof Dam. One of its basic tenets was the simple principle that the more water you use, the higher the cost. In other words, bigger users pay more for their water. Through this simple water conservation strategy we reduced water usage in the area by thirty-two per cent. We also introduced an insurance cover for people who had major leaks so that poor people would not suddenly find themselves with a massive water bill. However, the town was then under the control of the National Party, and they were not completely enthusiastic about our plans. My aim to introduce the concept of free basic water within an escalating block-rate tariff fell on deaf ears in Hermanus.

It was left to the city of Durban to be the first to introduce free basic water, and to be the forerunner of the new policy for water in the country. We achieved this at a meeting where my adviser and I came together with the mayor of Durban and the head of Durban Water to discuss the problem of water theft. We agreed to help them combat this on condition that they introduced free basic water. It took some persuading but we had the ever-practical head of water supply on our side. When he explained to the mayor that it cost more to bill for the first six kilolitres per month than the revenue received, the argument was won. Though my own departmental officials were less than enthusiastic, this step launched us in a direction that was not to be reversed.

The person behind Working for Water and other water conservation initiatives was Guy Preston. I had first met him when he accosted me at Cape Town International Airport, interrupting my inevitable smoke break with a firm but polite request that I look at the posters he happened to have with him featuring the work he had been doing at the University of Cape Town on reducing water and energy usage in the Kruger National Park. I had to step outside the smoking zone, trying to clutch his posters with one hand while determinedly hanging on to my cigarette with the other, holding it at arm's length to keep it within the smoking section. It took quite a while – Guy insisted I look at six posters!

I encountered Guy again at a public meeting that I convened in March 1995 to gather public views on the controversial plans to build a dam on the Palmiet River deep in the heart of the unique Kogelberg biosphere – to the bemusement of my officials, who were not used to ministers soliciting public opinion before acting. Guy spoke out strongly against the building of the dam. At that moment I ducked out of the meeting for my inevitable smoke break, but I didn't go far. I was intrigued by what I heard, listening to the whole debate just out of sight, and the very next day I called Guy in. At our first meeting he declined a drink (being a teetotaller) and a snack (being a vegetarian). Though I couldn't help looking quickly under my desk to see if he was wearing sandals as well, I knew I had encountered someone with a deep commitment to environmental issues and asked him to join my department as one of my advisers. He readily agreed although at first he had to find his own funding for the post.

I sought support from the Reconstruction and Development Programme (RDP) to kickstart the Working for Water programme and approached the minister at the time, Jay Naidoo. He obviously required business plans – so we produced these virtually overnight – but initially I asked him to just trust me. He committed R25 million and we launched Working for Water on 16 October 1995 at the Theewaterskloof Dam outside Cape Town. Wearing the unmistakable yellow T-shirt (the production of the T-shirts with Working for Water logos later became a job-creation programme in itself), I set to work, with slasher in hand, to remove the first invasive alien tree in the programme – a black wattle from Australia. It was a tough plant and took several attempts on my part. But at last it lay on the ground and, with a wink at my staff and the television crew standing by, I stood up proudly and declared myself 'One Slash Asmal', a name that stuck for many years.

I recall at one of the first meetings of Working for Water, in the Western Cape, I faced an audience made up probably equally of black African and coloured workers. They had seated themselves in separate groups. I decided there and then – and said it to them – that I never wanted to see that again. We set out to overcome barriers: language barriers and geographical divides. That was what I wanted to achieve in our programmes, for our aim went well beyond water provision. The initial R25 million, which was allocated for six months, turned into R60 million the next year, and today stands at over R1.5 billion for the various programmes.

Working for Water became the biggest water conservation programme in Africa and its spin-offs were considerable: empowerment and training of workers, industries for productively using alien wood, even the provision of crèches and reproductive health education programmes for the women who spent their days engaged in the highly labour-intensive, and often dangerous, task of hacking the invasive alien vegetation. We worked closely with those members of the communities who were affected by the improvements in resources as well as those directly engaged in the programme, providing education on HIV/Aids and distributing condoms, and even intervening in cases of domestic abuse and other social problems. One of the most satisfying achievements of this innovative programme was the way it developed the workers' skills and expertise. We took particular pleasure in saying goodbye to a few of our employees who left us to start up their own business, clearing alien trees from farmers' land, an initiative of their own making but built on the skills they had gained while employed by Working for Water. We even had staff members whose growing interest in environmental issues, combined with what they had learnt from climbing mountains to work on dangerous terrain, empowered them to undertake a different sort of journey altogether: they successfully climbed Mount Kilimanjaro.

Make no mistake, it was hard, back-breaking and often dangerous work. We felt a strong responsibility as employers for the well-being of those working on the programme. Injuries, even deaths, although in many ways inevitable in dangerous work of this kind, were always devastating. Nevertheless, by the end of 1998, the Working for Water programme was employing forty-two thousand people, of whom, as I insisted, more than half were women, in more than three hundred projects across the country. Their task was to clear invading alien plant species, which robbed South Africa of up to seven per cent of its rainwater 'runoff', overwhelmed the most productive land and threatened the country's biological diversity.

Obviously I have my team of advisers and all the many individuals who worked on and supported the water conservation programmes to thank for the unprecedented success of this initiative. These were the new brand of South Africa's civil servants. I was moved when told recently by one of the programme managers, Dr Christo Marais, that I was 'the parent' of water conservation work in South Africa. His words were: 'Without you they would not have happened.'

The Working for Water programme was really one of the few outcomes that the government could confidently claim as a success story for the RDP. We were the only project at the time that actually spent its whole budget. In fact, we had to do a little juggling with the budgets when we realised that Working for Water had just about run out of money. I was determined to keep this project alive. We used to produce a weekly newsletter recording achievements, which was distributed to the entire Cabinet, I suspect to the chagrin of some members who could not so clearly demonstrate accomplishments in their own spheres. We also produced a video on Working for Water and showed it to Cabinet, where it got enthusiastic applause from people like Jay Naidoo. Someone told me that there were graffiti in the women's cloakrooms in Parliament that read: 'Turn off the tap. Kader Asmal is watching you.'

Within the Working for Water programme we dealt with wetland conservation and wildfire management, and these in time became the fully functional and highly successful Working for Wetlands and Working on Fire programmes. Since then, further programmes have been developed under the banner of the Natural Resources Management Programmes. It has indeed been humbling and inspiring to see what has been achieved out of that risk taken by Jay Naidoo when I asked him to trust me and in return he gave me the first investment from the RDP.

All this left me with the question: What was I to do with the engineer-led officials in my department who remained unconvinced by my focus on conservation? I called in Larry Farwell, a water specialist whom Bruce Babbitt, the inspirational Secretary for the Interior in the United States, sent out to assist the National Water Conservation Campaign. He did a most revealing experiment. Larry measured water use in our department's headquarters. To my great perturbation, he found that ninety per cent of the department's water was being lost to leaks. This clearly showed the advantage of consulting outsiders who came with a fresh outlook.

In April 1996 the department hosted a major conference, the National Shared-Vision Consolidation Conference, which we called 'Grasdak' after the name of the conference venue. The Grasdak programme embodied all my passions: human rights, social justice and environmental sustainability. It was the product of two years of intense work, and it signalled for me that the department had finally 'arrived'. The Grasdak conference was an emotional occasion, with poetry, music and art presented at the opening dinner by the affected communities. No eye remained dry when the Mpumalanga team danced in, with a white director, and rendered their beautiful Mpumalanga song 'Vision of Life'. It seemed to encapsulate the department's vision.

Out of the presentation came the call to arms for a transformed water sector in South Africa: 'Ensuring some for all … forever'. The idea behind this slogan, first heard at Grasdak, was to recognise that water resources in South Africa were finite and limited ('some'); that their benefits should be accessible to all and shared equitably by all ('for all'); and that they can be managed as renewable resources, provided their environmental sustainability is not compromised ('forever'). These were the values enshrined in South Africa's national Constitution, but now translated into a vision for the water sector. This was in sharp contrast to the slogan I often used to refer to the principles behind apartheid water provision: 'all for some, for now'.

What we did in the water portfolio had never before been considered. A United Nations Human Development Report made mention of the fact that we were one of the very few countries that spent less on their military budget than on water and sanitation. In 2000 I was awarded the tenth Stockholm Water Prize by the Swedish king, Carl XVI Gustaf, at a moving ceremony marked by the glorious singing of a South African choir and colourful fireworks that exploded into a brightly shining South African flag. It meant a lot to me to be the first non-scientist to have been so honoured. Desmond Tutu, one of those who nominated me for this award, wrote: 'Kader Asmal's integrity and vision, coupled with a well-developed conservation ethic, has put him in a state of creative conflict with the conventional and non-sustainable thinking around water management that pervades so many bureaucracies. He has given impetus to a conservation-based approach to water management in South Africa.' Tutu was one of many who came to understand what we were trying to achieve in the department.

Given the legacy of apartheid and the massive backlog in water provision, I had begun the process of revising legislation in the sector at the very start of my tenure. Work started in 1994 on the Water Supply and Sanitation White Paper and the following year we produced a white paper for forestry. At the same time, I ordered a complete review of the law around water, which was published in 1995 under the title 'You and Your Water Rights: South African Water Law Review'. A discussion document on the legal principles of water was produced in 1996 and a national forestry action plan was published by 1997. By 1997 a white paper on a new national water policy had been finalised, and at an International Workshop on Best Management Practices for Water Conservation (a closed workshop for leading management experts) South Africa's then draft water legislation was acclaimed as the most 'comprehensive and visionary' in the world. This white paper became a draft bill and finally, in 1998, the groundbreaking National Water Act, the jewel in the crown of my time at the department.

At the root of the Act was the intention to undo the notion that South Africa was awash with water and to reorient our national outlook towards one of scarcity. We also had to shift the prioritisation of water supplies away from the farms and industry and towards ordinary people, especially in the rural areas. We had to do this very carefully and as part of a process of reconciliation and change, but at the same time it had to be community-based, because the world's experience shows that otherwise there is no sustainability.

There were four main principles underpinning the National Water Act of 1998. Firstly, the concept of a 'water reserve' was a world first: in terms of this, water for basic human needs and water for basic ecological functioning have first priority, and only once these needs have been met can water be put to commercial or other use. The second principle was the acknowledgement that South Africa has a duty to ensure its neighbouring states have an equitable share of water from international (shared) rivers. Third was the change from 'water rights' to 'water-use rights', which implied that major water-users would be charged most for their consumption, an extremely unpopular notion at the time among some, but crucial for equity and efficiency. Finally, the new legislation introduced the notion of 'catchment management agencies', which saw the delegation of decision-making and power to interested and affected parties so that people could make decisions in their joint enlightened self-interest. I believe this last principle was unprecedented.

The preparatory work for the National Water Act took four years of intense research, consultation and participation. Nothing like it had ever been attempted in South Africa. In order to research and design the legislation, I assembled a team of young people, many of them women, who had never before been involved in social policy. They contributed a completely fresh approach and produced legislation that would change the lives of millions. I knew that so much of the success of the process depended on winning over the old guard as well. When within the department itself officials began to enjoy themselves and take pride in their work, I knew there would be no stopping us. Many were people who felt their careers – and aspirations – had been curtailed in the previous ministry. It is worth relaying the experience of one of them as he got caught up in the preparations ahead of the new national legislation:

'I experienced this exciting period personally from the groundwater side. Groundwater, the forgotten resource, was regarded as of very little value in terms of the past priority of commercial agriculture and urban–industrial development and was classified as "private water" in the old Act, meaning that government had basically no interest in its development and protection. It had remained the domain of the hydrogeologist and the driller and it still took years before it became part of the armoury of water resources planners. Not so for the new minister. He soon defined surface water as the "masculine resource", the resource of engineers, concrete, dams and pipelines, whereas groundwater he saw as the "feminine resource", the resource of women with their daily water-bearing burden and of children desperately in need of a daily supply of life-giving water. And that is what groundwater became in a matter of years, now serving 60–90 per cent of communities with domestic water in the different provinces.

'By 1998, groundwater was defined as a "significant water resource" in the National Water Act, with no difference from surface water in its treatment in law … Many other middle managers experienced this as one of the most fruitful periods of their careers. Science for development thrived, with the best of external and DWAF [Department of Water Affairs and Forestry] professionals working hand in hand. In all this, the Water Research Commission and its network of water academics were able to play a major and pro-active role.'

The openness of the process of drawing up the National Water Act was apparent in the number of international experts who were consulted and contributed enthusiastically. Many long-term international water management ties were created during this period. I remember fascinating discussions with Hector Garduño, now an international water consultant, who had played a leading role in water law reform in Mexico; Willi Struckmeier, head of the Mapping Commission of the International Association of Hydrogeologists; and the Finnish ambassador to South Africa, who arrived at my ministerial house in Pretoria with a doctor in attendance and medical tubes protruding from his chest.

The Water Act fundamentally reformed the law concerning water and access to water in South Africa. One of its provisions stipulated that the country should provide twenty-five litres of potable water free of charge for everyone within two hundred metres' walking distance. The centrepiece of the Act was the establishment of equitable, fair and open decision-making on all matters to do with water.

We were the first country in the world to say that water is a public trust, administered on behalf of the whole community by the government, and therefore there is no ownership of water. Water allocations were to be fixed for a period of forty years, not forever. Our concept of a water reserve meant that no longer could farmers, municipalities or anyone else build a dam if it meant that the river ran dry in other places where the water was desperately needed.

Reflecting on these challenges, I wrote a paper on water and ethics in 2004 for Unesco, in which I argued that it was essential that countries hammer out an ethical solution, together, and that this would have to be done in collaboration with civil society. The notion of 'togetherness' is a powerful notion for me and underpinned my work in reshaping the water sector in South Africa and globally. It lay at the root of a number of important local initiatives such as Working for Water, the River Health programme and the Masibambane water services programme. All of these were organised around the principle of togetherness, as without the joint decision-making, collaborative participation and collective ownership that togetherness implies, no programme – in water, forestry or otherwise – can ever be fully realised.

I also grew to appreciate the great strength and resilience of our people in the rural areas. Dumped there by apartheid, they were 'surplus people', often resettled where there was no water. When I asked them to help, to participate in this project of mine, to take responsibility for decisions on how water should be sourced and distributed, they never flinched. I remember a visit to a newly installed tap in a far-flung rural area. The women there explained carefully to me that they would damage the tap by resting their heavy buckets on it. I could see the problem, but before I could comment they proposed a solution. They needed a perch from which they could transfer the heavy buckets onto their heads. Such a simple yet wise solution deeply impressed me; I immediately got my department to build it. This was a salient reminder of the innate wisdom of the people in the rural areas despite their lack of education and facilities.

Throughout my ministry, I strived to get out as often as I could to see conditions on the ground. During apartheid, ministers very rarely had any interaction with the public. This must have compounded their isolation and made even more remote any possibility for collaboration and joint decision-making. For the ANC ministers in Mandela's government, there was an enormous amount of goodwill and pride from the people toward *their* ministers. The result was a cascade of letters, requests for appointments and, crucially, demands for visits.

One of my first forays into the heartlands of South Africa was anything but congenial. This was a so-called bridge-building exercise with primarily white business figures, involving a weekend visit to the Wood Fair at Sabie, an annual event of importance to the forestry industry. We arrived late at the guest house as my driver got lost. Our hosts were very generous in postponing their dinner until our arrival. Theirs was a beautiful house and we were presented with a *cordon bleu* meal. Over coffee, with my usual curiosity about names and background, I enquired about my hosts' surname. I had not acclimatised myself to the South African habit of using first names. I remembered that his first name was Gerard. What was his surname? He replied, 'Ludi.'

'My God,' I said aloud, 'are you *the* Gerard Ludi.' His wife asked: 'Does it make a difference?' I felt a tightness around my chest and could not breathe easily. Ludi was the informer who had entrapped the anti-apartheid hero Bram Fischer and others by infiltrating himself into the Johannesburg committee of the Communist Party. Ludi proceeded to 'explain' his virulent anti-communism on the basis of his opposition to authoritarianism, but all I wanted to do was leave – immediately. I debated with Louise whether we should return to Pretoria that night, but an obligation to the organisers of the fair prevailed. I made the mental note to find out in future who my hosts were going to be on any further 'bridge-building' visits. Needless to say, we didn't do much bridge-building on that occasion.

Another disquieting experience was an encounter with an elderly woman in KwaZulu-Natal. I was in the Mvoti River district near Stanger, finding out how we could assist small black farmers. In that area, the farmers were sugar-cane growers and we had been asked to find the money to build a small retaining dam to help them. I had to discover who would be affected by the construction of the dam. There were a small number of huts made of clay whose occupants were prepared to move upstream into more substantial brick-built houses, except for one elderly woman who refused to move. I went to see her. We began with the traditional greetings. I then explained to her the benefits (which, of course, had not been quantified or measured) that could flow from building the small dam. She held my gaze. I grew uncomfortable. When

I pointed out the advantages of taps in the house, proper sanitation and land for growing vegetables, she looked at me very calmly and took my hands into hers. 'Look', she said, 'at the cobwebs at the corners of the house. You can see the cobwebs, but you can't see the spirit of my son and husband who built this house for me. You can take my pots and pans to the new house you are promising. But you can't take my tears and my cries with me. Please, Mr Minister, I would like to die in the house of my family!' I didn't pursue any further attempts to secure money for the dam.

During my time as minister, much work was done in the area of forestry as well as water. Just as I believed water was a communal, shared asset, so I believed that our forests were part of the community, to be enjoyed and used sensibly by all. But the forestry industry was powerful and a very large source of foreign income, and the apartheid government had a lot of financial interests in forestry when I took over the ministry. Forestry uses enormous amounts of water, and it came as a shock to the industry when they realised they could no longer bully their way to get what they wanted. Certainly within the department the new state of affairs led to some dramatic conflict between the water conservation projects on the one hand and the forestry officials trying to promote forestry on the other. I had to fight hard with the departmental old guard, who used fairly illogical arguments to defend what they believed was their God-given right to water. They pointed to the sugar industry and other water-intensive crop industries to argue that they were being singled out. Despite evidence to the contrary, many remained convinced that forests cause rain – which they do, but not for South Africa. That rain falls into the ocean.

Until 1994, when I took the helm as minister, commercial forest plantations in too many places were zones of exclusion where authorities made sweetheart deals, promising timber to strangers from outside, and often allowing the planting of trees too close to a riverbed where no plantation should ever be. By 1999 we had done much to change this paradigm. We set out with an ambitious programme to achieve no less than a green revolution in South Africa.

Our forestry policy was based on the belief that, within a framework provided by government, the private sector could and would play a vital role in achieving the benefits, not only for itself but for the nation, of commercial forestry. The commercial forestry sector, despite its small local resource base, has achieved a great deal in the international market, creating jobs and bringing in much-needed export earnings. There is a shortage of forest land in South Africa and we need the industry, but it must be well managed.

The provision of wood to industry was not meant to be a government function. Even if the land remains in the hands of the state, it is naturally a responsibility of the private sector. It was these principles that guided the restructuring of the South African Forestry Company Ltd (Safcol) and my own department's commercial forests. As I left the ministry, preparations were being made to dispose of seventy thousand hectares of smaller plantations owned by the department. This not only brought in revenue but also created many opportunities for small and medium enterprises to enter the forest and timber business. The disposal also lifted the daily operational burden of running a big, and loss-making, business and enabled us to concentrate on those activities that were clearly government's concern.

Here we focused on issues of equity and sustainability in rural areas where wood is such an important source of energy. We could not stand by while poor communities were forced to choose between slowly but inexorably destroying their environment and going to bed without cooked food. This required placing ordinary people at the centre of our forestry effort and allowing them to take ownership of woodlots in rural areas to provide fuel wood. Urban forestry and the greening of our cities, an important focus of Arbour Week, also became essential parts of our community forestry work. Finally, the disposal of plantations gave us the time and resources to start tackling the conservation of our country's fast-dwindling natural forests.

A new National Forests Act, together with a National Veld and Forest Fire Act, laid firm foundations for the sustainable management of South Africa's natural forest resources. The new law stated that contracts for timber from state forests could no longer be in perpetuity, thus ending a relic of the past which had protected access to state timber for selected sawmillers for all time. The commercial forests will in future be managed in a way that brings the maximum benefit to the rural communities around them. For those communities surrounded by forests, there is now finally the prospect that they will share in the bounty. Access to them, for firewood and herbs, is secure but regulated. No longer will people be forced to plunder the forests of their ancestors for firewood. The saplings will grow. The endangered birds of these forests will keep on singing.

Dams came to represent an extremely important and rewarding dimension of my work at the department and internationally. In 1999 I was appointed chairman of the World Commission on Dams, an independent organisation developed by both proponents and opponents of large dams. In fact the membership of the commission was evenly balanced between these diametrically opposed viewpoints, often leaving it to me to break any deadlocks. The commission's goal was to develop international ethics and guidelines for all parties interested in building, operating or closing large dams.

In a world in which two billion people have no access to electricity, the hydropower that dams potentially generate might seem a clean alternative, especially in countries with running rivers. However, dams can also put strain on a country. As a commission member commented: 'Often, budgeted construction costs are massively exceeded, and the countries in question end up with unexpected debt. Due to the construction of dams, four million people are relocated each year. Environmental damage not initially foreseen can have a detrimental effect as a result of negligent studies and predictions, for example in biodiversity, lost forest areas and entire ecosystems. And often, the ratio between costs and benefits is unbalanced.'

When I chaired the World Commission on Dams we developed an approach to decision-making in development projects that I called 'globalisation from below', a notion I adopted from my friend Professor Richard Falk. Within a human rights framework, this approach not only considered the rights and risks of global investors but it also insisted on highlighting the human rights of, as well as the considerable risks to, people who were most directly affected by the project. As we brought peasants, workers, women's groups and representatives of indigenous people into the debate, we saw the tremendous potential of grassroots globalisation for advancing human rights in transnational negotiations. In many other areas, I believe the future of human rights will also depend upon 'globalisation from below'.

Globalisation from below has the potential to promote what I have called the public good, something that would ultimately be in everyone's interest. The public good is not just another word for human rights. It directly engages the global economy as an alternative to the commodification of all values and goes to the heart of Amartya Sen's call to clarify 'the values and ethics that shape our conception of the global world'.

I believe this sentiment was expressed in the Lesotho Highlands Water Project. This had been initiated by the apartheid regime to supply water to South Africa, and at the time was directly in contravention of international sanctions. When I inherited this distasteful project, I turned it into a partnership with our Lesotho neighbours, so that by the time it was completed under my ministry I believe it had come to serve a very different purpose, one much closer to Amartya Sen's idea of engaging the global economy in pursuit of the global good.

I recall the opening in April 1997 of the tunnel to bring water from the Katse Dam in Lesotho to the Ash River near Clarens in the Free State as one of the most dramatic events during my tenure as Minister of Water Affairs. Two tunnels, one from the South African side and one from Lesotho, had to be drilled through basalt rock and meet absolutely precisely. It was obviously difficult to predict the exact time the two would meet, but Louise and I and various officials of the Department of Water Affairs and Forestry walked half a kilometre or so along the tunnel and settled down, champagne glasses at the ready, on chairs set out for us in front of a solid wall of rock. The engineers and officials of the Trans-Caledon Tunnel Authority (the body charged with administering the scheme) looked rather anxious as we waited. I admit I had a moment or two of doubt. Would the tunnel-boring machine complete its task on time? Would the two tunnels meet up perfectly? The answer came in the form of a roar, distant at first as the machine approached, that grew steadily thunderous. The earth seemed to shake, and then the machine gradually emerged, shattering the rock wall and spraying clouds of dust over us all and our champagne glasses. It was huge, and completely dwarfed the workers who emerged from between its drilling spokes. You could say it was a truly earth-shattering occasion. Only after the drama and applause had subsided did I have time to think of the significance of this mammoth task, and the satisfaction to be gained from working in co-operation with our neighbour, Lesotho. I remembered those times in exile when I had written to various foreign ministers to oppose this apartheid venture, which had been proposed ostensibly to support Lesotho, though in reality it would aid only South Africa. Now we had achieved it, as partners, to the mutual benefit of both countries.

One of the major issues that occupied my time as chairman of the World Commission on Dams was that of water scarcity and water security. Though our planet is blue, less than 2.5 per cent of our water is fresh, less than 33 per cent of fresh water is fluid, less than 1.7 per cent of all fluid waters run in our streams. And the world has been stopping even these. In the last hundred years we have dammed our rivers at unprecedented rates; since 1950, we have built forty thousand dams each more than four storeys high.

As one who authorised the next stage of one of the largest dams in Africa, I can say that nations continue to build dams for sound reasons. Dams store, use and divert water for consumption, irrigation, cooling, transportation, construction, mills, power and recreation. Dams remove water from the Ganges, Amazon, Danube or Columbia rivers to grow cities on their banks. When it comes to parting – or imparting – the waters, dams are our oldest tool. Yet are dams our *only* tool, or even our *best* option?

Pursuing that question, the World Commission on Dams, during my chairmanship, undertook an independent, comprehensive global review. We found that just as water scarcity drove the construction of dams, scarcity also drove the commission's work. There is no substitute for the water that sustains us; even my *uisce beatha* (Irish for 'water of life', better known as whiskey) must be offset with real H_2O. We daily deplete what water remains, and it is no overstatement to call it 'a crisis of biblical proportions'. In Ecclesiastes, recall the passage:

> One generation passeth away,
> and another generation cometh:

but the earth abideth always ...
All rivers runneth to the sea,
yet the sea is not full ...

The words are beautiful, haunting and, suddenly, anachronistic, for they are not true, thanks to growth, change and developments during our lives. In some years our mightiest rivers – Africa's Nile, China's Yellow, America's Colorado, Australia's Murray – no longer even reach the sea. As rivers shrivel, freshwater ecosystems can't abide. As another generation comes more people suffer from hunger and thirst. An estimated 1.2 billion people, or one in five worldwide, lack access to safe drinking water. Three billion, or half the world's population, lack sanitation; millions pass away from waterborne disease. Farmers compete with booming cities for water. In a decade we drain aquifers that took centuries to fill. In dry regions, saltwater pollutes groundwater miles from the sea. In China, Mexico and India, water tables fall a metre a year, and the earth above subsides upon them. Worse, in 2025 we must find a fifth more water for three billion more people, shoved against the hard wall of finite supply. By then, one in three will struggle just to find water to drink and bathe, to say nothing of growing food.

This scarcity sounds bleak, and it is. Never before have stakes been higher, players more numerous, the field more complex. Mark Twain wrote what may have been the first and certainly the most eloquent words on the topic of environmental scarcity and water security. Twain lived in a frontier state, California, that was then hot, drought- and flood-prone, mosquito-ridden, politically unstable and economically stagnant – a condition closely resembling many nations today. 'In the West', he wrote, 'whiskey's for drinking, and water's for fighting over.' A century later, the notion that 'water's for fighting over' echoes loudly. But, I have to ask: *Have* battles been fought over water? Is water scarcity a *casus belli*? Does it in fact divide nations? My own answer is no, no and no. The idea that 'water's for fighting over' shifts energy and resources from local priorities to foreign affairs. It scares off investment where it is most in need. It inverts priorities, delays implementation of policy. And it forgets that water management is, ultimately, about real people.

We must develop bottom-up national strategic policies based on the needs of our critical transnational waters. Twain, in other words, was not exactly wrong, even if he was speaking with his tongue firmly in his cheek. We may walk to the bar to do something about a scarcity of whiskey. As for water, it was never in the past, is not now and must not be in the future for fighting over. Water is for conserving. Water is for bathing. Water is for drinking. Water is for sharing. Water is the catalyst for peace. Today, when we rest by the river and hear it dance through the reeds, it tells a new story, how it serves all, not only the few.

In a few short years as Minister of Water Affairs and Forestry, I feel I was able to introduce some far-reaching changes, changes that have genuinely improved people's lives and particularly the lives of South Africa's women. For this I will for ever be grateful and proud. If, in the fullness of time, anyone cares to remember my time as head of this portfolio, I should like to be viewed not as the minister who provided taps and toilets, who planted a few trees, and opened a dam or water scheme here and there. I should like to think that I helped contribute to a more hopeful future, expressed by Philip Larkin's astute words:

> If I were called in
> To construct a religion
> I should make use of water.

10

Education

The little township of Groutville lies not far from where I grew up in Stanger. The main secondary school in the town is Nonhlevu High, which by 1999, the year I became South Africa's Minister of Education, had deteriorated into an appalling state of disrepair. Five years into South Africa's new democratic dispensation, the school was a travesty of learning. Almost every window in the school was broken, the buildings were neglected and the schoolyard was overgrown. The *average* age of the students was twenty-one. Teachers and students arrived late for school. Once they got there, there was hardly any teaching during school hours. The pass rate for the Senior Certificate was a lamentable four per cent.

By 2003, the school had completely turned around. The Senior Certificate pass rate was just under eighty per cent. On my last visit, not a single window was broken; the buildings had been repaired and new toilets had been built; there were well-kept lawns and newly planted flowers; a sports field had been laid out through sponsorship from the private sector; teachers and students arrived on time; there was clear evidence of learning and teaching; and the community was closely involved in the life of the school. This was the kind of outcome that gave me the most pleasure in my new job at the head of South Africa's complex education system.

I had started my working life as a school teacher at Darnall in KwaZulu-Natal and I taught for almost thirty years at Trinity College Dublin before returning to South Africa in 1990. So teaching young people has always been an important activity to me. Education is such a crucial – and often controversial – portfolio because it directly touches every family. Education is not only about the well-being of children. As Es'kia Mphahlele said, 'The highest goal of education is enlightenment that leads to true emancipation.'

I heard about my appointment as Minister of Education in Thabo Mbeki's Cabinet in the early hours of the morning. It was about five thirty, and I immediately phoned my special adviser and told him to get the offices ready for me. I felt I had no time to lose. On my very first day in office I had him call in all the members of what was then known as the 'broad management' of the department for a first meeting. There I probably spent a disproportionate amount of time raising objections about the furniture, the curtains, the lighting: I found my new office dark and gloomy and I wanted sunlight and fresh air. I suppose I was spelling out my need for a fresh, new approach.

The result was that not all relationships with my senior management in the education sector started off well. I am often reminded of the stand-off I had with one of my chief directors, Ahmed Essop, when I announced my intention to introduce improvements to the dress code in the department. I insisted that all the men wear ties. This was anathema to Ahmed, and after a period in which we both dug in our heels, I gave way. I realised I had met my match in Ahmed when it came to determination. Maybe I also realised the work my staff produced was more important than whether or not they wore a tie. In the years that I spent with Ahmed our working relationship grew from strength to strength, even though he never once wore a tie.

I think the staff were rather shocked at the stark contrast between my style and that of my predecessor, Sibusiso Bengu. A former teacher, he was a true gentleman with a low-key style of management. Oversight came from the parliamentary Portfolio Committee on Education, chaired at the time by Blade Nzimande, and Bengu tended to rely very much on his officials to develop policy frameworks. His Director-General was Chabani Manganyi, a former Vice-Chancellor of the University of the North, whom I first encountered when I served as the chairperson of the university's Council. A qualified psychologist but at the same time very highly regarded in education circles, he was a quiet, dignified man whose style and tempo were probably similar to Bengu's. My staff were at first rather nervous of me, and not without cause. After becoming used to working for a quietly spoken and fairly reserved minister, they were rather worried about what they were in for when I stepped into the ministry. I probably didn't set their minds at rest either.

One of my staff has said of my arrival in the education ministry, 'Kader literally shook the building.' I know my staff found me exceedingly energetic, but I trust I am not capable of creating an earthquake. All the same, I accept I did shake the staff, at least those who had not worked with me before.

When I arrived in my office there was a change of guard. Chabani soon left the department – perhaps our styles of operating were just too different. In his place Thami Mseleku, a former South African Democratic Teachers' Union (Sadtu) officer who had been special adviser to the former minister, was proposed to the Cabinet as the Director-General. He and the other top officials were all deeply committed to the transformation of education in the country. They infused their work with an energy that made this a distinctive experience for me.

My first instruction to my senior management team was to invite every one of them to write to me directly about what they considered were priority issues. Actually, I think they found this rather disconcerting, as they were used to communicating through the 'appropriate channels'. They certainly were not used to having direct access to the minister and being called upon to interact with me. We all had to get to know each other, and there was some tension at the beginning, but it didn't last very long.

Once I began work, there were never enough hours in the day to deal with the injustices I saw around me, even though I insisted that my department start at seven o'clock and continue until all hours of the night. Sometimes my staff were on call even after that in case I thought of something that needed immediate action or if I read a letter or newspaper article late at night that so incensed me I couldn't wait until the next morning to draft a reply. I must say that it sometimes happened that once I had calmed down by the next day I could be persuaded to toss a particularly fiery response into the bin. One of my senior assistants became so adept at this I called her the 'chief censor'.

Never one for technology, I liked to dictate my letters into a tape recorder. I knew the typists sometimes struggled to understand my accent, and I believe they found it even more difficult at times to make sense of my choice of words. Because I liked to rattle these off at great speed, punctuation also proved something of a problem for them.

There was simply so much work to be done to meet the massive needs of the children of South Africa. I found it hard to sit still and wait for something to happen. I learnt in time that my staff's nickname for me during those years was 'Papa Action'. Papa Action was a character in the television soap opera 'Yizo Yizo 2'. He appeared to have limitless energy, which he put to use by getting personally involved in everyone's business. That was my style: a hands-on personal engagement with every project (and person) for which (and for whom) I was responsible.

Around that time, when I was diagnosed with a variety of cancer, one of my former colleagues from Water Affairs took to sending me vitamins, which he believed to have great restorative powers. My staff members used to threaten to withhold the pills. They joked that I didn't need any more energy; it was they who needed the vitamins.

I think my staff came to dread Wednesday afternoons when I would return from Cabinet meetings and call them together for what they called the War Council. I liked to gather them around my desk where I would give something of a report-back, while simultaneously issuing instructions and orders. I valued that personal contact with the team. It was always impromptu, rarely had an agenda and sometimes, I think, created considerable confusion among my staff. Often they had to go away and try to interpret or make sense of my many and sometimes apparently contradictory requests, especially the written instructions in my notoriously incomprehensible handwriting. Yet in time most rose to the challenge admirably and developed their own styles of working.

My staff in the Ministry of Education knew that they could expect to be called upon at any time to respond to all manner of projects, from the World Commission on Dams, to the Cabinet arms control committee, to the Masifunde Sonke national reading campaign, or any other of the campaigns or committees I was engaged in during my tenure as Minister of Education. Before every Cabinet meeting I expected them to brief me on all agenda items, even though I read every Cabinet document and proposal. It was essential to me that I was prepared and able to speak my mind on any and all debates if need be. I have to pay the staff credit for always being on call and so willingly. Some have told me that I inspired them, 'energised' and 'galvanised' them. Others have said that I 'touched their lives' in many ways and that they learnt much from me.

This pleases me immensely. I like to think that I never really stopped being a teacher.

As minister I was determined to keep my finger on the pulse of public opinion. After all, education affects almost every citizen. I studied the media obsessively, every night pouring over the day's newspapers at my kitchen table, and I would cut out reports, articles, even letters to the editor, that were relevant to my department. These I would hand out to my staff and request some kind of response. My staff also came to expect from me verses of poetry that I found inspiring. In particular I reminded them often of the words of Bertolt Brecht: 'When the difficulty / Of the mountains is once behind / That's when you'll see / The difficulty of the plains will start.'

During my first five weeks as Minister of Education, I engaged in a structured 'listening exercise'. I invited all the key constituencies to come and meet me or submit written representations if they wanted to. It was a wonderful mission of discovery. I read dozens of documents and my officials gave me copious briefings. In meetings unprecedented in their intensity and frankness, I met the leading representatives of every national education structure. We talked, we argued and we found common ground. Finally, to cap this listening campaign, I consulted with the provincial MECs for education who together formed an important structure known as the Council of Education Ministers. This resulted in my departmental Plan of Action, called Tirisano, meaning 'working together', which aimed at the national mobilisation of education and training resources. Tirisano matched President Mbeki's call for 'A nation at work for a better life for all'. That was what we had to do in education, together.

Following my whirlwind campaign to meet and engage with those in my department as well as a broad range of stakeholders in education, I came to three important conclusions. Firstly, the leadership of our education and training system embodied remarkable qualities of patriotism, talent, experience and commitment. We had the essential human resources for the next phase of our education revolution. What is more, they were eager to get on with it.

Secondly, I was told by everyone I met that we had created a set of policies and laws in education and training that were at least equal to the best in the world. I was proud that our young democratic government was able to build a national consensus around the main education policy positions of the mass democratic movement, so soon after taking power, while simultaneously reorganising the entire structure of education administration and provision.

Thirdly, the national education leadership was unanimous that our system of education and training had major weaknesses and carried deadly baggage from our past. Large parts of the system remained seriously dysfunctional. It was not an exaggeration to say that there was a crisis at each and every level of education.

At the first Cabinet meeting of the new government, President Thabo Mbeki posed the question 'Is our education system on the road to the twenty-first century?' The South African public, I knew, had a vital interest in the answer. Having consulted virtually the entire leadership corps of the education and training system, I was able to give him and everyone else my reply. My answer, in 1999, was ambivalent, at best. In fact I believed that the education of the majority of people in our country amounted to a national emergency, which required an exceptional response from the national and provincial governments.

When I took over the education ministry in 1999, South Africa had been a democratic state for five years, and while considerable progress had been made by my predecessor, there were many areas of deep debate and controversy within this portfolio. Perhaps that was why I enjoyed it so much. Few subjects stir strong attitudes or invite engagement more effectively than the education of one's children. The language of instruction, the place of religion in schools, the syllabus, corporal punishment, the merging of tertiary institutions and the correction of race-based distortions in the sector were but a few of the areas that I had to deal with. Each elicited profound and heated deliberation among South Africans, and rightly so.

Despite the huge challenges facing the sector, I made sure to focus on what are sometimes known as the 'Cinderella areas of education' – special needs schooling, early childhood development and adult literacy. When I became Minister of Education, I discovered that nearly twenty per cent of South African adults and young people could not read or write in any language, and millions more were functionally illiterate and innumerate. To meet this need, a new Adult Basic Education and Training (Abet) programme was conceptualised. The government introduced the skills levy, an income-related fee imposed on employers to be used for upgrading the skills of their staff, and established Sector Education and Training Authorities (or Setas) in every industry and occupation in South Africa to monitor and manage learnerships, internships and apprenticeships. The government's aim was to encourage employers, including national, provincial and local governments, to run or support Abet programmes for their employees. I also extended an open invitation to all religious, political, social, educational and community bodies to help us design a major programme of voluntary service on behalf of literacy and numeracy, and make facilities available to run it. Despite our best efforts, however, we were never really able to make much of an impact on the scourge of illiteracy in our country, and our efforts in the Abet exercise were very largely a failure, something I will always deeply regret. Too much bureaucracy at provincial and national level, too much focus on examinations and not enough creativity were the reasons I identified for this malaise.

I also recognised the urgent need to address the HIV/Aids emergency in the education and training system. This was a priority, especially when research showed the shockingly high prevalence of the virus among our teachers. We opted to work alongside the Ministry of Health to ensure that the national education system played its part in stemming the epidemic. I appointed an adviser specifically on the subject and made sure that the subject of HIV/Aids became part of the revised curriculum: stemming the growth of this pandemic required informing the upcoming generation of its dangers. Part of this initiative was a very important conference we held in 2002 on sexuality and education, focusing on the theme of the right of girls and women to be taken seriously when they say no. By bringing the issue of HIV/Aids into the ambit of the Education Department, I also wanted to be sure that no children were discriminated against or excluded on the grounds of being HIV-positive.

I was driven to this conclusion by a most unusual meeting I had with two Afrikaans-speaking women, one in late middle age, the other in her thirties. They had carried out a representative though selective survey of sexual behaviour among pupils at Indian, coloured, African, white English and white Afrikaans schools. My staff told me that I should not 'waste my time' in meeting these two people, who had no organisational backing. But they intrigued me. The older woman had even used her pension money for the survey. Their findings showed that there was very little difference among the schools, whatever their race or class. What they did reveal was that sexual activity at all the schools surveyed was pretty extensive and started at the early age of between ten and twelve. The figures were alarming. Though the reasons were in many cases different, the consequences were the same. I felt that no one should ignore these two women's findings because of some religious or cultural reason.

Another key priority for me was infrastructural development. It was essential to end the physical degradation in South African schools. Although the government was to contribute more than R1 billion to the National Schools Building Programme, it required twelve times that amount to meet the backlog. It was impossible to contemplate this situation with complacency: it cried out for remedy. We produced a video for Cabinet to demonstrate conditions in some rural schools. These were so shocking that when I previewed the video it was hard to stop myself breaking down and crying. I couldn't bear to see the conditions in which so many of our children were trying to gain an education.

I used every opportunity to press for public spending on repairing or, if necessary, replacing dangerous and dilapidated schools, and providing water and sanitation services where they did not exist. I envisaged schools as centres of community life. I wanted the facilities of the schools to be put to use for youth and adult learning, community meetings, music and drama, sports and recreation. I saw this as a way of addressing crime and degradation in the poorest areas. In my opinion, an idle school was a vulnerable place, inviting vandalism. A busy school, on the other hand, was a place that the community would protect, because it was theirs.

Whenever possible I made a point of joining my staff when they visited schools or campuses so that I could see the conditions for myself, although that wasn't the only reason for my visits. I didn't just want to talk to the staff or officials; I got real pleasure from talking to the young people I encountered and tried to arrange walkabouts at every opportunity. I aimed to invigorate and galvanise both teachers and learners, build morale and create some kind of shared energy in schools. At the beginning of the academic year I would travel from one province to another, making impromptu visits to schools, to see for myself that teachers were there on time, that schoolbooks had been delivered, children were registered and in their classrooms, and schools were functioning properly. Once, in 2002, the principal of a school and I rolled up our sleeves and joined a teacher who was painting his classroom in advance of the school's reopening.

Of course, one of the most contentious areas I encountered as Minister of Education was the curriculum. In 1994 we had inherited an outdated, racist and sexist curriculum. Soon after we wrested power from the apartheid regime, the Minister of Education, Sibusiso Bengu, set out to replace what existed then: Christian National Education for whites, Bantu Education for Africans, Coloured Education for coloureds and Indian Education for Indians. He proposed a system known as Outcomes-Based Education (OBE) and this received the backing of the parliamentary Portfolio Committee for Education, chaired by Blade Nzimande. OBE, together with a proposed new curriculum, was adopted by our schools. This took place before I was appointed minister in 1999. From the start it was controversial. Some members of the public felt that government had imported OBE and imposed what amounted to an alien philosophy on an unwilling and unwitting populace. Many people, including teachers and parents, often simply couldn't make sense of the concept.

When I became minister I knew that one of the first things I had to do urgently was familiarise myself with the principles of OBE. Among my earliest instructions to my chief adviser was to ask him to identify three experts in the department who would provide me with one-page explanations of the meaning of OBE. I put to them a simple question: What do I say to parents who want an explanation of OBE? When their answers were handed in, we both read them through carefully. After a moment's silence we looked at each other and burst out laughing. The jargon was such that we were still none the wiser.

Strangely I received much criticism for OBE, even on several occasions from Nzimande himself. This was ironic, given the genesis of the policy and his own role in its creation. Still, it rankles a little that a policy that I inherited and had no option but to pursue became the source of such opposition and criticism. I was accused of things in which I had played no part, and what I actually did set out to do was often forgotten. There were some tense moments in Cabinet, where my approach to OBE was seen to challenge policies that had been set in place by the ANC. In the broader world, there was little understanding of the debate about OBE that was taking place within government and how I resolved to deal with it during my term of office. My main concern, following my listening campaign, was to move decisively to correct whatever needed correction, without losing sight of our overall vision of moving away from the previous stultifying, divisive and regressive approach to the curriculum.

My starting point was that learning for the majority of children in the townships and rural areas was by rote and that we needed an alternative to this kind of learning. This alternative was spelt out very clearly in the ANC's 1994 policy document on education known colloquially as the Yellow Book. Though the Yellow Book did not mention OBE, it had a vision of a school curriculum that would be democratic, non-racist and non-sexist and that would work towards national unity through recognising diversity and enabling the fulfilment of individual potential. In line with this, I wanted a common, national curriculum that would help us overcome the passivity and lack of interest in education that a history of inferior education had bred. And this meant tackling a curriculum that was under heavy pressure.

In 1999, when I took office, the Deputy Director-General of Education, Ihron van Rensburg, was in the throes of phasing in OBE – then termed Curriculum 2005, to indicate that it would be completely and fully implemented by 2005. (Implementation was to be phased in between 1998 and 2005 over a seven-year period.) Van Rensburg had presented a report to the Heads of Education Departments Committee and the Council of Education Ministers that was concerned mainly with whether we should continue to plan for implementation in two grades in 2000 or only one. In my view we were clearly at a critical turning point with this curriculum and I needed to take decisive steps to deal with it.

Van Rensburg's report observed that resistance among teachers had diminished and there was now considerable confidence and enthusiasm among them for the curriculum, but there were also troubling references to the competence of teachers and the capacity and understanding of the district officials who had to drive the change. Most significantly, OBE was resource-hungry and we simply did not have adequate resources for the learning support materials, professional development and support personnel required to make it a success.

There were also ongoing headaches in the process of procuring and distributing textbooks. Orders weren't placed on time by the provinces; there were tender difficulties and problems with small business suppliers; publishers ran out of stock; communications problems occurred all along the chain; and difficulties arose with the management of the process in the provinces. We sent a team to the provinces and met with officials of the Department of State Expenditure and the Finance Department, with publishers as well as provincial education departments, but the problems seemed to remain intractable. In 2000 I asked the British government for assistance in this complex area of ordering books.

While we as a ministry acknowledged the far-reaching problems with OBE, there was never any intention to abandon the model. In fact it was made clear that a 'chop and change' approach would simply compound and reinforce difficulties and that substantial change was more likely to succeed than small-scale innovations. Therefore, along with a schedule for phasing in Curriculum 2005, we proposed the establishment of a Review Committee to monitor the process and prepare a report on what was needed to ensure the successful future implementation of OBE. I requested this report after my 'listening campaign', which had indicated there was a need for substantial review of the curriculum.

As the year progressed, the strain was felt at all levels. There was a lack of a culture of learning and teaching in many schools. We had inherited poorly qualified and badly trained teachers and also faced the uncertainty and instability created by the process of teacher rationalisation, retrenchment and redeployment introduced under Bengu. This had left a swathe of demoralised and cynical teachers in its wake. Not surprisingly, it was proving difficult to train teachers for the introduction of Curriculum 2005 in grade seven in 2000.

I began doing spot visits to schools and found in some cases indolent teachers not teaching and children not in class. My approach to low morale and indiscipline was to try to improve teachers' physical conditions of work, turn schools into community centres supported by teacher development, reward good teachers and emphasise the dignity of the profession. To motivate teachers, I introduced the National Teacher

Awards to reward those who were making a difference to their schools, though implementation of this was delayed for a year by Sadtu, who argued that teaching was not an individual but a collective matter. We did eventually introduce the awards on Teachers' Day in October 2000 and I made it an annual event, addressed by the President. It is now an institutionalised part of the department's activities and a great success.

This was not my only experience of Sadtu obstructing progress. Actually, throughout my term and beyond, Sadtu hampered every effort to raise the standards and improve the professionalism of teachers. The union insisted on being involved in the approval of staff and fought every step I took in implementing the school evaluation system introduced to assess shortcomings and make improvements at school level. Sadtu saw its role as that of a trade union, and a very militant and active one at that, whose responsibility was to protect and defend the rights and working conditions of its members. The quality of teaching remained a disputed issue.

It was around this time that Bill Spady, the American whose ideas were most influential in shaping the notion of OBE taken up in the Department of Education, came to South Africa. I met with him and we had a rational conversation. His ideas were plausible, though he distanced himself from what was passing for OBE in South Africa. I invited him to address a gathering of our key officials, role-players and intellectuals in education at the Council for Scientific and Industrial Research (CSIR). His reception was a stormy one. By lunchtime I was ready to close the discussions and call off the afternoon's proceedings. His somewhat evangelical style did not go down well with the intellectuals, although it clearly spoke to others who were inspired by the OBE vision.

Despite the continuing dispute, by the end of 1999 we had decided on the terms of reference for the Review Committee. I asked my provincial colleagues to send progress reports for their respective provinces and also to indicate whether there was a need for an external agency to assist with a review. Though the national department did not want an external review, I knew we had to have one. We needed a review to consider all the key sticking points: the structure and design of the curriculum, professional development, learning and teaching support materials, district support as well as implementation of time-frames – and all within three months, by March 2000. Our terms of reference were framed not as a review of OBE as such but of its implementation, so that we could improve and strengthen what we had already set in place, fully aware of all the difficulties being faced.

The team I decided on was headed by Linda Chisholm, Professor of Education at the then University of Natal in Durban. Working with her were not only the best brains we had in education, but also key leadership figures in ANC education. Despite differences over OBE, all the members of the Review Committee were committed to overcoming the divisions of the past. They produced a brilliant report. Before its completion, they did not share the report with me or anyone in the department and it did not go through the usual bureaucratic approval processes. Chisholm was fiercely determined to produce an independent review.

On 31 May 2000 the report of the Review Committee was handed to me at a press conference in Pretoria. It made substantive recommendations on changes to the structure and design of Curriculum 2005, some of which underpin curriculum implementation to this day. In fact, a more recent review, undertaken in 2009, hardly added anything new; it simply brought the story up to date since the first. I am very proud that the approach we adopted in the 2000 review had a major international and regional impact.

The report was a major critique of the path we were set on, by an external, highly credible group of people. While the original plan for OBE called for sixty outcomes – an absurd demand – the review called for only six, which was much more manageable. But it also provided strategic guidance on what was to be done in the short, medium and long term. After this report, there was no going back and continuing with the implementation of Curriculum 2005. While the report did not recommend ending OBE, its recommendations were radical enough to halt all plans for putting in place Curriculum 2005. Teacher development, textbooks in preparation and district plans were stalled as the nation held its collective breath about where to next. Of course this caused a sensation, with the media declaring in headlines, 'OBE is dead!' The *Pretoria News* went so far as to say 'Asmal has abolished OBE'.

I had to maintain a difficult balancing act. I had a report that had captured the public imagination and given a new direction, which was endorsed by my provincial colleagues. But its implicit challenge to

Curriculum 2005 also meant that my head was on a block. The old OBE curriculum had had the full support of the ANC's Alliance partners and Sadtu, which had participated in its implementation. Indeed, the report generated shock-waves among my colleagues. My presentations to the parliamentary Portfolio Committee and to Cabinet were heated and intense. Questions were asked as to whether this represented a challenge to the ANC and its vision or whether it was in line with what the ANC wanted. I argued that the implementation difficulties necessitated revision. The report was helping rather than hindering us in achieving our goals. I believed then, as I do now, that the basic principles underlying OBE were not at fault; it was our readiness for and implementation of it that had proved faulty. I still hold that at the heart of any OBE curriculum should lie the values of social justice, equity and development, and the development of creative, critical and problem-solving individuals.

At its meeting on 25 July 2000, Cabinet endorsed the need to develop a Revised National Curriculum Statement that would detail in clear and simple language the curriculum requirements at various levels. The immediate way forward was to implement the recommendations for changing the design of the curriculum. Curriculum 2005 provided curriculum development tools that were far too onerous for the majority of our teachers and assumed that they had the time, skill and resources to use them. The Review Committee recommended simplifying the content of each learning area.

I agreed that the curriculum should be simplified in this way and appointed Linda Chisholm to drive the revision process. By the end of 2000, a plan had been produced, funding was found, and a ministerial project committee and task team were established to manage the process. In January 2001 I officially launched their work.

Even as this process was under way, provinces continued to signal difficulties with OBE. One provincial head of education came to the Council of Education Ministers saying that teachers wanted a return to teaching and learning formats with which they were familiar and which they understood. It was clear to me that some provinces were placing an excessive emphasis on bureaucratic approaches to education: this was done in the name of OBE but was entirely against the spirit of the OBE with which I associated myself. In particular, one of the key principles of OBE was to de-emphasise content in education, at a time when the absence of textbooks made teaching virtually impossible.

When the Scottish Qualifications Authority visited South Africa and benchmarked our Senior Certificate examination in 2001 against theirs, they found our standards comparable to the best in the world. But one of their main recommendations was to reform the mathematics and physics syllabuses to include topics that lend themselves to problem-solving in real situations. This was precisely the aim of an outcomes-based curriculum, and it confirmed our move in this direction and away from rote learning.

By 30 July 2001 the draft National Curriculum Statement was completed and we sent it out for public comment. Most of the more than two hundred serious submissions we received – an exceptional number – began with an opening statement about what a major improvement this represented. There was overwhelming support from all the major stakeholders, including the unions and major religious bodies. However, it provoked a storm among Christian National Education groups, mainly around the proposed Life Orientation curriculum. There was also an orchestrated and bizarre opposition campaign conducted by a home-schooling movement and an organisation called the Pestalozzi Trust run by a former University of Pretoria academic. On some days we would find the department fax machine blocked by their responses. We were accused of everything from unconstitutional indoctrination to the work of the devil or the anti-Christ. Nevertheless, the Revised National Curriculum Statement was approved by the Council of Education Ministers in April 2002 and gazetted for implementation, starting in 2004. For me, this represented a considerable accomplishment in the field of education.

One of the most significant of all my achievements as minister, perhaps, was my engagement of religious leaders and scholars to develop a policy on religion in education. I established a commission under the chairmanship of David Chidester, Professor of Religious Studies at the University of Cape Town, to investigate the whole question of religious instruction in schools, and appointed a Standing Advisory

Committee on Religion and Education. During these deliberations I met and spoke personally with all the leaders of the different faiths in the country. I posed to these leaders the notion that religious instruction was anomalous in a school system populated by children from many different religious backgrounds and beliefs.

The revised policy for religion and education was launched on 9 September 2003 in Cape Town. Based on the constitutional values of citizenship, human rights, equality, freedom from discrimination, and freedom of conscience, religion, thought, belief and opinion, it distinguished between religion education and religious education. Religion education is education about religions that affirms religious diversity – and therefore should be treated and taught like any other subject – whereas religious education or instruction teaches the precepts of a specific religion, usually to members of that faith. We agreed this was not the task of the curriculum. In other words, religious instruction was a matter for the church, not for the state. While I agreed that school premises could be used for this instruction, I insisted that religious instruction in state schools be removed from the compulsory schedule. This pleased groups like the Zion Christian Church, South Africa's largest faith community, which had been routinely discriminated against as falling outside the Christian establishment's notion of mainstream orthodoxy.

Many countries still allow a state-designated religion to dominate the education system. We had lived through this, and I rejected it. Instead I adopted a co-operative model, with the state and church in harmony, existing separately in our specific spheres, and working collectively in shared spheres of interest such as education. I chose this approach because South Africa is not a secular nation – the Preamble to the Constitution implores God to bless Africa, and our inspiring national anthem opens with the words 'Nkosi Sikelel' iAfrika' (God bless Africa) – but nevertheless embraces many different religions.

The policy on religion and education which I implemented stated that school prayers could continue but should be non-denominational. Though I never encouraged children to opt out of religion, I did feel that compulsory religious instruction that favoured one group over another was antithetical to our Constitution and contrary to the principle of equality. Children should learn about the major religions of our country; about Eid al-Fitr, Yom Kippur, Christmas and Diwali. This kind of instruction could only support tolerance and embrace diversity.

The new policy was also in keeping with international developments in the field of religion and education. Under the auspices of the High Commissioner for Human Rights, the United Nations convened a conference on religion in school education in Madrid during November 2001. This affirmed our policy's distinction between the teaching of religion, which is the responsibility of the home, family and religious community, and teaching about religion and religions, which is the responsibility of the school. In the school, as the UN Special Rapporteur for Freedom of Religion or Belief put it, education about religion 'should be conceived as a tool to transmit knowledge and values pertaining to all religious trends, in an inclusive way, so that individuals realise their being part of the same community and learn to create their own identity in harmony with identities different from their own'. Such teaching about religion, he concluded, 'radically differs from catechism or theology, defined as the formal study of the nature of God and of the foundations of religious belief, and contributes to the wider framework of education as defined in international standards'. Our policy, therefore, accorded with international developments and standards. But it was also an innovative South African solution.

Yet, despite the logic of the policy and its recognition as accepted international practice, the response of some people, organisations and groups to my proposed removal of religious instruction from South African schools was surprisingly hostile. I realised once again how divisive the issue of religion could be. It was one of the few issues that drew criticism in my more than ten years of addressing the ANC's parliamentary caucus. Beyond the caucus, I was also in trouble at my ANC branch in Rosebank in Cape Town. Some members even called on me to apologise publicly for my attempt to abolish religion from our schools. This reaction of my fellow ANC cadres to my proposed reforms depressed and disappointed me. I recalled in particular the strong faiths of both Oliver Tambo, who was a very committed Anglican, and Albert Luthuli, who was a trained Methodist minister. Their faiths never intruded either on their public discourse or on their personal relations. Nelson Mandela and Walter Sisulu, both of whom were Communist Party leaders in their day, also had particular religious affiliations, but these never controlled their public policies.

If my own party was hostile on the issue of religion in schools, further afield the response from some quarters verged on the apoplectic. Right-wing Afrikaner groups called my policy 'Asmal's New Ageism'. I didn't know what this meant, but it sounded bad, so I went to talk to one of the leading spokesmen for the Afrikaner establishment, the Western Cape Premier and leader of the New National Party, Marthinus van Schalkwyk. I will never forget the vehemence with which he responded. Barely concealing his anger, Van Schalkwyk insisted that Christianity was the faith of the majority of people in the Western Cape, and he would not accept any other form of religious instruction in schools. I walked away from that meeting with the impression of an overwhelming intolerance and religious chauvinism.

Eventually, after two or three years, the opposition and protests petered out. All the churches I had met raised no objections to the new policy. The policy document was adopted and attracted considerable interest internationally, particularly in multicultural societies. Not every country agreed with our approach. I remember meeting the prime minister of a foreign country and being told that, multicultural or not, his country would remain Catholic for as long as he was around. But at least in South Africa children would no longer be forced to remain silent while being instructed on matters of faith with which they could not identify or agree or be excluded on the ground of not being a member of the dominant faith.

Much of my work on the revised Curriculum 2005 was based on my personal antipathy towards exclusion of any kind. This is why I made sure that the revised curriculum covered diversity, tolerance, sexual orientation and other subjects that had been taboo in the past.

Of course, attention to the curriculum was only one of many issues I had to deal with. I soon realised that what was needed to redirect South Africa's education system went well beyond changing the curriculum. We had to determine priorities. The first challenge was making our provincial systems of co-operative government work, in itself a major challenge. According to the Constitution, the overall responsibility for the management of the education system rested with me, the Minister of Education, while the nine provincial departments were responsible for the day-to-day running of schools and the implementation of national policy in their provinces. This structure sometimes made me feel like

Pontius Pilate. The Minister of Education carries all the responsibility, but none of the power. I didn't want to feel like the court eunuch and I intended to fulfil my responsibility as minister within the letter and spirit of the Constitution.

As national minister I worked closely with the provincial Council of Education Ministers, applying the national norms and standards identified in the Constitution. My aim was to identify individual problematic schools, sometimes by making unannounced visits to institutions, and working with the provincial authorities to decide how to rectify these weaknesses. I used to report regularly to Parliament on the state of education in the provinces – for me the processes of accountability were critical – and a good deal of my time was spent dealing with problems in provincial education.

While working with the provincial ministers I was genuinely amused by being referred to as 'sir' by someone I had always thought to be a redoubtably tough woman. Helen Zille, later to become Premier of the Western Cape, was then MEC for education in that province. I had trouble in getting her to drop this salutation. Not every MEC worked as hard or had as much control over his or her portfolio as Zille did. Though her manner did occasionally put people off, I had no difficulty in working with her.

As minister I was not prepared to hand over responsibility to the provincial departments and leave them to face the challenges without national ministerial support. I felt strongly that I was responsible not only for educational policy, but also for the nitty-gritty workings of the education system on the ground.

Also on my radar was the need to develop the professional quality of South Africa's teaching force. All the evidence provided to me indicated that there was a real malaise in the teaching corps of the country. Under apartheid, the provision of teachers in schools resulted in two serious social distortions. One was the extreme inequality in learner–educator ratios, which was sustained by unequal budget allocations based on racial and ethnic discrimination. The second distortion was the racially defined qualification structure, linked to racially defined opportunities for training, which ensured that African teachers, taken as a whole, were less qualified than other teachers. As Minister of Education, I was deeply concerned about teacher development, especially given the demands of outcomes-based education. Major research later indicated that teacher supply was not keeping pace with demand and I appointed a committee to investigate what should be done about teacher education to support the curriculum. As with the curriculum, the committee's work had long-term implications and its impact has been felt to this day. I wanted to insert dignity back into the teaching profession, for good teachers are vital agents of change and growth in our schools and communities.

When I think back on those years of spearheading education policy in South Africa, I realise that probably the most contentious project of all was the reform of the higher education system. In 1997, during my tenure as Minister of Water Affairs, the Cabinet approved the policy and legislative framework for the transformation of the higher education sector. This was introduced by my predecessor, with the White Paper on Higher Education. The Higher Education Act itself was passed at the end of 1997. I took more than a passing interest in the Cabinet discussions. Prior to entering Parliament I had spent my entire working life in higher education, and it was one of my great passions. At least in this case I could not be accused of pretending to be an expert on matters that fell outside my Cabinet portfolio.

I had an insider's understanding of the inner workings and rhythms of higher education institutions and an abiding appreciation of the role that higher education could play in creating a more just and equitable society based on the values of non-racialism and non-sexism. However, if the state was to contribute to a new South African identity, it was imperative to ensure that it remained at a distance. The white paper and the Higher Education Bill had struck a delicate and, in my view, appropriate balance between the imperative of institutional autonomy and the need for public accountability. However, it did not find favour with some of my Cabinet colleagues, especially at a time when the pressure for transformation was at its height. I mounted a vigorous defence in support of institutional autonomy, which in the end carried the day.

I looked forward to the opportunity to oversee the implementation of the agenda outlined in 'Education White Paper 3: A Programme for the Transformation of the Higher Education System'. This set the scene for investigating the number and type of institutions needed, which led to the rationalisation of the institutional landscape of the sector on a scale not attempted before, as far as I am aware, anywhere else in the world. I have no doubt that it left Hendrik Verwoerd, the chief architect of Bantu Education, turning and squirming in his grave.

Democratic South Africa inherited thirty-six higher education institutions, universities as well as technikons. The spatial geography of the institutions was based on race and ethnicity rather than social and demographic need. In our Tirisano programme we used to refer to this as the 'geopolitical imagination of apartheid planners'. Its logic was dictated by the apartheid fallacy of 'separate but equal development' linked to the grandiose smokescreen of 'independent' states. In this the ideologues of apartheid were following in the well-worn path trodden by post-colonial states in Africa and in South Africa's bantustans, where 'independence' was symbolised by the building of a parliamentary complex, an airport and a university.

The apartheid higher education system, the foundations of which were laid by the infamous Extension of University Education Act of 1959, was certainly separate but it was far from equal. There were huge inequalities both in resources and in quality between the white higher education institutions – some of which could hold their own with the best in the world – and those for black students. This legacy continues to haunt South Africa today and impedes the post-apartheid higher education sector in fulfilling its role in meeting the country's human resource needs and acting as the engine-room and catalyst for the creation of new knowledge, innovation and critical discourse.

I had had discussions with leaders of these institutions as part of my listening campaign – the vice-chancellors as well as the Council on Higher Education (CHE), which was established in 1998 as an advisory body to the Minister of Education. As a result I was convinced that the prerequisite for developing a national plan for higher education that would meet the human resource and research needs of South Africa as a middle-level developing economy was an investigation into the size and shape of the higher education sector.

I invited the CHE, which had first raised the issue during the listening campaign, to undertake the investigation. This was the first major piece of ministerial advice sought from the newly formed body. Little did I know at the time that what seemed to be a rational and objective first step in reshaping the apartheid-induced spatial geography of higher education would prove to be one of the most difficult and controversial issues I had to deal with during my five years as Minister of Education.

The CHE discharged its mandate with intellectual rigour and a keen sense of the social, economic and cultural context and the role of higher education in it. This was not surprising, given the composition of the task team established to undertake the investigation. Chaired by the formidable Mamphela Ramphele, it consisted of senior leaders from within higher education and leaders from business like Bobby Godsell and Wiseman Nkhulu, as well as from labour, including Ebrahim Patel, later to become the Minister of Economic Development.

The CHE's report, 'Towards a New Higher Education Landscape: Meeting the Equity, Quality and Social Development Initiatives of South Africa in the 21st Century', was released in June 2000. In my view, aside from its restructuring proposals, its lasting contribution centred on two key issues that underpin the values I hold dear. First, it made a compelling case for higher education as a 'public good'. Second, it contributed to the debate on redressing past inequalities by arguing that in the context of the changing student demographic composition of universities, with ever-larger numbers of black students enrolling in the erstwhile white institutions, social redress – which includes both the provision of student financial aid for poor students and the provision of resources to universities to deal with the learning needs of under-prepared students – cuts across the past divide between the historically black and historically white institutions. This implied – and this is its real import – that the focus and end result of any restructuring project must be to create South African higher education institutions which are neither white nor black and which, as the CHE stated, must be 'put to work for and on behalf of all South Africans'.

The CHE's restructuring proposals were far-reaching. The report made a compelling case for the creation of a diverse and differentiated higher education system and for a reduction in the number of institutions through 'combination' to ensure the sustainability of the system. It argued for the differentiation of institutions, based on a distinction between teaching and research universities. The differentiation proposals

275

were contentious and in the end were roundly rejected by the higher education sector on the grounds both that teaching and research could not be separated and, more importantly, that they would perpetuate past inequalities and forever consign the historically black universities and the technikons to the bottom of the institutional pecking order. The merits or otherwise of the CHE's proposals were lost in the fog of racial essentialism.

This inability to transcend the divides of the past and to imagine South African institutions free from the racial divides of the past was to re-emerge later in response to my proposals for the rationalisation of the institutional landscape of higher education.

Opposition was widespread and the CHE's proposals were stopped dead in their tracks. This did not unduly perturb me, as I too did not agree with the proposals. In my view, research is an integral component of higher education and a university that did not offer research programmes was not worthy of the name. Ironically President Mbeki, who was at best lukewarm about my subsequent restructuring proposals, in part because they too were criticised by some black bodies, was actually not opposed to the idea of a solely teaching university, I discovered later. After the Cabinet discussion on my proposals, in a moment that revealed his own approach to the role of universities, the President asked me why it was necessary for them to carry out research; surely teaching alone was adequate.

My response to the CHE's proposals was contained in the National Plan for Higher Education (NPHE), which was released in February 2001, with the 'full and enthusiastic support and endorsement of the Cabinet', as I indicated at the time. I accepted the need for a diverse and differentiated higher education system which would enable institutions to determine the type and range of qualifications offered, based on the relevance and responsiveness of the academic programmes on offer to their location and context, including regional and national priorities, as well as their capacity to offer such courses. The advantage of not locking institutions into a predetermined institutional category, as the CHE had proposed, was that it allowed them to identify their own niche areas as focal points for building institutional capacity in research.

My proposals were well received by the higher education sector in general. However, the technikons were miffed, as the NPHE indicated that universities and technikons would continue to be treated as different types of institutions in the medium term. The less onerous entrance requirements for diploma programmes at technikons played an important role in facilitating access to higher education; at the time there was also a dire shortage of middle-level technicians in the country. That they would play an important role in contributing to the national policy and development agenda did not pacify the leaders of the technikons. They had a chip on their shoulders, due in large part to the common perception of technikons as second-class institutions: 'real' higher education institutions offered degrees, not diplomas. I should add that this was not far off the mark, as some technikons were little more than glorified technical colleges.

However, I recognised that the technikons had the potential to mobilise support, which could impact on the broader institutional restructuring proposals that were to come. Thus against the advice of my officials – the only time this happened as far as I can recall, and on the assumption that winning the war was more important than losing a battle along the way – I acceded to the demand of the Committee of Technikon Principals to replace the name 'technikon' with 'university of technology'. This enabled them to lay claim to the titles and honorifics associated with universities – vice-chancellors, professors and so on – while their programme profile, which I determined through funding, ensured that their primary focus as diploma-granting institutions would remain.

The CHE's proposals for reducing the number of institutions was less contentious largely because they were not firmly rooted in concrete schemes and instead simply indicated that further investigation was necessary. The sector was not keen on further investigations and argued that any process for reducing the number of institutions should be left to the sector itself. This, as I suggested, was the equivalent of asking turkeys to vote for Christmas. I agreed in principle with the CHE's proposal, and an initial analysis of the available data by my officials clearly supported the case for rationalisation. However, I was aware that institutional rationalisation was a political hot potato and that its success depended on a clear and empirically grounded case. It was against this background that I announced the establishment of a national working group (NWG) to advise me on the 'feasibility of reducing the number of institutions and establishing new institutional and organisational forms through a more rational arrangement for consolidating the provision of higher education'.

Given the high stakes involved and the political minefield that would have to be navigated, I chose the members of the NWG carefully to ensure an appropriate balance between political savoir-faire and weight and an understanding of the higher education system. The NWG was chaired by Saki Macozoma, former political activist and MP turned businessman, with the Deputy Governor of the Reserve Bank at the time, Gill Marcus, serving as his deputy. Many of its members were retired senior higher education leaders, which was important to avoid any accusation of bias linked to institutional interests.

The NWG's report, 'The Restructuring of the Higher Education System in South Africa', which was released in December 2001, proposed reducing the number of institutions from thirty-six to twenty-one. This unleashed a storm of controversy, which I had anticipated, as the lobbying and teeth-gnashing began as soon as I announced the establishment of the NWG. The question of which institutions would go, which would be absorbed, how this would be done, and what the new merged institutions would be called, consumed the entire sector. It soon became clear that while the goals of transformation might perhaps not be in question, the strategies for achieving them or the application of agreed strategies would inevitably result in policy contestation, conflict and resistance. Indeed, it was obvious that all the institutions supported restructuring as long as it did not affect them. They were happy to support change as long as nothing changed. The dominant *leitmotif* was institutional survival at all costs, whatever the national interest, and a sanitised conception of 'transformation' came to prevail – one that entailed no pain, loss or disruption of long-standing traditions, behaviours and practices.

Behind the scenes, the lobbying grew more and more intense. This was brought home to me when I proposed a provisional moratorium on the intake of new students at the University of Transkei (Unitra) in Mthatha in 2002 (excluding students of the faculty of health sciences). Unitra seemed to be falling apart, and I said that no new students should be enrolled while a decision about its future was being made, based on the recommendations of the NWG. This fuelled the rumour, which had already started to circulate, that I intended to close Unitra. I was certainly thinking about it, or rather about using its infrastructure for other educational purposes, but Trevor Manuel, the Finance Minister, whose political judgement I trusted implicitly, said to me, 'You can't close Unitra.'

This became evident when Nelson Mandela called me on Christmas morning in 2001. 'Kader,' he said, 'what are you doing with Unitra? Why are you closing it down?' Mr Mandela's home in Qunu was not far from Unitra, and it was very much in the heart of his clan home-base and at the centre of his political heartland. 'I'm not closing it down, Madiba,' I told him. 'But there are huge problems at Unitra. The university far exceeds its income and is in deficit. We have to have proper management at Unitra. There are more deserving causes for public funding, such as health and welfare services and universities that are trying hard to meet black students' needs.'

After our discussion, Madiba seemed placated, for the time being at least. But he continued to lean on me to ensure that Mthatha retained at the very least a university teaching hospital. I also subsequently heard that the University of Venda was quietly lobbying behind the scenes for President Mbeki to take over the decision-making process altogether and bypass me when it came to the rationalisation of the tertiary sector.

The NWG's proposals were well argued and based on a careful consideration and analysis of the available data. I agreed with the overall thrust of their report and proposals with some exceptions, which I knew would be politically difficult to sell. This included the proposals to incorporate Unitra's Medical School into the University of Fort Hare (difficult because of Madiba's objections), and the proposed merger of the University of the Western Cape (UWC) and the Peninsula Technikon (likewise difficult because of the role played by UWC in the anti-apartheid struggles in the 1980s under the leadership of Jakes Gerwel).

My revised proposal resulted in the reduction of the number of institutions from thirty-six to twenty-three, two more than proposed by the NWG. I was aware that I would have to seek the approval of Cabinet for my proposals, given their far-reaching implications, including the funding required to facilitate implementation. However, my officials, in particular the Director-General, persuaded me that prior to going to

Cabinet I should engage with my political constituency in the ANC and the Alliance to ensure political support, in view of the on-going lobbying, which had intensified and could potentially derail the process. I agreed and undertook meetings with provincial ANC and Alliance structures across the country. The reception in general was positive, especially as it seemed that I was taking their concerns seriously. More importantly, it enabled them to get a better understanding of the underlying basis of the proposals, including the supporting data, free from the often myopic information provided by institutional lobby groups.

It was in the Eastern Cape that the mood was antagonistic and it was clear that daggers had been drawn. The Premier, Makhenkesi Stofile, supported by senior national Cabinet colleagues, made it clear that any attempt to merge historically black with historically white institutions would be opposed. Stofile was adamant that the formerly white Rhodes University should be taken over by the almost exclusively black University of Fort Hare. I was astounded by the fact that their objections seemed to be based on fear, the fear that the black institutions would not be able to measure up to their white counterparts. I also arranged for Saki Macozoma to brief a selected group of ministers and MPs from across the political spectrum in Cape Town, but not with much success. One minister was all for changing the name of the University of Cape Town to the University of Table Mountain, presumably in recognition of its geographical situation.

Parallel to the political consultations, I engaged with Trevor Manuel to secure the funding required for the restructuring, which was in the region of between R3 billion and R4 billion. I wrote him a letter but didn't get any reply from him for some weeks. Eventually, I privately approached the Director-General of the Treasury, Maria Ramos, and asked her to intervene, as without funding the mergers would not work. Manuel did eventually come back to me and agreed to fund the rationalisation, but over a period of three or four years.

I was now ready to go to the Cabinet. I had laid the groundwork and did not anticipate any further pitfalls. But I have to admit that at the last moment I got cold feet. Although I was convinced of the imperative of restructuring and the merits of the merger proposals, I was concerned about the scale, which had not been attempted anywhere else in the world. There had been concerns raised by institutions about the capacity of the department to manage the implementation and I was beginning to think that we might have been biting off more than we could chew, and that an incremental approach would be better. It was my officials who persuaded me to stand my ground, at a mid-morning meeting at my home where I was recuperating after a short spell in hospital. They convinced me that it was either all or nothing. If I made a concession to one institution, it would be the first step down a slippery slope of compromise. Fortified by a stiff whiskey, against doctor's orders (I got them to wash out the glass so Louise wouldn't know), I made my final decision. There was no going back.

However, the battle was not over. I tabled my proposals for the first time in a memorandum to Cabinet in June 2002. The proposals were not initially accepted by the Cabinet, ostensibly on the ground that the rationalisation of institutional structures was focused on the 'hardware' of restructuring, but the 'software of transformation' was missing. I decided not to point out that the software was covered in the National Plan for Higher Education, which had been discussed and approved by the Cabinet. I have always known that policy and law cannot be made by reference to other documents, and after a lengthy discussion in which the President expressed his unhappiness with the lack of transformation at the University of the Witwatersrand, he indicated that the proposals should be resubmitted, with the software issues integrated. I said, 'Quite right, Mr President,' and left to inform my officials, who were waiting in the ante-room. In passing I should add that this was not the first example of an attack on Wits University, which had arguably contributed considerably to renewal and transformation.

The Association of Vice-Chancellors of Historically Disadvantaged Tertiary Institutions had clearly got to the President. His office provided me with a copy of a submission the Association had made to him, which required my response. In August 2003 I placed the amended Cabinet memorandum back on the agenda of the next Cabinet meeting along with a document that set out in some detail the rationale for each of the proposed mergers and incorporations. This time, however, President Mbeki was out of the country and I was asked to chair Cabinet. I obviously could not table the proposals, possibly the most dramatic reform of a higher education system anywhere in the world, without the President being present. So the memorandum was withdrawn and immediately placed on the agenda for the meeting two weeks later.

This next gathering was barely quorate as most of the ministers were meeting a foreign state visitor, together with the President. Once again, I couldn't table such an important and controversial policy document when so many ministers were absent. The document was again withdrawn. I was now beginning to wonder whether Cabinet would ever discuss the plan, let alone actually approve it. It felt as if the lobbyists were getting their way. With the general elections of 2004 not many months away, it seemed as if the whole three-year rationalisation episode might be shelved.

Finally, in October 2003 the rationalisation proposal was listed on the agenda of the following Cabinet meeting, and a full Cabinet, including President Mbeki, was expected to be present. Here, at last, was my chance. But at the very moment when I was about to present my policy, President Mbeki stood up and left the room. He apparently had an urgent phonecall to take from another head of state.

On his departure Deputy President Jacob Zuma moved into the chair and, almost immediately, Trevor Manuel – with a twinkle in his eye – said to Zuma, 'Excuse me, chair, but I think we've all heard Minister Asmal speak on these proposals at length. I suggest we accept them.' Zuma agreed. There were mutters of agreement all round the table and the most far-reaching educational policy ever adopted in South Africa was through. There had not even been a vote. 'Can I dismiss my officials?' I asked Zuma, as I had various members of my staff on hand in the annexe to answer any queries that Cabinet might raise. Zuma nodded and Cabinet prepared to go on to the next item. I got up and left the room, light-headed with what had happened.

As I walked down the corridor towards my staff, I saw the President, who had just finished his important telephone call. 'Kader, what are you doing here?' 'We've finished,' I said. 'Oh, have they? Good,' he replied. Then off he went.

On 20 October 2003, more than three years after embarking on this epic journey of transformation, I announced the changes that were to take place, the identity of the institutions that were to be merged, and the names that were to be given to these new institutions. Higher education now had a framework that, if comprehensibly implemented, would ensure the sector was affordable, sustainable and responsive to the needs for knowledge and human resources in a changing South Africa and a globalising world.

Underpinning the reform of the tertiary education sector was a commitment on my part to 'cultural justice'. The pursuit of non-racialism does not disregard differences that are cultural or linguistic in nature. These differences can be a source of vitality and strength; in itself difference is not the problem. The challenge lies in elevating and harnessing differences to the point that they are embraced in the diversity of South Africa. This was why I introduced the idea of cultural justice, a term I borrowed from David Chidester, in my ministry. I pointed out that many people still find higher education institutions alien environments, where they experience 'cultural injustice' in institutional failures to include their languages, orientations, values and other cultural resources. This was my perennial concern about exclusion, made all the more urgent in the context of the need for change in the demographics of South African universities.

For the same reason I made efforts to ban some of the more barbaric initiation practices at some institutions of higher learning. I believed these arose out of specific backgrounds and could be deeply alienating to students from different cultures – not to mention they could also become nothing more than sadistic bullying. In one instance I called in the Human Rights Commission to investigate an initiation ceremony at one of the more traditional Afrikaans universities that had resulted in the death of a student.

Since we could not sustain institutions in which the burden of the culturally unfamiliar is borne by many for the comfort of the few, we needed to find ways to establish more equitable terms of cultural inclusion. Cultural justice required expanding the scope of inclusion for our different languages, lifestyles and cultural orientations so that all of our people felt affirmed. It also required sharing the burden of the unfamiliar so that all our people, and not only those disadvantaged by the prevailing cultures of our institutions, would feel challenged to engage with a cultural formation they found unfamiliar. After all, one of the defining features of teaching and research in higher education is the capacity to make the strange familiar and the familiar strange. By committing our institutions to advancing cultural justice, therefore, we would also be realising the promise contained in the very idea of a South African university.

I visited many universities at that time. One of my most memorable experiences was a visit to the Potchefstroom University for Christian Higher Education, as it was called then. Potchefstroom is about a hundred and twenty kilometres south-west of Johannesburg in what is now the North West Province. Former President F.W. de Klerk was an alumnus of the university and, at the time the rationalisation process was under way, he was also the university's Chancellor. The university was considered by many to be a second-rate institution with few redeeming qualities. When I arrived there, I was astonished to see young Afrikaner men wandering about the campus with pistols on their hips. This was 2002. I felt totally alienated and unwelcome – terrible sensations to have in your own country.

How on earth could any black South African feel even remotely that this university was in any way part of them, or that he or she had any stake in it? The notion of 'cultural justice', the sense of being at home or being comfortable, would challenge such arrogance directly. It was a reminder to me that transformation was not simply about shifting administrations or changing names but about fundamental change at the heart of the institution.

Of course, this made the language of instruction in the tertiary sector one of the most controversial of all the areas I had to manage. According to the 1996 Constitution, every South African has the right to receive education 'in the official language or languages of their choice in public educational institutions where that education is reasonably practicable'. The exercise of this right cannot, however, negate considerations of equity and redress.

Though my predecessor, Sibusiso Bengu, had implemented a language policy for schools, I indicated in the Higher Education Act of 1997 that the Minister of Education was responsible for determining language policy for higher education. The time came to make that determination.

The challenge of a new policy for language in education was to ensure that all of South Africa's languages could be developed as academic or scientific languages, while at the same time ensuring that existing languages of instruction did not serve as a barrier to access and success.

Afrikaans is the language associated with the apartheid regime, but it is also spoken by a large number of coloured people in the Western and Northern Cape. Other than English, Afrikaans was the only other South African language employed as a medium of instruction and official communication in South African higher education institutions. Anticipating the looming controversy, I invited Professor Jakes Gerwel to convene an informal committee to provide me with advice, and I sought out as well the ideas and opinions of many others in the sector, not least the vice-chancellors of the historically Afrikaans institutions.

While the student population in higher education was linguistically diverse and it was not uncommon to find a variety of home languages represented in a single institution, the information I had obtained indicated that English and Afrikaans were the two most frequently reported home languages. This was despite the fact that half of total student enrolments in 1999 reported an indigenous African or other language as their home language. The evidence suggested that the majority of universities and technikons used English as the sole medium of instruction while most historically Afrikaans-medium institutions offered parallel or dual instruction in English and Afrikaans. This shift could be ascribed to the demographic changes in the student population in the 1990s and the increasing numbers of students for whom Afrikaans was not a first or second language. The decision by both universities and technikons to adopt a more flexible language policy had, in all cases, been voluntary and self-funded, reflecting in part a growing commitment to transformation. In fact, no requests were received by the ministry from such institutions to support their language strategies. Nevertheless, it was also evident that the implementation of parallel or dual language instruction was uneven, and the commitment of institutional leadership to it had not always translated into practice at departmental and individual levels.

In November 2002 I introduced the new policy for language in higher education. It stressed the shift towards multilingualism and the protection and nurturing of all the country's official languages. It also ruled out the possibility of sole-medium Afrikaans higher education institutions. This decision sparked heated debate. I was castigated for being another Lord Milner, who after the Anglo-Boer War had introduced a policy of anglicisation in all schools throughout South Africa. The new policy stated that Afrikaans would be retained as a medium of academic expression and communication in higher education, but not to the exclusion of all other languages. For me, the notion of Afrikaans-only universities ran counter to the end goal of a transformed higher education system whose identity and cultural orientation were neither black nor white, neither English- nor Afrikaans-speaking, but unabashedly and unashamedly South African.

Moreover, I agreed with the rectors of the historically Afrikaans institutions that the sustained development of Afrikaans should also not be the responsibility of particular universities, as this could have the unintended consequence of concentrating Afrikaans-speaking students in some institutions and, in so doing, setting back their transformation agendas where they had embraced parallel or dual medium approaches to promote diversity.

The new policy that I announced stipulated that Afrikaans as a medium of academic expression and communication would be assured through a range of strategies, including the adoption of parallel and dual language options. These strategies would cater for the needs of Afrikaans speakers and also ensure that the language of instruction was not a barrier to access and success. At the same time, I promised to examine the feasibility of different strategies, including the use of Afrikaans as a primary but not a sole medium of instruction, and agreed to consult with the historically Afrikaans medium institutions. From then on I was no longer a Lord Milner: I was accused by a fellow Cabinet minister of selling out to Afrikaners!

In all, my aim was to encourage tertiary institutions throughout the country to consider ways of promoting multilingualism, in line with global and, particularly, African trends. It is my strong belief that learning more than one language should be general practice. Being multilingual should form part of what it is to be South African.

Looking back now, I am particularly proud of my efforts to instil certain values in our education system. I have always believed education is a value in its own right, a public good that everyone can enjoy and no one can be denied. I wanted our education system to reflect the values of our new Constitution and, by doing so, contribute to the development of knowledgeable, skilled, responsible and *ethical* citizens, citizens who know what it means to be South African.

In his State of the Nation address to Parliament in 2001, President Thabo Mbeki clearly articulated these values. He said: 'Outwardly, we are a people of many colours, races, cultures, languages and ancient origins. Yet we are tied to one another by a million visible and invisible threads. We share a common destiny from which none of us can escape because together we are human, we are South African, we are African.'

As I listened to him, I recalled a speech that Albert Luthuli made to white South Africans in the late 1950s. He said: 'I believe that our vision of democracy in South Africa will be realised, because there is a growing number of people who are coming to accept the fact that in South Africa we are a multiracial community – whether we like it or not … And since we are all here, we must seek a way whereby we can realise democracy, so that we can live in peace and harmony in this land of ours.'

Going back and looking at that speech, I realised that Luthuli had done an extraordinary thing. He told his white audience, 'You cannot preserve your heritage by isolating yourself, or by isolating other people; you can only preserve human values by propagating them and creating a climate where these values will flourish.' His answer was to preserve certain human values, not by 'hoarding' them but by sharing them as the only way to preserve them.

We all have values, and the good of our society rests on our ability to integrate all these values into our definition of South Africanness. However, values cannot simply be asserted; they must be put on the table, debated, negotiated, earned. This process, this dialogue, is in and of itself a value – a South African value – to be cherished.

For generations the vast majority of South Africans have desired a non-racial, non-sexist society based on equality, freedom and democracy. Such a society must be based on inclusion, and the abandonment of unfair practices that discriminate against people. For instance, while minister I made an effort to ensure that parents were aware that according to the Constitution their children could not be excluded from school just because they couldn't pay the fees. I also once had to challenge schools that wanted to exclude Muslim girls whose religion required them to wear headscarves. I was not prepared to tolerate exclusion in any form wherever it appeared.

Not long after I took over the education portfolio, I established a Working Group on Values in Education to look into the question of values in our educational institutions. It was headed by Professor Wilmot James and comprised leading intellectuals of the time like Hermann Giliomee and the renowned writer Antjie Krog. The working group reported back to me in May 2000, identifying the values that we wanted young adults to embody: equity, tolerance, multilingualism, openness and accountability. This was the start of an intense debate. On the basis of this document, the department held a conference in Kirstenbosch in Cape Town early in 2001 called Saamtrek, an Afrikaans word meaning 'pulling together in the same direction'. One of the keynote speakers was the Palestinian intellectual Edward Said, whom I greatly admired.

The initiative I launched in Parliament under the title 'Our Values in Education' took anti-racism doctrine further and resulted in new classroom practices: innovative learning materials were produced and disseminated to schools throughout the country; diplomas were offered for teachers on teaching anti-racism; my department initiated events like Freedom Day art competitions, celebrations, camps to bring together schoolchildren from all provinces, the Tirisano Schools Choral Eisteddfods, and meetings for children with video links to children in Palestine and other countries that were going through the same kind of struggles. We wanted all South Africa's children to identify with our national symbols – the national anthem, the flag, the coat of arms – and we even talked about introducing an oath of allegiance to the country. Our emphasis was on bringing arts and culture back to the schools and, most importantly, focusing on the teaching of history. For this I set up a departmental South African History Project, which I was passionate about, especially the history of our struggle with its principles of non-racialism, non-sexism, social cohesion and equality. In particular, we wanted these values to be disseminated throughout the provinces.

The initiative 'Our Values in Education' was dedicated to realising the central value of education as a public good. My purpose came from a very simple premise indeed: if we were to live our Constitution in our everyday life, we had to distil out of it a set of values that were as comprehensible and meaningful to grade ones and grade twos as they were to the Chief Justice of the Constitutional Court or the chair of the Human Rights Commission. I wanted to find a way of teaching our children what it means to be South African.

The school-based research into values conducted by the James Committee cut to the heart of the dilemma we faced. When asked about which values they found important in education, teachers identified, overwhelmingly, the need for old-style authoritarian discipline and control in the classroom. Indeed, they went further. A large majority, nearly eighty per cent of them, thought that the government put too much emphasis on children's rights, which led to problems in their classrooms. The research concluded: 'Until educators experience the concept of "child-centred" learning as a mechanism to gain (rather than to lose) respect and discipline in their classrooms, the tension between repressive and rights-centred interpretations of values is likely to continue.' In other words, unless we nurtured a value system in our schools that was workable, owned by everyone, and in line with the principles not only of our Bill of Rights but of our curriculum, school governance policy and legislation, we ran the dangerous risk of turning our classrooms into a battleground between an anarchic freedom that masquerades as 'human rights' and an authoritarian backlash that masquerades as 'moral regeneration'. This kind of understanding underpinned the thinking in our process of revising the national curriculum and was strongly reflected in our new curriculum, with its emphasis on history and culture.

Values – I repeat – cannot simply be asserted. This much is made clear in the James Committee's school-based report. Their research suggested that all stakeholders – parents, students and teachers – were unhappy with the value systems they perceived to be in operation in our schools. All felt that communication and dialogue were sorely lacking, and they craved the opportunity for more of it. For this reason, the research warned against 'an emphasis on value-prescription'. Values, it said, 'are not changed by prescription, but through dialogue, experience, new knowledge and critical thinking'. I should add that setting an example by individual behaviour might speak more than any prescription or even dialogue.

This is why, when it came to drafting a programme for values generation within our education system, I found myself, once more, reaching back into South Africa's history – right back to the model of the Freedom Charter.

President Mbeki described what he called 'the new patriotism' as 'a common recognition of the fact that all of us stand to gain from the transformation of South Africa into a non-racial, non-sexist and prosperous country'. Out of the new patriotism come the values of tolerance and acceptance, of equality and democracy, of dialogue, negotiation and conflict resolution that make us uniquely South African in the uniquely global universe of the twenty-first century.

A Mamelodi teacher once wrote to me the following lines: 'Apartheid had one good thing. It kept us together. We had a common enemy to fight. We helped each other. When the common enemy went, we were suddenly left alone and can't find the same powerful thing to hold us together. Each one for himself. And this has ruined a sense of community.'

When I was Minister of Education, my bravest hope was that we would work, together with that Mamelodi teacher, to find something even more powerful to hold her community together; something so powerful that it would not only rebuild the sense of community she felt had evaporated, but would bond her community of Mamelodi into the larger community of South Africa. My hope was that this bonding would come not out of the battle against a common enemy, but out of a battle for a common destiny.

At the end of the investigation into values in 2001, we produced a seminal document on values in education entitled 'Manifesto on Values, Education and Democracy'. This served as the lodestar for the initiative and it listed ten values that we should instil in our children: democracy, social justice and equity, equality, non-racism and non-sexism, *ubuntu* (human dignity and humaneness), an open society, accountability, the rule of law, respect and reconciliation.

Acknowledging that values can't be imposed, the document listed a number of strategies that would help to instil these values in our children. They included bringing arts, culture and history back into the curriculum, encouraging commitment to and awareness of the values of the Constitution among teachers and students, and promoting multilingualism and non-sectarian religious education. The document argued that diversity should be encouraged and valued. This meant allowing children to dress in ways that reflect their social or religious affiliations. This tolerance of outward appearance allows for diversity to be valued, not only because it promotes tolerance itself but also because it enables our children to work and live in an environment in which all can demonstrate their affiliations equally.

The manifesto also emphasised the values of openness and the development of inquiring and critical young minds. We hoped this new values-based perspective on education would help nurture a new, positive form of patriotism, promote anti-racism and serve to build a common citizenship. We wanted to help develop children who were not ignorant of their country's difficult past, but who grew up knowing that history and appreciative of the lessons that could be drawn from it.

As I look back over the five years I spent at the Ministry of Education, I believe the fire of learning in our country was faithfully tended. For teachers and learners, our Revised National Curriculum Statement, with its clear outcomes, was dedicated to setting minds and hearts alight. Abandoning the rote learning of the past, in which pupils' heads were filled like buckets, our curriculum was designed for critical thinking and creative imagination. It was designed for unleashing the energy of new skills and new human capacity. It was designed to advance human freedom and human fulfilment.

As a government the ANC created a single system of education. We moved from nineteen racially and ethnically based departments, with varying levels of effectiveness, into a co-ordinated, unified system. We undertook a similar task in higher education, with a national plan being implemented that reduced the number of universities and technikons from thirty-six to twenty-three stronger and more viable institutions.

We made significant strides in ensuring free and compulsory education for all. We placed emphasis on teachers as the key drivers of quality. By 2003, we had upgraded half of the sixty thousand unqualified teachers we had inherited and introduced a new career path, so a senior teacher could remain in the classroom and still be promoted. I am proud that most schools, by the time I had left the ministry, started on time, continued for seven hours a day and did so for at least 196 days a year. Very few schools were doing that before 1996.

At a deeper level, we took an expansive interpretation of inclusive education, and our policy on removing barriers to learning went well beyond traditional understandings of 'special needs education'. The Values in Education programme I initiated promoted values in our schools that flowed from our Constitution. This was complemented by the work of the South African History Project, which worked to ensure we wouldn't forget or lose our history.

We banned corporal punishment and declared all schools 'safe zones' with weapons and illegal drugs prohibited. We did not permit protests or political meetings on school premises. We outlawed harmful initiation practices at schools and universities. We lightened the burden on poor families through a funding model in which the poorest receive more resources than those less poor; through setting school fees at annual general meetings of school communities in which parents can participate; through partial or complete exemptions from fees; through school feeding programmes; through the National Student Financial Aid Scheme, which assists more than a hundred thousand deserving students annually to enter higher education.

Certainly the five years I spent as Minister of Education were among the most exciting of my life. Being the custodian of education in South Africa was a challenging and exhilarating experience. It was an enormous trust, of course, and success was vitally important to the future of our country. Keeping this trust required resources. It took money. Throughout my term as minister I had a sticker on my office door which highlighted the immortal words of Harvard University's former head Derek Bok: 'If you think education is expensive, try ignorance.'

The story of the transformation of South African education is a never-ending one. It is a story of perseverance and systematic struggle, a story of the triumph of the human spirit. But it is especially a story of joy when we make a difference to the lives of thousands of children. There were times, however, during those five years when I wondered whether any sane person would subject themselves to the pressures and controversies of the education sector. It makes me think of those memorable lines by Lewis Carroll: 'You are old, Father William,' the young man said / And your hair has become very white; / And yet you incessantly stand on your head / Do you think, at your age, it is right?' What would Lewis Carroll have made of the Ministry of Education at that time? Perhaps you need to be like Father William even to attempt, let alone survive, such a task. But my time as minister was an important part of my life: I learnt a great deal here and made, I hope, something of a difference.

11

Conclusion

While he was putting the finishing touches to his memoirs, Kader Asmal died on 22 June 2011. He left unfinished the final chapter of his book. In its stead, it seems fitting to end with the address that his wife Louise gave at a memorial service held in Cape Town at the end of June.

The memorial service for Kader in the Cape Town City Hall on 30 June 2011 was a truly amazing event. The hall was filled with family, friends and comrades – everyone from the Deputy President of South Africa to my fourteen-year-old granddaughter. In my Irish Anti-Apartheid days I had spoken to many small meetings, schools, trade union branches and so on, but never to such a large assembly. It could have been nerve-racking, but such was the love for Kader that emanated from everyone that my nervousness was dissipated. Over the weeks since Kader died, I have been absolutely stunned by the outpouring of affection for him and support for me and the family from people from all walks of life in South Africa, and from friends and colleagues who worked with Kader from all over the world. There was even a motion in the British Parliament.

As I told the audience at the City Hall, Kader would have revelled in the event. I went on to say:

It is difficult in a few brief paragraphs to do justice to the extraordinary breadth of Kader's interests, his empathy with people of all colours, creeds and beliefs, and his enthusiasm for causes that caught at his heart.

He was of course not perfect. As Fintan O'Toole wrote in the *Irish Times*: 'He was the bossiest man I ever knew – and the least authoritarian.' This meant he was a wonderful organiser, with a talent for inspiring others, plus a willingness to pitch in.

The Irish Anti-Apartheid Movement executive committee, for example, met every other Monday almost throughout the year in our house in Dublin. When we had to send out newsletters or prepare placards for a demonstration, Kader would sit on the floor with all of us and stuff envelopes or painstakingly paint slogans on placards – his teacher training for writing on blackboards came in useful. When all was done by the end of the night, he would bring out the whiskey bottle and ask someone to make tea for those who preferred it.

Years ago Kader told me that when he retired, we would spend the time reading poetry to each other. This never happened, as he was too caught up in the politics of the day and in trying to counteract the spreading corruption and the betrayal of the ideals of the ANC by some of its members.

Kader had been ill on and off for a year when he died. Such was his fighting spirit, though, that we never thought of him as frail or incapacitated. He missed the cut and thrust of debate when he resigned from Parliament, and he missed his wonderful staff – an absence which he took out on his family, making us run up and down, fetching and carrying or looking up material on the Internet, which he never mastered. Our sons called him a mechanical retard.

He was indeed demanding and, as Fintan O'Toole said, 'bossy ... but never authoritarian'. 'What makes Kader Asmal such an important figure in modern history', O'Toole continued, 'is that he was that rarest of things – a non-authoritarian revolutionary. Revolutionaries have to believe they are right, and Kader was no exception. Indeed, the struggle against apartheid was one of the most clear-cut causes you could imagine, dangerously close to being a war between good and evil. Such circumstances are perfect for breeding an intolerance of dissent, an impatience with formalities.

'Knowing you're right is an essential asset when you're struggling against an obscene power. It's a deep danger when you have become the power. Hence the tendency of revolutions to produce tyrannies.

'Kader was proud, occasionally imperious, always conscious of his own outstanding abilities. But he was deeply humble in the way that mattered most. He did not believe that any government, any authority, any movement could ever be good enough to dispense with accountability. He lived and breathed and loved the African National Congress and would certainly have given his life for it. But he didn't believe it could ever be infallible. He knew with all his heart that everyone with power – including, eventually, himself – should be accountable, open to dissenting opinions and subject to the rule of law.'

A few weeks after Kader's death, I still don't believe he has gone. But I hope – I know – that his spirit will live on, together with his love for freedom, equality, justice – all those ideals enshrined in the Freedom Charter and then in our Bill of Rights, which he helped write.

It is up to us now to take up the banner and forget our quarrels. We must march resolutely towards a South Africa which is free, non-racial, non-sexist, and in which the poorest of the poor can lift themselves up to share in the wealth of our country.

These are the ideals for which Kader lived. I hope we can work together to bring them to fruition.

Afterword
by Adam Asmal

Sadly, my father died shortly before he was able to complete this book. It was always his desire and intention that it contain a tribute to my mother. It would be a small but a dedicated and absolutely necessary acknowledgement of the enormous impact she had on him and his life.

In a way these memoirs are the final example of the contribution that she made to my father's life for fifty years. Within weeks of his death and despite the grief and pain she was enduring, my mother took it upon herself to finish his memoirs. She once again put her own needs aside to ensure that Kader's work was completed.

Those close to the family are fully aware of the role Louise played over the years, mainly in the background. To this day she has preferred to be behind the 'great man' and she was not bothered by the fact that her immense contribution to his life and, indeed, to this book would go untold. This would be an injustice, firstly to overlook her part in his life and, secondly, because Kader wanted a wider audience to know how devoted he was to her and how dependent he was on her. Louise was everything, from a sounding board, adviser, fierce critic and speech-writer to a lifelong friend, wife, carer, supporter and everything in-between. She held him together and, without her, if truth be told, he was often a little lost. On the rare occasions that she went away he would genuinely miss her and would not know what to do with himself, constantly asking, 'Shall we call her?' The thought had crossed my mind of what would happen in the unlikely event that she would die first: he would simply fall to pieces.

As the book recounts, Louise played a significant role in the Irish Anti-Apartheid Movement, serving on its executive and as honorary secretary for most of its life. She was a true political activist and a hard-working administrator, and as such she was the backbone of the Irish

Anti-Apartheid Movement for nearly three decades. She and Kader enjoyed a partnership forged both in struggle and in their personal lives.

In his last year Kader bravely battled his illness with the constant love, care and support of Louise and, to a much lesser extent, my brother and me. As Louise said in her speech at the official memorial service for Kader in Cape Town, 'Despite all, he still made me laugh,' recalling the story that shortly before his death whilst out in public he was asked how he was by a concerned stranger, to which he replied, 'Well, I can still stand on one leg and put on my underpants.' Of course, what he failed to mention was that he could no longer put on his own socks. This illustrates the closeness and depth of their partnership; for better for worse, in times of joy and in times of adversity. He was fully aware of the burden on her shoulders and wanted to make it a little less painful for her. He rejected the notion of other care-givers, and wanted only Louise at his side even though it was a most demanding task to look after someone in the throes of a terminal illness. And to his last day, she lovingly cared for him often at the expense of her own needs.

Kader would be the first to admit that without Louise he would not have risen to be the person everybody knew and would not have achieved all he did. More specifically, if it was not for Louise this book would not have come to fruition. The project started about six years ago and has seen several contributors come and go, from researchers to co-writers, editors and so on. The only person who has been a constant part of this book from its conception as an idea to the day it was handed over to the publisher has been Louise.

In Kader's final year he often didn't have the energy and concentration to work on his memoirs, but Louise would gently encourage and assist him. She painstakingly ensured that the project was kept alive, as she knew how important it was to him to document his life. From the beginning she has researched, written, rewritten, proofread and edited. She has now, as her final tribute to him, contributed a piece of her own.

Typewriters or computers were completely alien to Kader, so everything was handwritten with his beloved fifty-four-year-old fountain pen, and Louise is also the only person on the planet who can decipher his virtually incomprehensible handwriting with any degree of success. So it's fitting in many ways that, after almost fifty years of marriage and being by his side through all good times and bad, Louise has written the final chapter of these memoirs. This work presents a microcosm of their life, and now, finally, Louise has brought the book to its conclusion. No one else could have done it, and Kader would not have wanted anyone else to do it. The final word, however, goes to my father, taken from the seventieth birthday card that he gave to my mother:

Happy 70th Birthday

Darling Louise
You never stopped
growing!
With all my love
Thank you for nearly
five decades of a
loved life for us both
Keep growing your love
Kader

Sources

Appreciation by President Nelson Mandela. This comes from a citation in my honour on the occasion of my being made an Officer of the Légion d'honneur by the Government of France, 9 February 2006.

Chapter 1. I had previously published a tribute to my mother in the collection edited by Marion Keim, *UMama: Recollections of South African Mothers and Grandmothers* (Cape Town, 2009).

Chapter 2. For the history of the British Anti-Apartheid Movement, I have relied on Christabel Gurney's chapter 'In the heart of the beast: the British Anti-Apartheid Movement, 1959–1994' in South African Democracy Education Trust, *The Road to Democracy*, vol. 3: *International Solidarity*, part 1 (Pretoria, 2008). Roger Fieldhouse's *Anti-Apartheid: A History of the Movement* (London, 2005) is also useful.

Chapter 3. This chapter relies in part on the chapter written by Louise and me and Thomas Alberts on 'The Irish Anti-Apartheid Movement', which appeared in South African Democracy Education Trust, *The Road to Democracy*, vol. 3: *International Solidarity*, part 1 (Pretoria, 2008). We are grateful to Sadet for allowing us to reproduce parts of this chapter. For the section on Idaf I have consulted the chapter by Al Cook on the 'International Defence and Aid Fund of Southern Africa' in South African Democracy Education Trust, *The Road to Democracy*, vol. 3: *International Solidarity*, part 1 (Pretoria, 2008) and Denis Herbstein's *White Lies: Canon Collins and the Secret War Against Apartheid* (Oxford, 2004). The quote by Ruairi Quinn comes from his book *Straight Left: A Journey in Politics* (Dublin, 2005).

Chapter 4. The quotations in this chapter come from Luli Callinicos, *Oliver Tambo: Beyond the Engeli Mountains* (Cape Town, 2004); Albie Sachs, *The Strange Alchemy of Life and Law* (New York,

2009); and a paper by Enuga S. Reddy presented to the symposium 'The Anti-Apartheid Movement: A 40-year Perspective', London, 26 June 1999.

Chapter 5. I have quoted from three works by Albie Sachs, *Protecting Human Rights in a New South Africa* (Cape Town, 1990); *Advancing Human Rights in South Africa* (Cape Town, 1992); and *The Strange Alchemy of Life and Law* (New York, 2009). Some historical background to the chapter was provided by Rita M. Byrnes (ed.), *South Africa: A Country Study* (Washington, 1996).

Chapter 6. Some of Albert Luthuli's speeches have been recorded on the ANC website. His autobiography, *Let My People Go* (London, 1962), has recently been republished. See also the biography by Mary Benson, *Chief Albert Lutuli of South Africa* (London, 1963). For a biography of Luthuli's wife, see Peter Rule, with Marilyn Aitken and Jenny van Dyk, *Nokukhanya, Mother of Light* (Braamfontein, 1993). Other works referred to in the section on Luthuli are: F.W. de Klerk, *The Last Trek – A New Beginning: The Autobiography* (London, 1999); Alan Paton, *Ah, But Your Land Is Beautiful* (London, 1981); Studs Terkel, *Talking to Myself: A Memoir of My Times* (London, 1977); and Donal Brody, 'The Chief', part 4, *Great Epics Newsletter*, 3, 10 (1999). The section on Oliver Tambo draws on the essay I wrote for the collection edited by Pallo Jordan, *Oliver Tambo Remembered* (Johannesburg, 2007). The quote about Mandela by Stanley Greenberg comes from his *Dispatches from the War Room: In the Trenches with Five Extraordinary Leaders* (New York, 2009).

Chapter 7. Readers interested in a longer study of the TRC are referred to the book *Reconciliation through Truth: A Reckoning of Apartheid's Criminal Governance* (Cape Town, 1997), written by me, my wife Louise and Ronald Suresh Roberts. Other works on the TRC that I would recommend are Alex Boraine's insightful *A Country Unmasked: Inside South Africa's Truth and Reconciliation Commission* (Cape Town, 2000), and Antje Krog's evocative *Country of My Skull: Guilt, Sorrow and the Limits of Forgiveness in the New South Africa* (Cape Town, 1999). My inaugural lecture at UWC was subsequently reprinted in the *South African Journal on Human Rights*, 8, 4, 1992. I should also like to recommend Albie Sachs, *The Strange Alchemy of Life and Law* (New York, 2009).

Chapter 8. Useful background for the Mandela presidency was provided by Richard Calland, *The First Five Years: A Review of South Africa's Democratic Parliament* (Cape Town, 1999). The section on the Virodene story draws on a comprehensive series of articles by James Myburgh accessed from the website politicsweb. See also Myburgh's chapter in the book *The Virus, Vitamins and Vegetables*, edited by Kerry Cullinan and Anso Thom (Johannesburg, 2009) and, more generally on the subject of HIV/Aids, Nicoli Nattrass, *Mortal Combat: AIDS Denialism and the Struggle for Antiretrovirals in South Africa* (Pietermaritzburg, 2007).

Chapter 9. I have consulted Heather Mackay, *Water Policies and Practices* (http://assets.panda.org). The Philip Larkin quote comes with permission of Faber & Faber from his poem 'Water' in the collection *The Whitsun Weddings* (London, 1964).

Index

Asmal, Ebrahim (Mota) (brother) 11,
    19, 140
Asmal, Khatija (sister) 14
Asmal, Louise (Parkinson) 31, 32,
    37–9, 44–5, 54, 60, 65, 80, 115, 117
Asmal, Mohammed (Nullabhai)
    (brother) 11, 14, 19–20, 28, 140
Asmal, Rasool (mother) 8, 14–16
Asmal, Sonny (brother) 19
Association of Vice-Chancellors of
    Historically Disadvantaged
        Tertiary Institutions 281–2
asthma 8–9, 12
Atlantic Charter 13

B
Babbit, Bruce 241
Bantu Education 189, 262
Bantu Education Act 28
bantustans (homelands) 93, 107, 119
Beckett, Samuel 43, 57
Bedjaoui, Mohammed 87
Bengu, Sibusiso 255, 262, 264, 284
Bevan, Aneurin 35
Biko, Steve 29, 182
Bizos, George 120
Boipatong Massacre 127–8, 196–7
Boraine, Alex 178
Botha, Pik 195, 201
Botha, P.W. 81, 175
Boycott Committee 41
Boycott Movement 36, 40, 146
boycotts
    academic 70–2
    campaign 36
    economic 72
    international, of SA goods 42, 140
    of schools 15
    sports 61, 69
    Springbok rugby tour 60
Branagan, Geraldine 70
Brink, André 130
British Irish Rights Watch (BIRW) 59
Brody, Donal 143
Broederbond 208, 227
Burke, Edmund 123
Burnham, Margaret 171

Burton, Joan 53
Buthelezi, Mangosuthu 103, 123, 128,
    198–200
Byrne, Gay 81

C
Cabral, Amilcar 62–3
Callinicos, Luli 97
Cameron, Edwin 204
Campaign for Nuclear Disarmament
    46
Canon Collins Memorial Lecture,
    London 155
capital punishment 152–3, 161–2
Carolus, Cheryl 116
Castle, Barbara 41
Castro, Fidel 32, 193
Centre Against Apartheid 91
Centre for Applied Legal Studies 121
Centre for Development Studies 121
Chaskalson, Arthur 120
Chidester, David 268–9, 283
Chisholm, Linda 266, 267
Christian Action 35, 76–7
Christian National Education 28,
    262, 268
Christie, Renfrew 116–17
Churchill, Winston 13
Code of Conduct 151–2, 169–71
Codesa (Convention for a
    Democratic South Africa) 119,
    124, 127, 133–4, 177–8
Coetsee, Kobie 182
Colleges of Medicine of South Africa
    222
Collins, John 35, 76–7, 79
Commercial Cricket Club, Stanger
    club secretary 12–13
Committee of African Organisations
    35, 36, 41
Committee of Technikon Principals
    277
Committee on the Review of State
    Institutions Supporting
        Constitutional Democracy
        221
Communist Party of Ireland 65

Professor of Human Rights Law
176
University of the Witwatersrand
(Wits) 281
University of Transkei (Unitra) 278–9
University of Venda 279
University of Zambia 111

V

Van Rensburg, Ihron 263–4
Van Schalkwyk, Marthinus 271
Verwoerd, Betsie 233–4
Verwoerd, Hendrik 28
Viljoen, Constand 126–7
violence 93, 154
   and inhumanity 167
   'necklacing' 154
Visser, Olga 214–16
Visser, 'Ziggie' 214–16
Vorster, B.J. 141

W

water
   and women 224–5
   conference on dams, Durban 233
   drought and deprivation 225
   Gariep Dam 233
   sanitation 225
   Theewaterskloof Dam 237, 238
   virulent illnesses and indignity
   225
Water Affairs and Forestry, Minister
   of 224–53
   desertification and deforestation
   234
   environmental policy 235
   mining sector 234–5
Water Research Commission 231
White Paper
   on Higher Education 273
   on Water Supply and Sanitation
   242
Williams, Tennessee 43

Winter, Jane 59
Wolpe, Harold 54
Women's Charter 100, 106, 156
Woodberry Down School, London
33–4
Working for Water programme 236,
238–40, 245
Working Group on Values in
Education 288
World Campaign for the Release of
South African Political Prisoners
53, 57
World Commission on Dams 233,
249–51, 257
World Conference to Combat
Racism and Racial
Discrimination 93
World Trade Centre negotiations 181,
182, 196–7
World Wide Fund for Nature SA 237
Gold Medal for Conservation 237

X
Xuma, A.B. 13

Y
Yengwa, Percy 141

Z
Zalaquett, José 187
Zamchiya, David 171
Zapiro 222–3
Zeesen radio service 9
Zille, Helen 272
Zimbabwe
   freedom struggle 218–19
   Zanu-PF 219
   Zapu party 62, 218
   see also Mugabe, Robert
Zulu, Prince Sifiso 198
Zulu, Thami 170
Zuma, Jacob 120, 208, 282
Zwelithini, King Goodwill 198